FIRM FOUNDATIONS

A FAITH FOR TODAY'S CHURCH

A STUDY MANUAL ON THE WESTMINSTER CONFESSION OF FAITH

REV. WILLIAM McKEOWN B.Sc., B.D., M.Th.

'This book was formerly published by the Presbyterian Church in Ireland'

First published in a shorter form as "Firm Foundations: A Faith for Today's Church" by the Board of Evangelism and Christian Training, The Presbyterian Church in Ireland.

Edited and enlarged edition published by © The Oaks 2015.

British Library Cataloguing in Publication Data available.

Paperback edition	ISBN:	0-9548784-2-6	978-0-9548784-2-9
Hardback edition	ISBN:	0-9548784-3-4	978-0-9548784-3-6

Unless otherwise indicated quotations from The Westminster Confession in this publication are from The Westminster Confession of Faith, an Authentic Modern Version by Douglas F. Kelly, Hugh W. McClure, III and Philip Rollinson – Summertown Texts, PO Box 453, Signal Mountain, Tennessee, 37377-0453, 1 (800) 742-5710 and used throughout (hereafter for expediency when a paragraph needs to be distinguished it is referred to as Kelly) Fourth Edition 2004. ISBN: 1-893009-08-4 Copyright © 1979, 1992, 2004 The Summertown Company, Inc.

The Westminster Larger and Shorter Catechisms, (hereafter referred to as WLC and WSC respectively) in this publication are from The Westminster Confession and Catechisms in Modern English. Paragraphs of the Confession, from this publication are also used, and for clarification purposes are distinguished hereafter, by being referred to as Ward. Copyright © by Rowland S. Ward 1996, 2000, Special edition for distribution in Malawi – 2001, New Melbourne Press, 358, Mountain Hwy, Wantirna, Victoria, 3152, Australia. ISBN 0-9586241-4-3 All rights reserved.

"Unless otherwise indicated, all Scripture quotations are from The Holy Bible, English Standard Version Anglicised® (ESVUK®), copyright © 2001 by Crossway, a publishing ministry of Good News Publishers. Used by permission. All rights reserved."

Scripture quotations marked (NIV) are taken from the Holy Bible, New International Version®, NIV®. Copyright © 1973, 1978, 1984 by Biblica, Inc.™ Used by permission of Zondervan. All rights reserved worldwide. www.zondervan.com

Typesetting by The Oaks Secretarial Services, 028 25878 125, danielmckee@btinternet.com

Front cover: A meeting of the Westminster Assembly in the Jerusalem Chamber, Westminster Abbey, on 21st February, 1644.

Cover Design by Alex Grey of Greyjones Studio. www.greyjonestudio.co.uk greyjonestudio@gmail.com; alex.bm.grey@ntlworld.com

Printed by: Antrim Printers, Steeple Industrial Estate, Antrim, BT41 1AB.

Published by: The Oaks,
51, Glebe Road, Ahoghill, BT42 2QW,
Co. Antrim, Northern Ireland

CONTENTS

Foreword

This book has had a long gestation, commencing in the late seventies as notes to teach newly elected elders. Then when I was serving on the Christian Training Committee in the late eighties I was allocated the task to prepare a simple manual on the Westminster Confession of Faith that was published in 1994 by the Board of Evangelism and Christian Training.

I wish to thank all who served on the committee at that time for their guidance, criticisms and suggestions. To Victor Patterson, the Convener, for his encouragement and Ossie McAuley for providing the original questions. The idea of a revised version was mooted by Daniel McKee and I thank him, his urging of me when I was slacking, and the massive work in typesetting this publication. Thanks is also due for the encouragement from those within the local Ballymena Presbytery.

In this revised edition it was decided to use a modern English version of the Confession. Another difference is that modern versions of the Shorter and Larger Catechisms are included. This manual is designed as a simple introduction to the Confession for elders and members of Presbyterian churches; and I hope for others, who wish to discover what Presbyterians believe. It is not intended to replace the well-proven larger commentaries. It is sent forth with the prayer that it will help many and bring much glory to our great Triune God.

A special thanks to Rev. Dr Douglas F. Kelly for allowing us to use this modern version, (published by Summertown Texts); also to the Rev. Dr Rowland S. Ward for allowing us to use some paragraphs of his modern version of the Confession and especially his Catechisms included in the appendix of this volume.

Finally, it must be emphasized that while these modern versions give an excellent understanding of our subordinate standards, it is the 1647 version which is legally binding and which ministers and elders subscribe to in the Presbyterian Church in Ireland.

William McKeown

December, 2014

PREFACE

When you opened the Confession for the first time, you probably thought that it was complicated, out of date, and ought to be replaced. An attempt below has been made to answer the most common questions.

This book is to enable you to understand the Westminster Confession of Faith, which is accepted by the Presbyterian Church in Ireland as a statement of what it believes. This statement of belief is often called 'a subordinate standard'. The Bible is the supreme standard, with the Confession and the Catechisms as subordinate standards.

The Scripture Proof footnotes are, where possible, taken from the Confession of Faith as adopted by the Church of Scotland in the Act of 1647. They have been matched as closely as possible from the original but it is sometimes difficult to match text from the Old to the Modern versions. The Scripture proofs are given to back up this teaching in the Confession. The compilers added these proofs after the Confession was completed, although many had been discussed during the compiling of the confession. This may be the reason why a few of the Scripture proofs, in the author's opinion, are not the best choice for the doctrine being expounded. This is not to say that the doctrine itself is unbiblical, but that a more apt choice of Scripture references could have been chosen. This, however, is a minor flaw in the Confession as a whole.

The order of the Confession has been followed, apart from 'Confession chapter four', paragraph two, God's special creation. This has been moved from the 'Doctrine of God' and placed before 'Confession chapter six' under the 'Doctrine of Man'. 'Confession chapter nine' on freewill is discussed also under the 'Doctrine of Man' rather than under the teaching of the Mediator, as they are in the Confession. The Contents above give a clear logical outline of this six fold major doctrinal division being followed:

- The Doctrines of God and Man
- Salvation
- Person and Work of Christ and man's response
- Living the Christian life
- The Church
- The Last Things

The modern version used in this manual is "The Westminster Confession of Faith, an Authentic Modern Version" by D.F. Kelly, H.W. McClure, III and P. Rollinson – Summertown Text and is used throughout (hereafter for expediency when a paragraph needs to be distinguished it is referred to as Kelly). Each Confession Paragraph is placed within a border for clarity. When another version of the Confession is used, a different style border is employed with the Author's identity, but where the Confession is quoted in the text it is italicized.

Basic Questions Answered

WHAT IS A CONFESSION OF FAITH?

The word confess means to acknowledge or to declare. It is used in the New Testament in various ways, such as, to confess sin,

> *"If we confess our sins, he is faithful and just to forgive us our sins and to cleanse us from all unrighteousness"* (I John 1:9),

or to confess Jesus as Lord, that is, a personal confession of faith in Christ,

> *"because, if you confess with your mouth that Jesus is Lord and believe in your heart that God raised him from the dead, you will be saved"* (Romans 10:9).

It is employed to confess truth in the sense of a set of beliefs

> *"Fight the good fight of the faith. Take hold of the eternal life to which you were called and about which you made the good confession in the presence of many witnesses"* (I Timothy 6:12).

It is this latter sense that is used with respect to a confession of faith.

A confession of faith is a statement of what the church believes Scripture teaches on certain doctrines and practices. It is longer and more detailed than a creed, which is short, personal and is often used verbally to confess basic beliefs in a worship service.

A confession being longer, more detailed and precise, is not used in worship, but as a teaching aid.

WHY DO WE NEED A CONFESSION?

Many people claim that we do not need man-made documents, all we need is the Bible. "No book but the Bible, no creed but Christ" is their cry. This sounds very good, but no church or sect practices this. Every church or sect has a confession of faith, it has a set of beliefs. Often they are not written. They may be mental or oral, contained in their preaching or hymns. As an example of this, another Christian assembly might not have a written confession, but try advocating infant baptism or even denying the secret rapture in their assembly, and watch what happens!

A written confession serves as a witness to the world. It says this is what we believe the Bible teaches. At the same time it defines doctrine for the church and serves as a bond of unity for those who share similar beliefs. It is also a means of correcting those who deny certain matters of doctrine.

A written confession is useful since it leaves neither the church member nor the outsider in any doubt as to what the church claims to believe in the major areas of doctrine and practice. Just to say we believe the Bible is not sufficient. Since a sect like the Jehovah

Witnesses does the same, we must state clearly and precisely what the Bible teaches.

WHAT IS THE WESTMINSTER CONFESSION OF FAITH?

The Confession originated in the conflict between Charles I and Parliament. Charles wished to impose high Anglicanism on the people while the Puritans within the Church of England wished to have its creeds and practices revised in order to bring them into conformity with the Word of God. Parliament called together a group of over 150 Christian leaders, the vast majority being ministers of the Church of England, most of whom were of the Puritan persuasion. The Scottish Presbyterians were represented by four ministers and two elders, known as commissioners.

The Westminster Assembly, as it was known, met from July 1643 to February 1649. In that period it produced the Confession of Faith, the Larger and Shorter Catechisms, the Form of Church Government and the Directory for Public Worship.

A version of the Psalter was also approved for use in public worship. The Westminster Confession was adopted by the Church of Scotland in 1647 as a subordinate standard. Presbyterian churches throughout the world have followed its example.

The Savoy Declaration (1658) used by Congregational churches and the Baptist Confession (1689) are largely based on the Westminster Confession.

The content of the Confession is that of post-reformation Calvinism. It is a superb document for precision and clarity, without being over dogmatic in some disputed areas. It covers the main doctrines of the Christian faith, the only obvious omission is that of the Mission of the Church.

SHOULD THE WESTMINSTER CONFESSION BE CHANGED?

It has often been said that the Confession is out of date and needs to be changed. It must be remembered that its compilers believed it was an accurate summary of what Scripture taught on certain matters of faith and practice. If they were correct, then what was true in the 17th century is also true today, for God's Word does not change. This leaves the onus on us to prove from the Bible any teaching of the Confession which we claim is incorrect. It is not a matter that we do not like what it says, the issue at stake is, "Is this particular teaching unscriptural?" Unless we can prove it is unbiblical we must not alter the Confession.

This does not mean that we do not need to supplement the

Confession in some areas. Most would suggest additions covering the missionary duty of the Church and on the Holy Spirit. (It is unfair to say that the Confession has nothing to say on the Holy Spirit and his work, as there are many references to him scattered through the various chapters).

It is true that the English in the Confession is archaic, but modern translations (some from the original manuscripts as we have used here by Kelly) are now available. (Details of these and other books are given in the Further Reading list at the end of this manual).

WHAT IS MEANT BY SUBSCRIPTION?

When ministers and elders are ordained they are asked to subscribe to the Confession. In doing so they are saying that they agree with the teaching of the Confession taken as a whole. It is generally accepted that subscription does not bind a person to every minute detail in the document. However a person who would reject a doctrinal theme in the Confession could not sign it, since the rejection of such a doctrine would cause the whole Confession to collapse. No one could sign it who denies the Doctrine of Election, since in the Confession's teaching, man's salvation depends on it. No one can sign it who denies the validity of infant baptism for this is based on the Doctrine of the Covenant and it is a denial of a basic deduction from Scripture. Not to believe that the Pope is the antichrist (25.6), however, does not invalidate any major teaching in the Confession.

Teaching and ruling elders only are required to subscribe to the Confession, but not ordinary members. It should however be expected of a person applying for its membership to have a profession of saving faith backed up by a godly life. Not every member is required to take up office in a church, but if they do, it is only reasonable to expect them to agree to the teaching of that church. Otherwise he is dishonest and cannot fully support the work of the church in which he holds office.

While explanations in this manual are based on a modern version of the Confession, ministers and elders in the PCI subscribe to the original version as adopted by the Church of Scotland in her Act of 1647 *(See Code Chapter 1 Section 3 Paragraph 13).* For practical purposes there is little difference.

To think over and discuss:

1. *Do you think a church needs a written confession of faith? Give your reasons for and against.*
2. *What are your initial impressions of the Westminster Confession?*
3. *What would you do if you knew a leader within the church was actively promoting doctrines contrary to the Confession? (for example Adult baptism by immersion only).*

Chapter I

Our Great God

He Speaks To Us

Ref. Confession Chapter 1 – Holy Scriptures

In this study you will discover:

- God speaks to us through his Creation
- God has given us his written Word
- The Bible is sufficient in all matters of belief and behaviour
- The Bible is the supreme judge in all matters of religion

The most basic question that a person can ask about religion is, "Is there a God?" After this must come, "If there is a God what is he like and what does he require of me?" To obtain an answer to these questions God must be able to speak to us clearly and in an accurate way. It is for this reason that the Confession commences with a chapter on how God speaks to us. The very fact that God is willing to speak to us, teaches that he is a God of love and grace.

God speaks to us through his Creation

Confession 1.1

> Our natural understanding and the works of creation and providence so clearly show God's goodness, wisdom, and power that human beings have no excuse.[1] However, these means alone cannot provide that knowledge of God and of his will which is necessary for salvation.[2] Therefore it pleased the Lord at different times and in various ways to reveal himself and to declare that this revelation contains his will for his church.[3] Afterwards it pleased God to put this entire revelation into writing so that the truth might be better preserved and transmitted and that the church, confronted with the corruption of the flesh and the evil purposes of Satan and the world, might be more securely established and comforted.[4] Since God no longer reveals himself to his people in those earlier ways,[5] Holy Scripture is absolutely essential.[6]

This section of the Confession teaches that God has revealed

1. Romans 2:14-15; Romans 1:19-20; Psalm 19:1-3; Romans 1:32 with Romans 2:1.
2. I Corinthians 1:21, 2:13-14.
3. Hebrews 1:1.
4. Proverbs 22:19-21; Luke 1:3-4; Romans 15:4; Matthew 4:4, 7, 10; Isaiah 8:19-20.
5. Hebrews 1:1-2.
6. II Timothy 3:15; II Peter 1:19.

himself in creation.

> *"The heavens declare the glory of God, and the sky above proclaims his handiwork . . ."* (Psalm 19:1ff).

and also speaks through conscience,

> *"For when Gentiles, who do not have the law, by nature do what the law requires, they are a law to themselves, even though they do not have the law"* (Romans 2:14).

This is a true *revelation* of God; but people, due to sinful thinking have suppressed the truth and refuse to recognise it.

> *"For what can be known about God is plain to them, because God has shown it to them . . ."* (Romans 1:19ff).

Each one, in his conscience, knows there is a God. Creation announces this clearly to him but he refuses to listen. He prefers to believe a lie. Both believer and unbeliever are confronted by the same facts, but they interpret them differently. One sees the glory of God while the other sees an accident of matter. The unbeliever is, however, without excuse. God has spoken in his conscience as well as in the universe, but he has failed to acknowledge it. The fault lies with us, not God. Hence the claim, "an undevout astronomer is mad" (Edward Young 1683-1755).

This 'General Revelation', as it is called, is not sufficient to declare the will of God to man. God must speak in words. Certain aspects of his character are declared in this general revelation, but his will must be declared in words. Even unfallen Adam in the garden needed the Word of God to direct him, how much more sinful man?

> *"And God blessed them. And God said to them, "Be fruitful and multiply and fill the earth and subdue it, and have dominion over the fish of the sea and over the birds of the heavens and over every living thing that moves on the earth"* (Genesis 1:28),

> *"And the LORD God commanded the man, saying, "You may surely eat of every tree of the garden . . ."* (Genesis 2:16ff).

This Word – '*revelation*' is called 'Special Revelation'. Without it we would not know the way of salvation.

God has given us his written Word

Confession 1.2

What we call Holy Scripture or the written word of God now includes all the books of the Old and the New Testament, which are:

The Old Testament:

Genesis	II Chronicles	Daniel
Exodus	Ezra	Hosea
Leviticus	Nehemiah	Joel
Numbers	Esther	Amos
Deuteronomy	Job	Obadiah
Joshua	Psalms	Jonah
Judges	Proverbs	Micah
Ruth	Ecclesiastes	Nahum
I Samuel	The Song of Songs	Habakkuk
II Samuel	Isaiah	Zephaniah
I Kings	Jeremiah	Haggai
II Kings	Lamentations	Zechariah
I Chronicles	Ezekiel	Malachi

The New Testament:

Matthew	Ephesians	Hebrews
Mark	Philippians	James
Luke	Colossians	I Peter
John	I Thessalonians	II Peter
Acts	II Thessalonians	I John
Romans	I Timothy	II John
I Corinthians	II Timothy	III John
II Corinthians	Titus	Jude
Galatians	Philemon	Revelation

All of these books are inspired by God and are the rule of faith and life.[1]

[1] Luke 16:29, 31; Ephesians 2:20; Revelation 22:18-19; II Timothy 3:16.

The Confession states that God has spoken to us at various times and in different ways,

> *"Long ago, at many times and in many ways, God spoke to our fathers by the prophets . . ."* (Hebrews 1:1).

Afterwards this *revelation* was committed wholly to writing. An example of this would be the call of Moses. God spoke to him at the Burning Bush and later under the guidance of God this account was recorded in writing by Moses and so forms a part of Holy Scripture. The Bible is therefore God's revelation to us. The reasons given for a written revelation include the preservation and propagation of the truth and the protection of the church. The Confession makes it abundantly clear that God no longer reveals himself as he did in biblical times. Those former ways of God revealing his will unto his people have now ceased. In other words, Scripture is sufficient and we do not have extra revelation such as prophecy today.

The Confession lists the biblical books which, given by inspiration of God, are the Word of God in written form. The authors of the Confession did not believe in partial inspiration, but that all of Scripture was inspired. It was the words which were God-breathed, (*inspired*) not merely the authors who were inspired,

> *"All Scripture is breathed out by God and profitable for teaching, for reproof, for correction, and for training in righteousness . . ."* (II Timothy 3:16),

> *". . . knowing this first of all, that no prophecy of Scripture comes from someone's own interpretation"* (II Peter 1:20).

Confession 1.3

> The books usually called the Apocrypha are not divinely inspired and are not part of the canon of Scripture. They therefore have no authority in the church of God and are not to be valued or used as anything other than human writings.[1]

The Apocrypha was not recognised as a part of Scripture. The term 'Apocrypha' refers to religious writings which were included in the Greek version of the Old Testament as well as the Latin Bible. The Jewish authorities and the Protestant church never regarded them as

[1] Luke 24:27, 44; Romans 3:2; II Peter 1:21.

part of Scripture, which is part of the Canon. Roman Catholicism has always included them in their list of Scriptures, but call them 'deuterocanonical'. These writings have no special authority – they are merely human compilations. For this reason they should not be included with the Bible or read in public worship as Scripture.

Confession 1.4

> The Bible speaks authoritatively and so deserves to be believed and obeyed. This authority does not depend on the testimony of any man or church but completely on God, its author, who is himself truth. The Bible therefore is to be accepted as true, because it is the word of God.[1]

In the fourth paragraph (1.4) the authority of Scripture is discussed. The reason why the Bible is accepted as the rule for our lives is because God is its author. We do not accept it because the church or some human authority says so. The Scriptures are above the church – they create it, not the reverse. Again it is not a scholar who comes to Scripture and tells us what parts we can accept, rather all scholarship must come under its authority. If an expert says that we cannot accept the story of Adam and Eve because modern science teaches that it is out of date, then the believer is to be ruled by the teaching of Scripture.

Confession 1.5

> We may be influenced by the testimony of the church to value the Bible highly and reverently,[2] and Scripture itself shows in so many ways that it is God's word; for example, in its spiritual subject matter, in the effectiveness of its teaching, the majesty of its style, the agreement of all its parts, its unified aim from beginning to end (to give all glory to God), the full revelation it makes of the only way of man's salvation, its many other incomparably outstanding features, and its complete perfection. However, we are completely persuaded and assured of the infallible truth and divine authority of the Bible only by the inward working of the Holy Spirit, who testifies by and with the word in our hearts.[3]

While many of the things listed in this paragraph (1.5) may convince us that Scripture is unique, they will not convince us of the

[1] II Peter 1:19, 21; II Timothy 3:16; I John 5:9; I Thessalonians 2:13.
[2] I Timothy 3:15.
[3] I John 2:20, 27; John 16:13-14; I Corinthians 2:10-12; Isaiah 59:21.

fact it is the Word of God. It is the Holy Spirit who convinces us of that. The Bible does not become the Word of God to us through the work of the Spirit, rather it is objectively the Word of God due to divine inspiration and we are convinced of this through the work of the Spirit in our hearts.

Confession 1.8

> The Old Testament in Hebrew (the native language of the ancient people of God) and the New Testament in Greek (the language most widely known internationally at the time the New Testament was written) were directly inspired by God and have been kept uncontaminated throughout time by his special care and providence.[1] They are therefore authentic and are to be the church's ultimate source of appeal in every religious controversy.[2] The original languages of the Bible, however, are not understood by all of God's people. But all of God's people have a right to and interest in the Bible, and God himself commands them to read it thoroughly with awe and reverence for him.[3] Consequently the Bible should be translated into the native language of every people to whom it is introduced.[4] Then, the word of God will live fully in everyone; everyone will be able to worship God in an acceptable way;[5] and all believers may have hope through the endurance and the encouragement of the Bible.[6]

The subject of 'inspiration' is taken up again in the eighth paragraph (1.8). The original documents of the Bible were given by the immediate inspiration of God. While we do not have the originals, God has in his providence kept the copies pure so they can be regarded as authentic and therefore reliable. It is also advocated that the Bible should be translated into the language of every nation. All believers have the right to read and search the Scriptures for themselves, so that they can live godly lives.

---

1. Matthew 5:18.
2. Isaiah 8:20; Acts 15:15; John 5:39, 46.
3. John 5:39.
4. I Corinthians 14:6, 9, 11-12, 24, 27-28.
5. Colossians 3:16.
6. Romans 15:4.

The Bible is sufficient in all matters of Belief and Behaviour

Confession 1.6

> The whole purpose of God about everything pertaining to his own glory and to man's salvation, faith, and life is either explicitly stated in the Bible or may be deduced as inevitably and logically following from it. Nothing is at any time to be added to the Bible, either from new revelations of the Spirit or from traditions of men.[1] Nevertheless, we do recognize that the inward illumination of the Spirit of God is necessary for a saving understanding of the things which are revealed in the word.[2] We also recognize that some provisions for the worship of God and the government of the church are similar to secular activities and organizations; these are to be directed according to our natural understanding and our Christian discretion and should conform to the general rules of the word, which are always to be observed.[3]

The sixth paragraph (1.6) teaches that Scripture is sufficient for all matters of belief and conduct. Note the wording: *The whole purpose of God about everything pertaining to his own glory and to man's salvation, faith, and life is either explicitly stated in the Bible or may be deduced as inevitably and logically following from it.* The Bible does not give in detail how to live in a technological age, but principles are set down which apply to every age. The Old Testament taught for example that if your enemy's donkey wandered off and you found it, you should take it back to him,

> *"If you meet your enemy's ox or his donkey going astray, you shall bring it back to him"* (Exodus 23:4ff).

The principle here being that you are to care for your enemy's property. So if his car is stolen and you find it, you are to ensure that it is returned to him. This is what the Confession means by: *is either explicitly stated in the Bible or may be deduced.*

Warning is given against adding to the Scriptures by: *new revelations of the Spirit or from traditions of men.* The Scriptures are complete and give us all the information we need to live for God in this

---

1 II Timothy 3:15-17; Galatians 1:8-9; II Thessalonians 2:2.
2 John 6:45; I Corinthians 2:9-12.
3 I Corinthians 11:13-14, 14:26,40.

world. We do not need so-called words of prophecy, nor are we to be bound by church tradition.

Authority is not 'the Bible plus tradition' but Scripture alone. The phrase, *'or from traditions of men'* is in the Confession because of the emphasis by Roman Catholicism on tradition.

While the Confession denies the authority of so called revelations of the Spirit, it does acknowledge the need of the Spirit to enable us to understand the Word of God, *we do recognize that the inward illumination of the Spirit of God is necessary for a saving understanding of the things which are revealed in the word.* It is worthy of note that the word '*saving*' is used here. Men can have a head knowledge of biblical teaching, but the Spirit is required if that knowledge is to be saving.

Not every detail of worship or church government for example, is included in the Bible. These finer details are to be worked out using common sense, under the guidance of the general rule of the Word. Examples would be that a church is to have elders, although the number is not set down in the Bible.

Again, we are to meet to worship God. The time of the service or the exact order of worship is not given in Scripture, but I Corinthians 14:40 must always apply!

> *"But all things should be done decently and in order"*
> (I Corinthians 14:40).

Confession 1.7

> The meanings of all the passages in the Bible are not equally obvious, nor is any individual passage equally clear to everyone.[1] However, everything which we have to know, believe, and observe in order to be saved is so clearly presented and revealed somewhere in the Bible that the uneducated as well as the educated can sufficiently understand it by the proper use of the ordinary means of grace.[2]

There are some things in the Scriptures which are difficult to understand, yet the way of salvation is clear. There is no need to be an expert to discover this for it lies on the very surface of Scripture. The phrase, '*use of the ordinary means*' (1.7) refers to reading the Bible, listening to preaching and so forth. We do not need lights from heaven, extraordinary signs, or visions. The inner illumination of the

---

[1] II Peter 3:16.
[2] Psalm 119:105, 130.

Spirit is all that is required.

Confession 1.9

> The infallible standard for the interpretation of the Bible is the Bible itself. And so any question about the true and complete sense of a passage in the Bible (which is a unified whole) can be answered by referring to other passages which speak more clearly.[1]

The subject of biblical interpretation is covered briefly in the ninth paragraph (1.9), where the principle of harmony is advocated. The Bible does not contradict itself. To understand Scripture we compare Scripture with Scripture, the difficult parts to be interpreted in the light of those passages which are clearly understood. A portion of Scripture has only one correct interpretation. It is not a matter of taking out of it what we want.

Confession 1.10

> The Holy Spirit speaking in the Bible is the supreme judge of all religious controversies, all decisions of religious councils, all the opinions of ancient writers, all human teachings, and every private opinion.[2] We are to be satisfied with the judgment of him who is and can be the only judge.

In the last paragraph (1.10) of this chapter we are told that the Scriptures are the final court of appeal and in all controversies of religion the church is to appeal to them. In any doctrinal disagreement, it is not even the Confession we go to as final judge, but the Scriptures. The Confession emphasises that all writers, creeds and church councils come under the judgement of Scripture. It is not the word of any General Assembly which is infallible, but the Bible.

The phrase, '*The Holy Spirit speaking in the Bible*' refers to the fact that God's voice is heard in the Bible, not through some special word of prophecy or the voice of the church. God speaks to his church through the Scriptures, not apart from them.

With this foundation laid, the Confession goes on to discuss other doctrines found in the infallible Word.

---

1 II Peter 1:20-21; Acts 15:15-16.
2 Matthew 22:29, 31; Ephesians 2:20 with Acts 28:25.

Cross references with the Catechisms:

Shorter: 2, 3. Larger: 2-5.

To think over and discuss:

1. How does the Confession's teaching on Scripture reflect the character of God in terms of his truthfulness, power and love?
2. How is the sufficiency of Scripture being denied today?

HIS CHARACTER

Ref. Confession Chapter 2 – God and the Holy Trinity

In this study you will discover:

- There is only one God and he is great
- God is the source of all things and does not need his creation
- God is Triune

This is a chapter of the Confession which should be read on our knees. It gives us an awesome picture of God which stands as a counterbalance to the chummy God in much of today's Christianity. In brief compass, the chapter seeks to reflect the biblical teaching on the character of God. This it does without the speculation of many of the mediaeval writers.

There is only one God and he is great

Confession 2.1

There is only one[1] living and true God,[2] who is infinite in being and perfection,[3] a completely pure spirit,[4] invisible,[5] without parts[6] or emotions,[7] unchangeable[8], immensely vast,[9] eternal,[10] beyond our full understanding[11] almighty,[12] completely wise,[13] completely holy,[14] completely free,[15] and completely absolute.[16] He works everything according to the purpose of his own unchangeable and completely righteous will[17] for his own glory.[18] He is completely loving,[19] gracious, merciful, and long-suffering. He overflows with goodness and truth. He forgives wickedness, transgression, and sin,[20] and rewards those who diligently seek him.[21] His judgments are completely just and awesome;[22] he hates all sin[23] and will not acquit the guilty.[1]

---

1 Deuteronomy 6:4; I Corinthians: 8:4, 6.
2 I Thessalonians 1:9; Jeremiah 10:10.
3 Job 11:7-9, 26:14.
4 John 4:24.
5 I Timothy 1:17.
6 Deuteronomy 4:15-16; John 4:24; Luke 24:39.
7 Acts 14:11, 15.
8 James 1:17; Malachi 3:6.
9 I Kings 8:27; Jeremiah 23:23-24.
10 Psalm 90:2; I Timothy 1:17.
11 Psalm 145:3.
12 Genesis 17:1; Revelation 4:8.
13 Romans 16:27.
14 Isaiah 6:3; Revelation 4:8.
15 Psalm 115:3.
16 Exodus 3:14.
17 Ephesians 1:11.
18 Proverbs 16:4; Romans 11:36.
19 I John 4:8, 16.
20 Exodus 34:6-7.
21 Hebrews 11:6.
22 Nehemiah 9:32-33.
23 Psalm 5:5-6.

The Confession teaches that God is unique. There are not several gods but only one. The gods of other faiths are false, only the God of the Bible is true. All religions do not stand on the same level. It is interesting to note that the Confession does not try to prove the existence of God. In this it follows Scripture and starts with the fact that God is. To seek to prove his existence reduces God to the level of creation and he only "exists by our proof"; that is the height of arrogance!

This God is without limit *infinite in being and perfection*. He is completely perfect! He is spirit, therefore he is *invisible* and is without a body.

> "*. . . God is spirit, and those who worship him must worship in spirit and truth*" (John 4:24).

When Scripture speaks, for example, of the eye or the arm of God, it is just using our limited human language to describe him. It is like baby talk and we are the babies whom Scripture is addressing. This method of speaking about God is called "anthropomorphism"[2]. To say that God is without emotion does not mean that God is unfeeling, he certainly has feelings,

> "*The LORD passed before him and proclaimed, 'The Lord, the Lord, a God merciful and gracious, slow to anger, and abounding in steadfast love and faithfulness . . .'*" (Exodus 34:6).

Rather the thought is that he cannot be hurt by his creation against his will. His will controls his emotions, the emotions do not rule his will.

Immutable does not merely imply that God does not change, but that he cannot change,

> "*Every good gift and every perfect gift is from above, coming down from the Father of lights with whom there is no variation or shadow due to change*" (James 1:17).

He is also everywhere and all creation is in his presence (*immensely vast*); he is outside of time and therefore has no beginning or end (*eternal*). While he is *beyond our full understanding*, it does not mean that we can understand nothing about God. Otherwise it would have been pointless of God to reveal himself. We can of course say things that are true about God, but we cannot say everything. He is God, we are creatures! He is, as the Confession teaches, Almighty God!

He is also *completely wise* and *completely holy*. Holy means to be separate, to be different. He cannot be compared to anything or anyone in creation. This is the reason for the second commandment. He is holy, therefore he cannot stand sin,

> "*In the year that King Uzziah died I saw the Lord sitting upon a throne, high and lifted up; and the train of his robe filled the temple*" (Isaiah 6:1ff).

He is also *completely free*, that is, nothing or no one controls him or forces

---

1 Nehemiah 1:2-3; Exodus 34:7.

2 The attribution of human characteristics and qualities to non-human beings, objects, natural, or supernatural phenomena. God, animals etc.

him to act in a certain way. He acts according to his own desire. *Completely absolute* implies that he is the foundation of everything, he depends on nothing. He works everything out in accordance with his own *righteous* and *unchanging* plan and all *for his own glory* (cf. Confession Chapter 3).

The Confession states, along with other aspects of his character, that God is *loving* and *gracious*. This maintains the biblical balance between the "otherness" of God and his nearness in love. He is also the rewarder of those who diligently seek him. Man's responsibility is emphasised here. There must be the diligent seeking after his salvation.

> *"You will seek me and find me, when you seek me with all your heart"* (Jeremiah 29:13).

At the same time God is just. He hates sin and must punish the guilty. God cannot turn a blind eye to sin. This stands in contrast to much popular thinking about God, that he will forgive everybody, for that is his business.

God is the source of all things and does not need his Creation

Confession 2.2

God has all life,[1] glory,[2] goodness,[3] and blessedness[4] in and of himself. He alone is all-sufficient in and unto himself, nor does he need any of his creations[5] or derive any glory from them. Rather, he manifests his own glory in, by, unto, and on them.[6] He is the only source of all being, by whom, through whom, and to whom everything exists.[7] He has completely sovereign dominion over all things and does with, to, or for them whatever he pleases.[8] Everything is revealed and completely open to him.[9] His knowledge is infinite, infallible, and does not depend on any created being,[10] so that to him nothing is conditional or uncertain.[11] He is completely holy in all his purposes, works, and commands.[12] To him is due whatever worship, service, or obedience he is pleased to require from angels, human beings, and all other creatures.[13]

It has been argued by some that God needed his creation, that he was in a

1 John 5:26.
2 Acts 7:2.
3 Psalm 119:68.
4 I Timothy 6:15; Romans 9:5.
5 Acts 17:24-25.
6 Job 22:2, 3.
7 Romans 11:36.
8 Revelation 4:11; I Timothy 6:15; Daniel 4:25, 35.
9 Hebrews 4:13.
10 Romans 11:33-34; Psalm 147:5.
11 Acts 15:18; Ezekiel 11:5.
12 Psalm 145:17; Romans 7:12.
13 Revelation 5:12-14.

sense incomplete without it. Our Confession exposes this as false thinking, *God has all life, glory, goodness, and blessedness in and of himself.* In other words God was complete and happy without any universe, he does not need it to complete his joy. He is perfect. His glory is declared in his creation but it does not add glory to him.

He is the source of all life, every creature from the smallest to the greatest owes its life to him.

> *"He set the earth on its foundations, so that it should never be moved.*
>
> *You covered it with the deep as with a garment; the waters stood above the mountains . . . You cause the grass to grow for the livestock and plants for man to cultivate, that he may bring forth food from the earth and wine to gladden the heart of man, oil to make his face shine and bread to strengthen man's heart . . .*
>
> *O Lord, how manifold are your works! In wisdom have you made them all; the earth is full of your creatures.*
>
> *Here is the sea, great and wide, which teems with creatures innumerable, living things both small and great . . ."* (Psalm 104).

They are his creation, therefore he rules over them. They are in his loving hand and he can do what he wishes with them.

Our knowledge is limited and subject to error. God's knowledge is total *(infinite)* and without error *(infallible)*. It is not conditional on our actions. God does not have to wait to discover our actions so that he can take counter actions, he is never taken by surprise. *His purposes,* or plan, *works, and commands* are all holy since they come from a holy God.

It is God who must have our *worship*, *service* and *obedience*. It is he who states what he requires in these areas. We are not free to serve or worship him as we wish, only in the way his Word demands. The Confession is teaching here that it is God, through Scripture, who regulates our conduct in every area of life. God is sovereign over everything.

God is Triune

Confession 2.3

> In the unity of the Godhead there are three persons, having one substance, power, and eternity: God the Father, God the Son, and God the Holy Spirit.[1] The Father exists. He is not generated and does not come from any source. The Son is eternally generated from the Father,[2] and the Holy Spirit eternally comes from the Father and the Son.[3]

The Doctrine of the Trinity has been the subject of much speculation. The Confession gives us a brief statement of the doctrine,

---

1 I John 5:7; Matthew 3:16-17, 28:19; II Corinthians 13:14.
2 John 1:14, 18.
3 John 15:26; Galatians 4:6.

which is in keeping with the Scriptures. This may be summarised as follows:

The phrase, '*unity of the Godhead*' teaches that there is one God, not three as some people think the doctrine of the Trinity teaches.[1] He expresses himself eternally in three Persons. The word '*person*' is difficult for it does not mean distinct individuals as is commonly used today, rather it refers to three self-distinctions within the divine being. Fellowship is possible between each person since each is self-conscious, yet they are *one substance, power and eternity*. The word "*substance*" is not a good choice because today it invariably means something material. God is Spirit and we must not think of him being physical "stuff". It is for this reason that it would be better if the word "essence" were used in place of '*substance*'.

Each person of the Trinity is fully God:

- *the Father* is God

  > *"yet for us there is one God, the Father, from whom are all things and for whom we exist, and one Lord, Jesus Christ, through whom are all things and through whom we exist"* (I Corinthians 8:6; cf. John 5:19ff).

- *the Son* is God

  > *"And the Word became flesh and dwelt among us, and we have seen his glory, glory as of the only Son from the Father, full of grace and truth . . ."*
  > (John 1:14, 20:28; cf. Philippians 2:6).

- *the Holy Spirit* is God

  > *"But Peter said, "Ananias, why has Satan filled your heart to lie to the Holy Spirit and to keep back for yourself part of the proceeds of the land?*
  >
  > *While it remained unsold, did it not remain your own? And after it was sold, was it not at your disposal? Why is it that you have contrived this deed in your heart? You have not lied to man but to God . . ."*
  > (Acts 5:3-4; cf. Jeremiah 31:31; cf. Hebrews 10:15).

In other words, all the things which we can say about God are true of each person of the Trinity, for example, holiness, eternity, total knowledge, love.

The Confession also teaches that the Father is the eternal origin of

---

[1] "Hear, O Israel: The Lord our God, the Lord is one" (Deuteronomy 6:4).

the eternal Son and Spirit. The Son is eternally begotten of the Father and the Holy Spirit proceeds from the Father and the Son. We stand here at the very border of human language in seeking to state the first great mystery of being.

The Confession enables us to avoid two great pitfalls that recur in the history of the church. One is to state that the Son and the Spirit are less than the Father, which denies their true divinity. The other is that Father, Son and Spirit are only successive revelations of the one divine being. This teaches that the Father manifested himself as the Son and then as the Holy Spirit, thus denying the self-distinctions within the divine being. This is, of course, at variance with the Scriptures where Jesus prayed to the Father and refers to the glory he had with the Father before the world was,

> *"When Jesus had spoken these words, he lifted up his eyes to heaven, and said, 'Father, the hour has come; glorify your Son that the Son may glorify you . . .'"* (John 17:1).

The doctrine of the Trinity is basic to our salvation. If it is denied then it means that Jesus was not God, and that at Golgotha, the Father did not pour out his wrath on his Son. If this is so, the doctrine of redemption falls to pieces.

Cross references with the Catechisms:

Shorter: 4-6; Larger: 6-11.

To think over and discuss:

1. What sort of errors and wrong ideas do we have which could be corrected by Biblical teaching on God?
2. How can we tackle the trend today, of treating God simply as a close friend at the expense of the reverence and awe which is due to God?
3. Can we have fellowship with groups that apparently preach the gospel and yet deny the historic teaching on the Trinity?

HIS GREAT PLAN

Ref. Confession Chapter 3 – God's Eternal Decrees

In this study you will discover:

- God has a master plan which includes all events in the universe
- God has chosen a multitude of men and angels to eternal life
- If a person is lost it is due to their own sin

This chapter of the Confession has been unpalatable for many, and an area of controversy for others. It has received a bad press, but unfairly so since it is only teaching that God made a plan. It seems that we expect people to make plans for the future, for example retirement or an army going into battle, but not God.

God has a master plan, which includes all events in the universe

Confession 3.1

> From all eternity and by the completely wise and holy purpose of his own will, God has freely and unchangeably ordained whatever happens.[1] This ordainment does not mean, however, that God is the author of sin (he is not),[2] that he represses the will of his created beings, or that he takes away the freedom or contingency of secondary causes. Rather, the will of created beings and the freedom and contingency of secondary causes are established by him.[3]

God has made an eternal plan which includes all events. The Confession is very careful in its choice of words, so these matters are worthy of close attention.

It starts with God. He is the origin of all things, nothing or no one is prior to him, and he alone is eternal. His plan is eternal, being made before the creation of anything including time. This is one reason why it must include all events.

The plan is *wise and holy*. If God had not made a plan, then that would have been foolishness, but our God is wise, therefore he made a plan for the universe which is the best possible plan. It is holy,

[1] Ephesians 1:11; Romans 11:33; Hebrews 6:17; Romans 9:15, 18.
[2] James 1:13, 17; I John 1:5.
[3] Acts 2:23; Matthew 17:12; Acts 4:27-28; John 19:11; Proverbs 16:33.

implying that nothing God has ordered is sinful since that would be a contradiction of his holy character.

The phrase, *'the completely wise and holy purpose of his own will'* refers to deliberation within the Trinity. In other words, God does not act unreasonably when he decides what will happen. The will of God, or what he decides will happen, is wise, holy and reasonable. We are not in the hands of an evil, foolish and capricious deity!

God also acts freely in making his plan. Nothing has forced him to plan it in the way he has. He acts according to his own desires. This rules out the whole business of fate, which is impersonal and underlines the fact that we are in the plan of a personal and loving God.

The Plan of God is unchangeable. This follows from the fact that God is perfect and perfection never needs change. It also covers all things, whatsoever comes to pass. If this were not so, it would mean that there are events which happen independent of God, over which he has no control. This would deny his sovereignty.

The biblical basis for this belief that God plans all things is in passages like:

> *"In him we have obtained an inheritance, having been predestined according to the purpose of him who works all things according to the counsel of his will . . ."* (Ephesians 1:11),
>
> *"O Lord, how manifold are your works! In wisdom have you made them all; the earth is full of your creatures . . ."* (Psalm 104:24ff),
>
> *"Your eyes saw my unformed substance; in your book were written, every one of them, the days that were formed for me, when as yet there was none of them"* (Psalm 139:16),
>
> *"But as he was speaking, the king said to him, 'Have we made you a royal counsellor? Stop! Why should you be struck down?' So the prophet stopped, but said, 'I know that God has determined to destroy you, because you have done this and have not listened to my counsel.'"* (II Chronicles 25:16),
>
> *"Are not two sparrows sold for a penny? And not one of them will fall to the ground apart from your Father"* (Matthew 10:29).

The objections which are often made imply that this type of teaching makes God the author of sin and destroys human freedom. The second part of the first paragraph (3.1) addresses this objection with its statement: '*This ordainment does not mean, however, that God is the author of sin (he is not), that he represses the will of his created beings . . .*'

While sinful things happen in the world, God is not their author. He is holy and therefore he cannot sin. Evil is allowed in his plan, yet it is not eternal and he did not originate it. Our tiny minds cannot reconcile these two great truths of Scripture that God is holy and yet evil, of which he is not the author, is interwoven in his plan. We must accept both by faith cf. Confession 6.1.

No one is forced to sin. If they do so, they do it freely, it is what they wish to do. No person can turn round and say God forced me to sin. It is included in his plan, but men are responsible for their sinful actions. In the death of Jesus his accusers were accountable for his death, although it was a part of the plan of God.

> *"this Jesus, delivered up according to the definite plan and foreknowledge of God, you crucified and killed by the hands of lawless men"* (Acts 2:23).

The phrase, '*or that he takes away the freedom or contingency of secondary causes. Rather, the will of created beings and the freedom and contingency* [dependence] *of secondary causes are established by him'*, is an important statement but requires some explanation.

God, being the "First Cause", may act directly or by the use of means. These means are "Second Causes". He may act for example directly and heal a person or he may heal through medical care, this care would be the *'secondary causes'*.

A matter is said to be contingent if it will only occur under certain conditions. It is dependent on certain happenings. Suppose a large rock was at the edge of a cliff, it will not topple over unless it gets a strong enough push. God's plan allows for the fact that X does not occur unless Y happens (the push). While God is in overall charge he is not the direct cause of all events, because God has given man the ability to make decisions. The plan says the rock will fall, but God does not push it, force Y does.

'Secondary Causes' are established by the plan of God. Why should this be? Clearly, it is only because God has made a plan, that we can be sure that event X (the rock falling) will always have been brought about by Y (the push). In other words, without the push the rock cannot fall, so God brings about the push (Y), a secondary cause, in order for God's plan to come to fulfilment. It is because the law of gravity is a part of God's plan that we can be certain that the rock when pushed will fall over the cliff. If we deny the plan of God, we are in the arms of chance and then nothing can be certain. The rock when pushed may as well float in the air. The plan of God alone makes science possible.

This does not mean that God is not free to act differently to the normal, as he does in miracles.

Confession 3.2

> Although God knows whatever may or can happen under all possible circumstances,[1] he has not ordered anything because he foresaw it in the future as something which would happen under such circumstances.[2]

The second paragraph of this section rules out the popular idea that God looked into the future and saw what was going to happen and made it his plan. The problem with this theory is that God is not in charge, he is a prisoner of events in his own universe. It denies him both his freedom and sovereignty. If this were the case, there would be no point in prayer since God would be the prisoner of the future. The Confession correctly rejects this popular misconception.

God has chosen a number of men and angels to eternal life

Confession 3.3

> In order to manifest his glory God has ordered that some men and angels[3] be predestined to everlasting life and that others should be foreordained to everlasting death.[4]

In this (3.3) and the following paragraphs it is taught that the eternal destiny of men and angels was included in the plan of God. The reason given is to reveal the glory of God. This is as far as Scripture will allow us to go and since God is wise, this must have been the best way to declare his glory. In this chapter the word *predestined* is used with reference to *life* and *foreordained* with reference to *death*. This is only in the interest of consistency. There is nothing in Scripture, or the meaning of the words, to require them to be used in this exclusive sense.

There is a difference in the purpose of the election, or predestination, of men and angels. Angels were chosen to prevent them from falling into sin, while men are chosen to rescue them from sin.

> *"In the presence of God and of Christ Jesus and of the elect angels I charge you to keep these rules without prejudging, doing nothing*

---

1 Acts 15:18; I Samuel 23:11-12; Matthew 11:21, 23.
2 Romans 9:11, 13, 16, 18.
3 I Timothy 5:21; Matthew 25:41.
4 Romans 9:22-23; Ephesians 1:5-6; Proverbs 16:4.

from partiality" (I Timothy 5:21).

Confession 3.4

This predestination and foreordination of angels and men are precise and unchangeable. The number and identity of angels and men in each group are certain, definite, and unalterable.[1]

The fourth paragraph (3.4) teaches that it was not only a number of men and angels which God chose but certain individuals. This is the force of the *precise and unchangeable* design. Election does not mean that our God deals with people in the mass but rather his dealing with people is personal and individual. Again it is important to realise that it is not a small number which God has chosen but *"a great multitude that no one could count"* (Revelation 7:9). Abraham was told that his offspring would be as the stars in the heavens.

Confession 3.5

Before the creation of the world, according to his eternal, unchangeable plan and the hidden purpose and good pleasure of his will, God has chosen in Christ those of mankind who are predestined to life and to everlasting glory.[2] He has done this solely out of his own mercy and love and completely to the praise of his wonderful grace.[3] This choice was completely independent of his foresight of how his created beings would be or act. Neither their faith nor good works nor perseverance had any part in influencing his selection.[4]

A number of important points are made in this paragraph (3.5) which discusses the election of men. This choice of men unto everlasting life is eternal and therefore occurred before creation. It is also *unchangeable* since God does not need to nor can he change his plan. It is secret, therefore we are not to pry into it. This is God's side, he alone knows the number and the identity of the elect. It is our duty to be guided by and obey the revealed will of God 'Scripture' and not try to discover what he has not revealed. In evangelism we seek to win others to Christ by declaring the gospel to all, with the certainty that God will call sinners to himself.

The reason God has chosen people is for his *good pleasure*. In other words God delights in saving sinners, it brings him joy. Election

---

1 II Timothy 2:19; John 13:18.
2 Ephesians 1:4, 9, 11; Romans 8:30; II Timothy 1:9; 1 Thessalonians 5:9.
3 Ephesians 1:6, 12.
4 Romans 9:11, 13, 16; Ephesians 1: 4, 9.

is in Christ. This means a person is **not** saved apart from Jesus. It gives the lie to the popular idea that if I am chosen I will be saved no matter what I do. No, a person is chosen in Christ and is saved through belonging to him[1]

> *"Blessed be the God and Father of our Lord Jesus Christ, who has blessed us in Christ with every spiritual blessing in the heavenly places, even as he chose us in him before the foundation of the world, that we should be holy and blameless before him. In love he predestined us for adoption as sons through Jesus Christ, according to the purpose of his will, to the praise of his glorious grace, with which he has blessed us in the Beloved. In him we have redemption through his blood, the forgiveness of our trespasses, according to the riches of his grace, which he lavished upon us, in all wisdom and insight making known to us the mystery of his will, according to his purpose, which he set forth in Christ as a plan for the fullness of time, to unite all things in him, things in heaven and things on earth"* (Ephesians 1:3-10).

The Confession underlines that there was nothing in sinners to cause God to choose them. It is not faith, works, perseverance or anything else. The popular idea of election that God looked forward and saw who was going to believe and chose them, is contradicted here. A moment's thought will show that the Confession is correct. Man is a sinner unable to do anything for his own salvation therefore God must act first if sinners are to be saved. He must choose, for sinners will not choose him.

> *"For to set the mind on the flesh is death, but to set the mind on the Spirit is life and peace. For the mind that is set on the flesh is hostile to God, for it does not submit to God's law; indeed, it cannot. Those who are in the flesh cannot please God . . ."* (Romans 8:6-8ff).
>
> *"The natural person does not accept the things of the Spirit of God, for they are folly to him, and he is not able to understand them because they are spiritually discerned"* (I Corinthians 2:14).
>
> *"Jesus answered him, 'Truly, truly, I say to you, unless one is born again he cannot see the kingdom of God'"* (John 3:3).

see Confession 6.4 p67,

> *"For those whom he foreknew he also predestined to be conformed to the image of his Son, in order that he might be the firstborn among many brothers"* (Romans 8:29).

---

1 "Do not labour for the food that perishes, but for the food that endures to eternal life, which the Son of Man will give to you. For on him God the Father has set his seal" (John 6:27).

"No one can come to me unless the Father who sent me draws him. And I will raise him up on the last day" (John 6:44).

Creator and Controller

Ref. Confession Chapter 4 – Creation and
Ref. Confession Chapter 5 – Providence

In this study you will discover:

- God created all things out of nothing
- God is in charge of all events
- God allows evil but is not the author of sin

God created all things out of nothing

Confession 4.1

> In the beginning it pleased God the Father, Son, and Holy Spirit,[1] to create the world out of nothing in order to reveal the glory of his eternal power, wisdom, and goodness.[2] He made everything in the world, visible and invisible, in the space of six days, and it was very good.[3]

Creation was the work of the Trinity; *Father, Son and Holy Spirit* were all involved. According to the Confession creation was to display *the glory of* God's *power, wisdom and goodness*. From this we can infer that God did not have to make the world because he needed it. He, as Triune God, was complete within his being. It was to show forth his glory that he created the universe.

It is because of this that creation tells us that there is a God, it is revelation,

> *"For his invisible attributes, namely, his eternal power and divine nature, have been clearly perceived, ever since the creation of the world, in the things that have been made. So they are without excuse"* (Romans 1:20).

We see in creation the eternal power of God. Some power had to bring it into being, and that power had to be eternal, for nothing produces nothing. The eternal God alone can create out of nothing. As we study the universe and discover more of its wonder, we are amazed at the wisdom of God. The goodness of God is displayed in how he has made provision for all his creatures,

> *"You make springs gush forth in the valleys; they flow between the hills; they give drink to every beast of the field; the wild donkeys quench*

---

[1] Hebrews 1:2; John 1:2-3; Genesis 1:2; Job 26:13, 33:4.
[2] Romans 1:20; Jeremiah 10:12; Psalms 104:24, 33:5 6.
[3] [Genesis 1] Hebrews 11:3; Colossians 1:16; Acts 17:24.

> *their thirst.*
> *Beside them the birds of the heavens dwell; they sing among the branches"* (Psalm 104:10-12).

Creation speaks,

> *"The heavens declare the glory of God, and the sky above proclaims his handiwork"* (Psalm 19:1ff),

but people refuse to listen, holding down the truth and preferring to believe a lie,

> *"For the wrath of God is revealed from heaven against all ungodliness and unrighteousness of men, who by their unrighteousness suppress the truth"* (Romans 1:18ff).

The Confession teaches us that God made all things out of nothing. It says this happened in the beginning. There had to be a beginning. Time had to be created. Only God is eternal, not the universe. It is subject to time, he is not. It was made out of nothing. There was nothing apart from God in the beginning, no energy, no matter, no space nor time, he created it all. To say that matter, or energy always existed is to place them on a level with God. But there cannot be two eternities. God not only made what we see, but also the invisible world of spirits. This would include the order of angels.

The phrase, '*in the space of six days*' (4.1) causes some people concern. There is no problem in believing that an all-powerful God could have created the universe in six, twenty-four hour days. Yet there is nothing in the meaning of the word or its context in Genesis 1 to say that it must have been twenty-four hours. The sun which governs the duration of a solar day was not created until the fourth day

> *"And God set them in the expanse of the heavens to give light on the earth, to rule over the day and over the night, and to separate the light from the darkness. And God saw that it was good"*
> (Genesis 1:17-18).

It is generally agreed that the word "day" as used in Scripture means our normal day. The Confession and Scripture do rule out, however, that the universe was produced by time and chance and just evolved over billions of years.

The Confession affirms that the creation was all very good, there was no evil or sin built into the universe. This is one thing which counts against God using the evolutionary process to make the world since it involves death which is a result of sin.

> *"Therefore, just as sin came into the world through one man, and death through sin, and so death spread to all men because all sinned . . ."*
> (Romans 5:12).

The second paragraph, of Confession chapter four (4.2) which deals with human creation, will be discussed later.

God is in charge of all events

God did not make his universe and then abandon it, as some taught at the time the Confession was written. He is not a remote, uncaring God and yet at the same time he is separate from his creation, not a part of it. The Confession avoids these two errors known as deism[1] and pantheism[2].

Confession 5.1

> GOD, who created everything, also upholds everything.[3] He directs, regulates, and governs every creature, action, and thing,[4] from the greatest to the least,[5] by his completely wise and holy providence.[6] He does so in accordance with his infallible foreknowledge[7] and the voluntary, unchangeable purpose of his own will,[8] all to the praise of the glory of his wisdom, power, justice, goodness, and mercy.[9]

This first section of Confession chapter five (5.1) teaches that everything is under the direction, disposal and rule of God. There is nothing even to the very edge of the universe which is not under his control. This control is exercised according to his plan the *unchangeable purpose of his own will*. He is free to act as he wishes, he is not at the mercy of the forces of his creation. He is not the cosmic chess player merely countering the moves of men, he is in charge of the board and will ensure the 'game' will finish in his way.

This governing of all things is for the praise of his glory. It is to make creation praise him. Its description includes **justice** (what he does is right), **goodness** (it is also good), **mercy** (even his frown is tempered with mercy).

This rules out two popular opinions, **fate** and **chance**. God is in personal charge and events happen according to his **wisdom**, **justice** and **mercy**, not some impersonal, unfeeling fate. Chance too is ruled out. **If chance occurs then God is not in charge, and cannot be sovereign.** The Confession and Scripture teach that **he is in charge**

---

1 Deism – God created the world but does not intervene within it.
2 Pantheism – all is divine.
3 Hebrews 1:3.
4 Daniel 4:34-35; Psalm 135:6; Acts 17:25-26, 28; Job 38, 39, 40, 41.
5 Matthew 10:29-31.
6 Proverbs 15:3; Psalms 104:24, 145:17.
7 Acts 15:18; Psalm 94:8-11.
8 Ephesians 1:11; Psalm 33:10-11.
9 Isaiah 63:14; Ephesians 3:10; Romans 9:17; Genesis 45:7; Psalm 145:7.

even of the smallest details,

> *"Are not two sparrows sold for a penny? And not one of them will fall to the ground apart from your Father"* (Matthew 10:29).

Confession 5.2

> God is the first cause, and in relationship to him everything happens unchangeably and infallibly.[1] However, by this same providence, he orders things to happen from secondary causes. As a result of these secondary causes, some things must inevitably happen; others may or may not happen, depending on the voluntary intentions of the agents involved; and some things do not have to happen but may, depending on other conditions.[2]

In the second paragraph (5.2) we are told that although God is in charge this does not deny *secondary causes*. The fact that grain ripens is due to the sun, it is dependent on the sun, that is, it is *contingent*. God allows this process to happen under his rule. When a boy meets a girl in an apparent chance occurrence and through time they are married, the marriage was *contingent* on that 'chance' happening, which was not chance but under the control of God. The fact that water boils with the application of heat is said to be necessary. It cannot get colder since this is the way God has made things. God works out his plan through the things he has made including us. We act freely but God overrules for his own purpose. Joseph's brothers plan was evil, they acted freely but the Plan of God for his people was interwoven within it,

> *"As for you, you meant evil against me, but God meant it for good, to bring it about that many people should be kept alive, as they are today"* (Genesis 50:20).

Confession 5.3

> God uses ordinary means to work out his providence day by day.[3] But, as he pleases,[4] he may work without,[5] beyond,[6] or contrary to these means.

God normally acts through the things he has made, but he is free to bypass his normal means of operation if he so chooses. He may

1 Acts 2:23.
2 Genesis 8:22; Jeremiah 31:35; Exodus 21:13; Deuteronomy 19:5; I Kings 22:28, 34; Isaiah 10:6-7.
3 Acts 27:31, 44; Isaiah 55:10-11; Hosea 2:21-22.
4 Hosea 1:7; Matthew 4:4; Job 34:10.
5 Romans 4:19-21.
6 II Kings 6:6; Daniel 3:27.

heal a person through doctors or he may allow a person to die and bring them back to life as in the case of Lazarus (John 11). When God acts without means it is said to be a miracle. Some teach that miracles are impossible because they contradict the laws of nature (dead men do not live). This is to misunderstand the so-called laws of nature. They are part of God's plan, they work the way they do because a God of order is in charge of them moment by moment. God is not a prisoner of his own laws, he can act apart from them if he wishes. These laws are just the way that God has chosen to operate his universe, they are not like the moral laws which are part of his character. God cannot lie, since he is truth, but he can make a dead person live since that does not contradict his character. Miracles are just a different way of God acting and they too are part of his plan as much as the so called laws of nature, which are really God's normal working rules for his universe. **God rules his universe at his good pleasure, not at the dictates of man.**

God allows evil but he is not the author of sin

The question that is always asked when this subject is discussed is, "Does this not make God the author of sin?" The answer of the Confession as well as Scripture is a resounding **"No!"**

Confession 5.4

> God's providence reveals his almighty power, unknowable wisdom, and infinite goodness. His providence extends even to the fall and to all other sins of angels and men.[1] These sins are not simply allowed by God,[2] but are bound,[3] ordered, and governed by him in the fullness of his wisdom and power so that they fulfil his own holy purposes.[4] However, the sinfulness still belongs to the creature and does not proceed from God, whose holy righteousness does not and cannot cause or approve sin.[5]

While the providence of God includes the first *fall and all* the *sins of men and angels* (5.4), he is not the author of sin. While it is correct to say that God permitted sin, this is not a bare permission. It is under the control of God, so that he can order and ensure that even the evil acts of men fulfil his plan.

1 Romans 11:32-34; II Samuel 24:1 with I Chronicles 21:1; I Kings 22:22-23; I Chronicles 10:4, 13-14; II Samuel 16:10; Acts 2:23, 4:27-28.
2 Acts 14:16.
3 Psalm 76:10; II Kings 19:28.
4 Genesis 1:20; Isaiah 10: 6-7, 12.
5 James 1: 13-14, 17; I John 2:l6; Psalm 50:21.

Men in sinning do what they desire to do, but God so overrules it that even evil can be used for his Holy Plan. He does not cause them to sin nor does he approve of it. Judas is an example. He freely betrayed Jesus. What he did was sinful, yet it was a part of the Divine Plan for the salvation of the world. We must hold these two things together, although our understanding of them will never be complete. God directs all things including the free evil acts of men, yet he is not the author of sin nor does he approve of it.

The next two paragraphs (5.5 and 5.6) deal with providence and the sin of the godly and ungodly.

Confession 5.5

> In the fullness of his wisdom, righteousness, and grace God often allows his own children to be tempted in various ways and for a time to pursue the corruption of their own hearts. God does this to chastise them for their previous sins and to reveal to them the hidden strength of corruption and deceitfulness in their hearts, so that they may be humbled.[1] In addition to various other just and holy results, believers are thereby raised to a closer and more constant dependence on God for their support and are also made more alert in detecting and resisting opportunities to sin.[2]

This fifth paragraph teaches us that temptation and the evil desires of a believer's heart may be used of God to bring about an increase in holiness. The Confession lists a number of reasons for God doing this.

1. Chastening. His children cannot sin without the chastening hand of God to show he disapproves,

    "In your struggle against sin you have not yet resisted to the point of shedding your blood. And have you forgotten the exhortation that addresses you as sons?"

    "My son, do not regard lightly the discipline of the Lord, nor be weary when reproved by him" (Hebrews 12:4-5ff).

2. To teach them that although they are changed by grace, they are not perfect. There is still sin within, and though it does not rule it still seeks to ruin. This humbles us and causes us to cry out to God as Paul did for deliverance.

    "What then shall we say? That the law is sin? By no means! Yet if it had not been for the law, I would not have known sin.

---

1 II Chronicles 32:25-26, 31; II Samuel 24:1.
2 II Corinthians 12: 7-9; Psalms 73, 77:1, 10, 12; Mark 14:66-72 with John 21:15-17.

For I would not have known what it is to covet if the law had not said, 'You shall not covet'" (Romans 7:7).

"Wretched man that I am! Who will deliver me from this body of death? Thanks be to God through Jesus Christ our Lord! So then, I myself serve the law of God with my mind, but with my flesh I serve the law of sin" (Romans 7:24-25).

3. This process of exposing believers to temptation within and without has the purpose of making them depend on God more and make them watchful of the many temptations which come their way,

   "So to keep me from becoming conceited because of the surpassing greatness of the revelations, a thorn was given me in the flesh, a messenger of Satan to harass me, to keep me from becoming conceited" (II Corinthians 12:7ff).

Confession 5.6

> It is different for the wicked and the ungodly. As punishment for their previous sins, God, the righteous Judge, spiritually blinds and hardens them in their own sinfulness.[1] From them God not only withholds his grace, by which they might have been spiritually enlightened,[2] but sometimes he also withdraws whatever gift of spiritual understanding they already had[3] and deliberately exposes them to the opportunities for sinning which their corrupt natures naturally seek.[4] He thereby gives them over to their own desires, to the temptations of the world, and to the power of Satan,[5] and so it happens that they harden themselves even under those circumstances which God uses to soften others.[6]

In this paragraph (5.6) the thought turns to the ungodly. The wicked here are those who have been given God's warnings but refuse to repent. God then will often withdraw his grace because of the hardening of their hearts. In some cases the judgement of God will soften people in a temporary way, but when the judgement is past, they return to their evil ways.

"When he killed them, they sought him; they repented and sought

---

1 Romans 1:24, 26, 28, 11:7-8.
2 Deuteronomy 29:4.
3 Matthew 13:12, 25:29.
4 Deuteronomy 2:30; II Kings 8:12-13.
5 Psalm 81:11-12; II Thessalonians 2:10-12.
6 Exodus 7:3 with 8:15, 32; II Corinthians 2:15-16; Isaiah 8:14; I Peter 2:7-8; Isaiah 6:9-10 with Acts 28:26-27.

God earnestly" (Psalm 78:34ff).

God gives up such wicked people to their sin and their destruction is certain. For some people the day of grace is shorter than their time on earth.

> *"For the wrath of God is revealed from heaven against all ungodliness and unrighteousness of men, who by their unrighteousness suppress the truth"* (Romans 1:18ff).

The Confession also observes that these people often harden themselves under the means that would soften others. The goodness of God, the judgements of God, the warnings and the Word of God will bring many to faith, but others reject and rebel against these tokens of mercy and are therefore hardened by them.

> *"And he said, 'Go, and say to this people: Keep on hearing, but do not understand; keep on seeing, but do not perceive'"* (Isaiah 6:9ff).

Confession 5.7

> Just as the providence of God in general extends to every creature, so, in a very special way it takes care of his church and orders all things for her good.[1]

The final paragraph of this chapter teaches that while there is the general care of God for all people, there is his *special care* for the *church*. Indeed he rules *all things for* the *good of his church*,

> *"And he put all things under his feet and gave him as head over all things to the church, which is his body, the fullness of him who fills all in all"* (Ephesians 1:22-23ff).

Cross references with the Catechisms:

Shorter: 9, 11; Larger: 14-16, 18, 19.

To think over and discuss:

1. Does it matter if we accept an evolutionary process controlled by God rather than creation?
2. How is the Doctrine of Creation of value in the ecology debate?
3. What comfort has the Doctrine of Providence brought to your life?

---

[1] I Timothy 4:10; Amos 9:8-9; Romans 8:28; Isaiah 43:3-5, 14.

CHAPTER II

MAN – THE CROWN OF GOD'S CREATION

THE GREATNESS OF MAN

Ref. Confession Chapter 4 – Creation

In this study you will discover:

- Man is a special creation of God
- Man is made in the image of God
- Man was given the Law of God

The doctrine of man is very important. To see man as a super-animal is to insult the one who is the crown of God's creation. This teaching is vital since a man's behaviour is governed by how he views himself. If you think that you are an animal you are apt to behave like one!

Man is a special creation of God

Confession 4.2

> After God had made all the other creatures, he created human beings, male and female,[1] with reasoning, immortal souls.[2] He endowed them with knowledge, righteousness, and true holiness in his own image[3] and wrote his law in their hearts.[4] God also gave them the ability to obey his law and the potential to disobey it; i.e., he gave them freedom of their own wills, which could change.[5] In addition to this law written in their hearts, they were commanded not to eat from the Tree of the Knowledge of Good and Evil.[6] As long as they obeyed God's law and kept this commandment, they were happy in fellowship with God[7] and had dominion over the other creatures.[8]

Man was created after all other creatures, he did not evolve from them. He, according to Scripture and the Confession, was a separate and distinct creation of God.

---

1 Genesis 1:27.
2 Genesis 2:7 with Ecclesiastes 12:7 and Luke 23:43 and Matthew 10:28.
3 Genesis 1:26; Colossians 3:10; Ephesians 4:24.
4 Romans 2:14-15.
5 Ecclesiastes 7:29.
6 Genesis 3:6; Ecclesiastes 7:29.
7 Genesis 2:17, 3:8-11, 23.
8 Genesis 1: 26, 28.

> *"Then God said, 'Let us make man in our image, after our likeness. And let them have dominion over the fish of the sea and over the birds of the heavens and over the livestock and over all the earth and over every creeping thing that creeps on the earth.'*
>
> *So God created man in his own image, in the image of God he created him; male and female he created them"* (Genesis 1:26-27).

Mankind was also made male and female. The sexual distinctiveness of man and woman is an imprint of the Creator, not just something that happened. It follows that to blur this distinction or to try to eliminate it altogether is rebellion against the purpose of God. This is the basic reason why homosexuality and other sexual deviations are wrong.

Man and woman are also special because they have *reasoning* and *immortal souls*. To be *reasoning* means that man has the ability to think and to analyse. The term soul describes the spiritual side of man. It is unbiblical to think of the soul as a 'thing' that exists inside a body rather like clothes inside a suitcase. The soul and body are both important. The soul does not exist without the body or the body without the soul. They form a unity which never should have been broken. Man is body-soul, not body and soul. It was the entrance of sin with the consequence of death, which severed soul and body. In the resurrection they will be united again. The Confession, as does Scripture, teaches two sides to man's nature, he is body-soul not body and soul and spirit. Soul and spirit for all practical purposes are used inter-changeably in the Scriptures.

When the soul is described as being immortal it does not mean that it has the power in itself to live forever. It is only immortal because that is God's plan and he grants it the ability to live forever. It does so only at his wish. Man is not an animal, he is unique in God's creation.

Man is made in the image of God

When the Scripture teaches that man is made in the image of God, it means that there are aspects of God's character which are reproduced in miniature in man. To use a modern term, man is an analogue of God.

Historically the meaning of the term 'image of God' has been divided into two:

- **those characteristics which were distorted, though remain, after the Fall,** and
- **those which were lost by the Fall.**

Of the former we think of reason, creativity, morality, spirituality and the ability to communicate in depth through the means of language.

The Confession concentrates on the latter sense, referring to those characteristics that were lost in the 'Fall' but are renewed, though imperfectly, by regeneration – *knowledge, righteousness and true holiness*. Man was **human** at creation but the fact that he lost these aspects of the image of God made him **sub-human**. The purpose of salvation is to make man **truly human**. This will only be completely fulfilled at the return of Christ.

When created, man had true knowledge of the world and God. His knowledge was not complete, there was room for progress as he lived in God's world, but what he had was perfect. He also had perfect righteousness and holiness, standing in a right relationship with God, his standards of morality were the same as God's. He was holy, no sin marred his soul. This was man in the image of God as he came from the hand of the Creator.

Man was given the Law of God

Man was given the law of God in two ways. It was written on his heart and he was also given external commands. These commands included labour, reproduction and management of the earthly creation as well as the command with respect to *the Tree of the Knowledge of Good and Evil,*

> *"Then God said, 'Let us make man in our image, after our likeness. And let them have dominion over the fish of the sea and over the birds of the heavens and over the livestock and over all the earth and over every creeping thing that creeps on the earth'"* (Genesis 1:26ff),
>
> *"but of the tree of the knowledge of good and evil you shall not eat, for in the day that you eat of it you shall surely die"* (Genesis 2:17).

It is important to note that even in the state of sinlessness man still needed divine revelation to guide him in the world. He did not know naturally what God required.

God gave man the power to keep all his laws. Man was not made with a defect so that he could not obey the commands of God. At the same time he was given the liberty to choose to keep or not to keep the law of God. He had perfect freedom.

If he kept God's law he would remain in fellowship with him and be truly happy. If he rejected it he would lose all this.

This paragraph of the Confession finishes with a little footnote that man *had dominion over the creatures*. This was part of the command which God gave to man,

> *"And God blessed them. And God said to them, 'Be fruitful and multiply and fill the earth and subdue it, and have dominion over the fish of the sea and over the birds of the heavens and over every living thing that moves on the earth'"* (Genesis 1:28).

Man is God's manager in creation, therefore he is not to worship it. No pet can become an idol! He was to rule but not ruin creation. Man is truly the crown of God's earthly creation.

Cross references with the Catechisms:

Shorter: 10; Larger: 17 & 20

To think over and discuss:

1. In what ways do you see the male/female distinction being destroyed in today's society?
2. Is this anti-biblical thinking influencing Christians?
3. Does the doctrine of the image of God help modern man who regards life as meaningless to discover purpose in life?

THE SIN OF MAN

Ref. Confession Chapter 6 – The Fall of Man, Sin, and the Punishment for Sin

In this study you will discover:

- Sin: its origin in the human race
- Sin: the effects of
- Sin: the consequences of

Sin: its origin in the human race

Confession 6.1

> Our first parents were led astray by the cunning temptation of Satan and sinned in eating the forbidden fruit.[1] It pleased God to allow them to sin, because in his wisdom and holiness he planned to order their sin to his own glory.[2]

The Confession does not speculate about the origin of evil. Where Scripture does not speak the Confession is silent.

> *"The secret things belong to the LORD our God, but the things that are revealed belong to us and to our children for ever, that we may do all the words of this law"* (Deuteronomy 29:29).

In this chapter the 'Fall' of man and its consequences are discussed. The Confession, as does Scripture, accepts the 'Fall' as something which happened in history and not as a mere symbol teaching a truth about sin. This must be the case, for the whole biblical doctrine of sin depends on the 'Fall', as does the biblical teaching on salvation. If we deny the biblical 'Fall' we deny biblical redemption.

The sin of Adam and Eve was eating the fruit of the tree of the knowledge of good and evil. There was nothing special about the tree, it was the command of God which was important. The essence of sin was the fact that they doubted the Word of God and disobeyed his law. Unbelief and rebellion were the key elements in the original sin and these marks out the true nature of sin.

It was Satan who tempted Adam and Eve. Satan is a real person who is totally opposed to God and his ways. We can either over-estimate Satan or under-estimate him. He cannot make us do evil, he can only tempt us to break God's law. If we sin it is our fault. It was the fault of Adam and Eve, they listened to and obeyed Satan rather

---

1 Genesis 3:13; II Corinthians 11:3.
2 Romans 11:32.

than God. In this they were wholly responsible, and although Eve tried to move the blame to the serpent, they were guilty.

> *"Then the Lord God said to the woman, 'What is this that you have done?' The woman said, 'The serpent deceived me, and I ate'"* (Genesis 3:13).

Their rebellion is even more remarkable when we consider that they were holy and were not in tune with Satan's evil desires. Whereas in our case, we are sinners and are in tune with the suggestions of the evil one.

The Confession states that God allowed the 'Fall'. It was part of his plan and he was to order these events for his own glory. We cannot understand the "*whys*", God alone knows the true reason. It should be remembered however, that we would not have known the mercy of God if the 'Fall' had not occurred.

Sin: the effects of

Confession 6.2

> By this sin they fell from their original righteousness and fellowship with God,[1] and so became dead in sin[2] and completely polluted in all their faculties and parts of body and soul.[3]

In this second paragraph (6.2) the immediate effects of the 'Fall' are explained.

Man is no longer righteous. He has broken the Law of God and as a consequence he has lost fellowship with God. He is described as dead in sin. The idea of death is separation. When a person is dead they have no contact with the world in which they once lived. Adam and Eve were spiritually dead, they now lived in the world of sin out of *fellowship with God*. Death also suggests that they could not act in a true spiritual way, being incapable of true spiritual action.

Sin has extended its tentacles to every human faculty. Man's whole person was affected; – mind, will, emotions – even the very body was now subject to sickness and death.

The next section deals with the effect of the 'Fall' on succeeding generations. The fact that Adam and Eve were in a covenantal relationship with God (see Confession Chapter 7) and that they had been ordained as representatives of the human race, meant that their actions

---

1 Genesis 3: 6, 7-8; Ecclesiastes 7:29; Romans 3:23.

2 Genesis 2:17; Ephesians 2:1.

3 Titus 1:15; Genesis 6:5; Jeremiah 17:9; Romans 3:10-18.

had implications for the generations to come. Their failure meant that the human race had failed. Their wrong decision opened the floodgates of sin and allowed it to engulf humanity.

Confession 6.3

> Since Adam and Eve are the root of all mankind, the guilt for this sin has been imputed to all human beings,[1] who are their natural descendants and have inherited the same death in sin and the same corrupt nature.[2]

Their guilt, that is their liability to punishment, was imputed or credited to the human race. To state it another way, the race became legally responsible for Adam's sin,

> *"Therefore, just as sin came into the world through one man, and death through sin, and so death spread to all men because all sinned"* (Romans 5:12ff).

The race was also subject to death and the corrupt nature of Adam. His bias to evil was passed on to his children forever.

Here the Confession (6.3) inserts an important proviso, *natural descendants*, which refers to the normal procreative act. This excludes Christ and thus ensures the start of a new race untainted by Adam's sin.

Confession 6.4

> This original corruption completely disinclines, incapacitates, and turns us away from every good,[3] while it completely inclines us to every evil.[4] From it proceed all actual sins.[5]

In the fourth paragraph (6.4) the subject of total inability is expounded. It is from this original sin of Adam that our actual transgressions proceed. The result for us is that, since we have a corrupt nature, we are opposed to and incapable of all good. At the same time our preference is for evil. This does not mean that man is not capable of kind acts such as showing compassion. It does mean that no action of his is wholly pure, because it is defiled by sin. It also teaches that man can do no spiritual good, he is by nature opposed to the ways of God. If he does try to keep the law of God and avoid evil, this is due to the hand of God upon him even in an unsaved state, often

---

1 Genesis 1:27-28 and 2:16-17 and Acts 17:26 with Romans 5:12, 15-19; I Corinthians 15:21-22, 49.
2 Psalm 51:5; Genesis 5:3; Job 14:4, 15:14.
3 Romans 5:6, 8:7, 7:18; Colossians 1:21.
4 Genesis 6:5, 8:21; Romans 3:10-12.
5 James 1:14-15; Ephesians 2:2-3; Matthew 15:19.

called Common Grace. If he attempts spiritual actions they have the wrong motive of trying to gain favour with God.

Confession 6.5

> During life on earth this corrupt nature remains in those who are regenerated,[1] and, although it is pardoned and deadened in Christ, yet it and all its impulses are truly and properly sinful.[2]

This section (6.5) deals with sin in those who are Christians, those who have experienced regeneration. Although the believer is a new person to the extent that the power of sin is broken in his life he still sins.

> *"What then? Are we to sin because we are not under law but under grace? By no means!"* (Romans 6:15ff).

There is no such thing as perfectionism in this life.

This section also underlines that the remnant of the corrupt nature in the believer and its action is truly sinful and serious. This is the implication of *all its impulses are truly and properly sinful*. Indeed sin in believers is very serious for they have the power to resist and they should know better, since they have the law of God in their hearts.

Sin: the consequences of

Confession 6.6

> Every sin, both original and actual, transgresses the righteous law of God[3] and brings guilt on the sinner.[4] Every sinner is consequently subjected to the wrath of God,[5] the curse of the law,[6] and death,[7] with all the resultant miseries, spiritual,[8] temporal,[9] and eternal.[10]

In this final paragraph of this chapter the terrible consequences of sin are expounded.

Both *original* sin *and actual* transgressions are a contradiction of the law of God and each makes us guilty before him. This implies that we are under his *wrath* and all that entails. The *curse of the law* refers to the sanctions of the law. These sanctions came upon those who

---

1 I John 1:8, 10; Romans 7:14, 17, 18, 23; James 3:2; Proverbs 20:9; Ecclesiastes 7:20.
2 Romans 7:5, 7-8, 25; Galatians 5:17.
3 I John 3:4.
4 Romans 2:15, 3:9, 19.
5 Ephesians 2:3.
6 Galatians 3:10.
7 Romans 6:23.
8 Ephesians 4:18.
9 Romans 8:20; Lamentations 3:39.
10 Matthew 25:41; II Thessalonians 1:9.

broke it and include *death, temporal and eternal* (physical and *spiritual*).

> *"For all who rely on works of the law are under a curse; for it is written, 'Cursed be everyone who does not abide by all things written in the Book of the Law, and do them'"* (Galatians 3:10).

The Confession mentions *miseries, spiritual, temporal and eternal,* which result from sin.

Spiritual misery is being out of fellowship with God and the struggle we have, even as believers, with sin and temptation. The writer to the Hebrews called it "*your struggle against sin*"

> *"In your struggle against sin you have not yet resisted to the point of shedding your blood. And have you forgotten the exhortation that addresses you as sons?*
>
> > *'My son, do not regard lightly the discipline of the Lord, nor be weary when reproved by him.*
> >
> > *For the Lord disciplines the one he loves, and chastises every son whom he receives'"* (Hebrews 12:4-6).

Temporal misery refers to the physical and day to day trouble we have because we live in a fallen world, the drudgery of work, the common sicknesses, the tired and weak body, the personal relationships and national disasters which fall in our way.

These all result from the 'Fall'. Some indeed are the result of personal sin as the second commandment would teach us,

> *"You shall not make for yourself a carved image, or any likeness of anything that is in heaven above, or that is in the earth beneath, or that is in the water under the earth"* (Exodus 20:4).
>
> *"For his invisible attributes, namely, his eternal power and divine nature, have been clearly perceived, ever since the creation of the world, in the things that have been made. So they are without excuse"* (Romans 1:20).
>
> "The punishments of sin in this world are either inward, such as blindness of mind, a depraved sense, strong delusions, hardness of heart, horror of conscience and shameful lusts; or outward, such as the curse of God on the creatures for our sakes, and all other evils that befall us in our bodies, reputations, possessions, relationships and occupations, together with death itself" (WLC 28).

Eternal misery is eternal punishment in hell, God's wrath without mercy upon those who turn their back on him.

> "The punishments of sin in the world to come are everlasting

> separation from the enjoyment of God in his presence, and extremely severe torments in soul and body, without any break, in the fire of hell for ever" (WLC 29).

The Confession leaves us in no doubt about the serious consequences of sin.

Cross references with the Catechisms:

Shorter: 13-19; Larger: 21-29

To think over and discuss:

1. What aspects of this teaching on sin do we need to emphasise today?
2. How should this teaching affect our evangelism and prayer life?

MAN'S FREEWILL

Ref. Confession Chapter 9 – Freewill

In this study you will discover:

- The true meaning of freewill
- The difference in man's ability before and after the Fall
- The ability of the believer in this life and the next

The subject of freewill is often an area of controversy between Christians. This statement of the Confession is admirable for its clarity and conciseness.

The true meaning of freewill

Confession 9.1

> God has given man a will, which by nature is free, i.e., it is not forced or necessarily inclined toward good or evil.[1]

The first paragraph (9.1) is true of the will of man before and after the 'Fall', as well as in the state of salvation. It refers to man as man, it is part of his make-up. The will of man is free to make decisions in accordance with his nature. The will is not independent of the man's nature, it is a part of it, and therefore it reflects his character.

The will of man is *not forced*, that is, controlled by external forces. It is not his environment nor Satan nor God which compel him to act contrary to his desire. He acts in keeping with his desire at the moment of the action.

Anything man does is done freely. He is not coerced by anyone or anything to do it. That is not the same as saying that man has the power to do anything in the spiritual realm. While he acts freely he has limited ability. In the physical realm, to use an illustration, man has the freedom to walk about this world; he has also the freedom to walk on the seabed but he has not the ability to do so. No one would say that man is not free because he cannot live under water or fly in the air without special apparatus. The choice of man's actions is limited because of his make-up, but within his limitations he acts freely.

---

1 Matthew 17:12; James 1:14; Deuteronomy 30:19.

The difference in man's ability before and after the fall

Confession 9.2

> In his state of innocence man had complete freedom and the natural ability to will and to do what is good and pleasing to God.[1] God also made man so that he could lose that freedom.[2]

The second paragraph (9.2) teaches that prior to the 'Fall' man had the ability to do good and to keep God's law perfectly. He could please God and had the power to do so. At the same time he was mutable, that is, it was possible for him to change and rebel against the law of God. Man, prior to the 'Fall' had the power of contrary and alternative choice, he could choose good action or he could choose evil.

Confession 9.3

> Man fell into a state of sin by his disobedience and so completely lost his ability to will any spiritual good involving salvation.[3] Consequently fallen man is by nature completely opposed to spiritual good,[4] is dead in sin,[5] and is unable by his own strength either to convert himself or to prepare himself for conversion.[6]

After the 'Fall', as this subsequent paragraph (9.3) teaches, man *lost* the *ability to* do *any spiritual good* with reference to *salvation*,

> *"For to set the mind on the flesh is death, but to set the mind on the Spirit is life and peace"* (Romans 8:6ff).

This natural man, man without the Spirit of God, suffers from inability. He can do nothing to aid his own salvation. The Confession refrains from saying that man can do no natural good. This is because he is made in the image of God and because of the non-saving 'common' grace of God to all men. Man is able to do natural good, such as care for his family, show concern for the poor and many other things. These actions, though good in a general sense, are tainted with sin, for sin has affected every part of man's being.

Man in the *state of sin* has the power of alternative choice. He can

---

1 Ecclesiastes 7:29; Genesis 1:26.
2 Genesis 2:16, 17; 3:6.
3 Romans 5:6, 8:7; John 15:5.
4 Romans 3:10-12.
5 Ephesians 2:1,5; Colossians 2 13.
6 John 6:44, 65; Ephesians 2:2-5; I Corinthians 2:14; Titus 3:3-5.

choose within a range of evil options, all corrupted by sin. He can act freely within his own nature that is sinful. He has not the ability to act outside his own nature, he has lost the ability of contrary choice, he is a slave to sin.

The ability of a believer in this world and the next

Confession 9.4

> When God converts a sinner and brings him into a state of grace, he frees him from his natural enslavement to sin.[1] By God's grace alone, freely given, sinful man is enabled to will and to do what is spiritually good.[2] However, since the old sinful nature also remains, the believer cannot consistently or perfectly will to do what is good but also wills evil.[3]

The fourth paragraph (9.4) considers the state of the true believer. He is a man in tension with the old way of life and the new age of righteousness. It is God who changes the sinner, and this is all of his grace. It must be due to grace since we have discovered the sinner is not able to do any spiritual good.

While the great change of regeneration breaks the dominion of sin, there is remaining corruption, it is not all wiped out in this life[4]. The Confession does **not** teach that a new nature is planted along with the old nature which remains untouched, or that the old nature is so removed that the person is perfect. The **Confessional and Biblical position is** that the dominion of the old nature is broken and a new nature is implanted as well. Man is no longer under the dominion of sin, he is under the kingship of Christ, he is a new creation!

Confession 9.5

> The will of man is perfectly free and permanently inclined to good alone only in the state of glory.[5]

The Christian is able to do spiritual good and desires to do so, though due to the sin within, it will not be perfect. At the same time he

1 Colossians 1:13; John 8:34, 36.

2 Philippians 2:13; Romans 6:18, 22.

3 Galatians 5:17; Romans 7:15, 18-19, 21, 23.

4 "What then? Are we to sin because we are not under law but under grace? By no means!" (Romans 6:15ff),

"Therefore, if anyone is in Christ, he is a new creation. The old has passed away; behold, the new has come" (II Corinthians 5:17).

5 Ephesians 4:13; Hebrews 12:23; I John 3:2; Jude 24.

may choose to do evil as is clear from David in the Old Testament (II Samuel 11&12). The believer has the power of alternative and contrary choice.

In heaven, *the state of glory*, the remaining corruption has been removed and he is now able to act perfectly. At the same time he has by God's grace been made immutable, he can no longer choose to do evil. He is free to do good, he only wishes to do good, he has the ability to do good but has not the ability to sin. He has the power of alternative choice but **NOT** contrary choice. He is now (in heaven) not able to sin whereas in Eden he was able not to sin.

Cross references to the Catechisms:

(Neither catechisms have a question on freewill, but the following questions are relevant).

Shorter: 18, 26, 35, 38; Larger: 17, 21, 25, 27, 45, 67, 75, 78, 86.

To think over and discuss:

1. Have we neglected this teaching on inability in our witness today?
2. Give illustrations of this teaching for use in witness.
3. In what ways does this teaching modify the way people should be counselled for salvation?

GOD'S COVENANT WITH MAN

Ref. Confession Chapter 7 – God's Covenant with Man

In this study you will discover:

- Man is bound to God in a Covenantal relationship
- The meaning of the term 'Covenant of Grace'
- The administration of this Covenant in Old and New Testaments

The theme of the covenant is crucial for understanding the Bible as well as the teaching in the Confession. In this chapter the covenant theme is used to describe God's relationship to man before and after the Fall.

Man is bound to God in a Covenantal relationship

The meaning of covenant

The word covenant in Scripture is used to describe relationships between men and between God and man and is sometimes called a 'treaty',

> *"At that time Abimelech and Phicol the commander of his army said to Abraham, 'God is with you in all that you do. Now therefore swear to me here by God that you will not deal falsely with me or with my descendants or with my posterity, but as I have dealt kindly with you, so you will deal with me and with the land where you have sojourned.' And Abraham said, 'I will swear'"* (Genesis 21:22-24),

> *"On that day the LORD made a covenant with Abram, saying, 'To your offspring I give this land, from the river of Egypt to the great river, the river Euphrates . . .'"* (Genesis 15:18ff),

> *"When Abram was ninety-nine years old the LORD appeared to Abram and said to him, 'I am God Almighty; walk before me, and be blameless'"* (Genesis 17:1ff).

It is the divine covenants with which the Confession is concerned. A covenant is basically a bond of life and death. To be in the bond or fellowship is life, to be out of it is death. In Scripture the various divine covenants have several common factors:

1. They are one-sided, that is, it is God who comes and sets down the conditions. They are not compacts or contracts which are bargained out by the two parties. (Genesis chapters 12, 15, 17).
2. They not only include the person with whom they are made but also the generations to come,

> *And God said to Abraham, "As for you, you shall keep my covenant, you and your offspring after you throughout their generations. This is my covenant, which you shall keep, between me and you and your offspring after you . . ."* (Genesis 17:9ff).

3. Obedience to the covenants brought blessing and disobedience, the covenant curse (Deuteronomy ch. 28).
4. After the Fall there was often a ceremony which inaugurated the covenant. This took the form of a binding oath and often involved death or the shedding of blood.

> *"He said to him, 'Bring me a heifer three years old, a female goat three years old, a ram three years old, a turtledove, and a young pigeon . . .'"* (Genesis 15:9ff).
>
> *"And Moses took half of the blood and put it in basins, and half of the blood he threw against the altar. Then he took the Book of the Covenant and read it in the hearing of the people . . ."* (Exodus 24:6-7ff).

One way of expressing the relationship established by a divine covenant is to say that God is King and Father and man is servant and son.

God's Covenant with man

Confession 7.1

> The distance between God and his creation is so great that, although reasoning creatures owe him obedience as their creator, they nonetheless could never realize any blessedness or reward from him without his willingly condescending to them. And so it pleased God to provide for man by means of covenants.[1]

The first paragraph sets the scene. The fact that God is the holy Creator and man is a creature implies that man must obey God because he is the creation of God. However, in order that man could *realize any blessedness or reward from* God, God entered into fellowship with man expressed by way of a covenant. The point being made is, that God does not owe man anything and the blessings, which he receives from God, are all of his goodness. Here we see the love of God. He wishes to enter into fellowship with the creature he made. This was not for God's good but the good of man.

---

1 Isaiah 40:13-17; Job 9:32-33; I Samuel 2:25; Psalms 113:5-6, 100:2-3; Job 22:2-3, 35:7-8; Luke 17:10; Acts 17:24-25.

Confession 7.2

> The first covenant made with man was a covenant of works.[1] In it life was promised to Adam and through him to his descendants[2] on the condition of perfect, personal obedience.[3]

This paragraph (7.2) refers to the first covenant made with man in Eden. The Confession calls this the covenant of works. This can be a misleading term implying that man earned this relationship with God. (The Shorter Catechism term, "covenant of life" is preferable WSC12). It is common today to deny that God made a covenant with man in Eden, yet all the factors of a covenant are present. It was God who set down the conditions, there was a bond of life and death, Adam had life, indeed he was the son of God,

> *". . . the son of Enos, the son of Seth, the son of Adam, the son of God"* (Luke 3:38);

to eat of the tree brought death, the covenant curse. Adam also was the representative of the generations to come

> *"Therefore, just as sin came into the world through one man, and death through sin, and so death spread to all men because all sinned —"* (Romans 5:12ff).

If we take this with the fact that Adam's disobedience is described as breaking the covenant,

> *"But like Adam they transgressed the covenant; there they dealt faithlessly with me"* (Hosea 6:7).

there can be little doubt that Adam was in covenant with God. If he was not in covenant with God, what relationship had he with his Creator?

If we accept the idea of Adam in covenant with God, it means that all men today are covenant breakers and are therefore under the curse of God. They owe allegiance to God not only as creatures but also because they are children who have chosen another father, the devil,

> *"You are of your father the devil, and your will is to do your father's desires. He was a murderer from the beginning, and has nothing to do with the truth, because there is no truth in him. When he lies, he speaks out of his own character, for he is a liar and the father of lies"* (John 8:44).

Life was promised to Adam and his posterity upon *the condition of*

---

1 Galatians 3:12.
2 Romans 10:5; Romans 5:12-20.
3 Genesis 2:17; Galatians 3:10.

perfect and personal obedience. The thought is that if Adam continued to obey, he would have reached a stage where God granted to him and his offspring eternal life and it would have been impossible for them to fall away. This is a deduction from the fact that if he disobeyed, then he and his posterity fell into sin. This idea of a testing or probationary period for Adam was a common idea at the time the Confession was formed. The question must be asked, "is it scriptural?" The answer would appear to be in the negative. The evidence is that Adam had life and there is no higher form of life than fellowship with God. There is no mention in the biblical text of a testing period. All we can say is that God gave Adam the gift of fellowship with himself which would have continued provided he did not disobey the law of God. This teaching is not new for it occurred at the time the Confession was written, for example Larger Catechism 20 states:

". . . entering into a covenant of life with him on condition of personal, perfect, and **perpetual** obedience . . ." (WLC 20 *emphasis added*).

However, for some it would seem strange if God would hold man in suspense forever and not at some point confirm eternal life so that Adam and Eve were "able not to sin".

The meaning of the term 'Covenant of Grace'

Confession 7.3

> By his fall, man made himself incapable of life under that covenant, and so the Lord made a second, the covenant of grace.[1] In it he freely offers sinners life and salvation through Jesus Christ. In order to be saved he requires faith in Jesus[2] and promises to give his Holy Spirit to all who are ordained to life so that they may be willing and able to believe.[3]

The remaining paragraphs deal with the covenant of grace. This is a term used to describe the second covenant which God made in order to save sinners. This covenant, we are told in the Larger Catechism

". . . was made with Christ as the Second Adam, and in him with all the elect as his seed" (WLC 31).

The Confession makes it clear that this salvation is by faith in Christ and faith is a result of the work of the Holy Spirit in the elect. The covenant is therefore unconditional, God gives the grace so that

1 Galatians 3:21; Romans 8:3; 3:20-21; Genesis 3:15; Isaiah 42:6.
2 Mark 16:15-16; John 3:16; Romans 10:6,9; Galatians 3:11.
3 Ezra 36:26-27; John 6:44-45.

man can walk in the way of the covenant.

Since the first Adam failed, God had planned that mankind could have fellowship with him through the last Adam, Jesus Christ. To Christ was given the elect for whom he lived and died so that they would be saved. There is only one covenant of grace that started in time with the promise to Adam in Eden,

> *"I will put enmity between you and the woman, and between your offspring and her offspring; he shall bruise your head, and you shall bruise his heel"* (Genesis 3:15).

and went through various administrations until the last Adam came when it commenced its final phase.

Confession 7.4

> This covenant of grace is frequently identified in Scripture as a testament, in reference to the death of Jesus Christ, the testator, and to the everlasting inheritance and everything included in that legacy.[1]

The fourth paragraph requires some comment. The statement: '*This covenant of grace is frequently identified in Scripture as a testament*', is open to question. The Greek word used in the New Testament which is translated covenant had a dual meaning of covenant and will or testament. At the time of the New Testament the common use was 'will' but the Greek version of the Old Testament used the word to translate the Hebrew word for covenant. There are only two occurrences in the New Testament where the Word could be translated will/testament and that is in Hebrews 9:16-17.

> *"For where a will is involved, the death of the one who made it must be established. For a will takes effect only at death, since it is not in force as long as the one who made it is alive"* (Hebrews 9:16-17).

The thought in Hebrews is that only when the maker of the will (the testator) dies does it come into operation. This ties up with the reality that when Christ died then the New Covenant was inaugurated and also that covenant-making was linked to the shedding of blood. The use of the word 'will' also highlights the unconditional nature of the covenant, the testator decides who will benefit without any consultations with the beneficiaries. They receive an inheritance for which they did not work. In the case of Christ, the Testator, he did it on their behalf.

[1] Hebrews 9:15-17; Hebrews 7:22; Luke 22:20; I Corinthians 11:25.

The administration of this covenant in Old and New Testaments

Confession 7.5

> This covenant was administered differently in the time of the law and in the time of the gospel.[1] Under the law it was administered by promises, prophecies, sacrifices, circumcision, the paschal lamb, and other types and ordinances given to the Jewish people, all foreshadowing Christ.[2] For that time the covenant administered under the law through the operation of the Spirit was sufficient and effective in instructing the elect and building up their faith in the promised Messiah,[3] by whom they had full remission of their sins and eternal salvation. This administration is called the Old Testament.[4]

In the fifth paragraph (7.5) the administration of the Covenant under the Old Testament is discussed. The purpose of this phase of the Covenant administration was to prepare the people for the coming of Christ, to instruct people until the Messiah came. Not only did it show people the need of salvation since they could not fulfil the law, it also taught about the coming Messiah and his work through the prophecies, ceremonies and sacrifices. The point is made correctly that the people under the Old Testament were not saved by works but through faith in the coming Messiah.

Confession 7.6

> Under the gospel Christ himself, the substance[5] of God's grace, was revealed. The ordinances of this New Testament[6] are the preaching of the word and the administration of the sacraments of baptism and the Lord's supper.[7] Although these are fewer in number and are administered with more simplicity and less outward glory, yet they are available to all nations, Jews and Gentiles,[8] and in them the spiritual power of the covenant of grace is more fully developed.[9] There are not then two essentially different covenants of grace, but one and the same covenant under different dispensations.[10]

---

1 II Corinthians 3:6-9.
2 Hebrews chapters 8-10; Romans 4:11; Colossians 2:11-12; I Corinthians 5:7.
3 I Corinthians 10:1-4; Hebrews 11:13; John 8:56.
4 Galatians 3:7-9, 14.
5 Colossians 2:17.
6 Luke 22: 20.
7 Matthew 28:19-20; I Corinthians 11:23-25.
8 Matthew 28:19; Ephesians 2:15-19.
9 Hebrews 12:22-28; Jeremiah 31:33-34; Hebrews 8:6-13; I Corinthians 3:9-15.
10 Galatians 3:14, 16; Acts 15:11; Romans 3:21-23, 30; Psalm 32:1 with Romans 4: 3, 6, 16-17, 23-24; Hebrews 13:8.

The final paragraph (7.6) deals with the fulfilment of the Old Testament promises when Christ came and the shadow became the substance. This was not a new covenant but a new administration of the same covenant of grace. Away went the complexity of the Old Testament system and in came the simplicity of the New Testament. The emphasis was on preaching, not ceremony, and the two sacraments of Baptism and the Lord's Supper, replaced circumcision and the Passover.

The other difference was that the covenant, which had been mainly restricted to one nation, now became international. It was for all nations both Jews and Gentiles. Here the Confession demonstrates that it is not unaware that the gospel has to be taken to the nations.

Cross references with the Catechisms:

Shorter: 12, 16, 20; Larger: 20, 22, 30-35.

To think over and discuss:

1. Why is the Covenant made with Adam important for understanding the Bible?
2. In what way is it important for us today?
3. How does the unconditional nature of the Covenant of Grace affect our evangelism?

CHAPTER III

OUR GREAT SALVATION

THE MEDIATOR

Ref. Confession Chapter 8 – Christ the Mediator

In this study you will discover:

- God appointed a Mediator to save his people
- The Person of the Mediator
- The work of the Mediator
- The work of the Mediator is effective

God appointed a Mediator to save His people

Confession 8.1

> In his eternal purpose it pleased God to choose and ordain the Lord Jesus, his only begotten Son, to be the mediator between God and man.[1] Jesus is the prophet,[2] priest,[3] and king,[4]the head and savior of his church,[5] the heir of all things,[6] and judge of the world.[7] From all eternity God gave him a people to be his seed[8] and to be in time redeemed, called, justified, sanctified, and glorified by him.[9]

The first paragraph (8.1) serves as an introduction to the rest of the chapter opening with the great statement that in God's eternal plan the Father chose his *Son, to be the mediator between God and man*. It was God who took the initiative so that man could be brought back into covenant fellowship with him.

The Father gave his Son, as Mediator, the authority to serve as *prophet, priest and king*. He is the one who is *the head of* the *church* and will *judge the world*. It was the Father, who in the great triune plan before the creation of the world gave *a people to* the *Son*. It was the Son who redeemed them and by him they are *called, justified, sanctified and gloried*. By this statement the Confession is teaching that the work of Jesus, applied by the Holy Spirit, actually secures and

1 Isaiah 42:1; I Peter 1:19-20; John 3:16; I Timothy 2:5.
2 Acts 3:22.
3 Hebrews 5:5-6.
4 Psalm 2:6; Luke 1:33.
5 Ephesians 5:23.
6 Hebrews 1:2.
7 Acts 17:31.
8 John 17:6; Psalm 22:30; Isaiah 53:10.
9 I Timothy 2:6; Isaiah 55:4-5; I Corinthians 1:30.

guarantees the salvation of his people. He did not come merely to make salvation possible, but to ensure the salvation of the elect.

The person of the Mediator

Confession 8.2

> The Son of God, the second person of the Trinity, is truly the eternal God, of one substance and equal with the Father. In the fulness of time he took on himself the nature of man,[1] with all the essential qualities and ordinary frailties of man – except that he was sinless.[2] Jesus was conceived by the power of the Holy Spirit in the womb of the Virgin Mary out of her substance.[3] These two complete, perfect, and distinct natures, the Godhead and the manhood, were inseparably joined together in the one person of Jesus without being altered, disunited, or mixed together.[4] The person Jesus is truly God and truly man, yet one Christ, the only mediator between God and man.[5]

The Confession underlines the Church's historic teaching that Jesus was fully God and fully human. He was not less than God. He was and is, *the second person of the Trinity,* being, *truly the eternal God, of one substance and equal with the Father*. This brief, but full statement stands in contrast to many of the cults who make the Mediator less than the Father. Jesus is truly God. The humanity of Jesus also receives full recognition. The Son of God took upon himself man's nature. It was **not** the reverse that man took upon himself divinity.

The humanity of Jesus never existed apart from its conjunction with the deity. This was human nature with all its infirmities, except that it was sinless. Sin is no part of true human nature, but weakness, tiredness, human needs and emotions are. The Mediator who was truly human experienced them all.

The fact that Mary conceived Jesus under the power of the Holy Spirit is taught, emphasizing the point that he was *of her substance*. The wording of the Confession could be better in this section. Strictly the Holy Spirit did not conceive him, it was Mary who conceived, and Jesus was begotten of the Holy Spirit. *"And behold, you will conceive in your womb"* (Luke 1:31, cf. Luke 1:35).

The unity of the two natures is taught at the end of the second

1 John 1:1, 14; I John 5:20; Philippians 2:6; Galatians 4:4.
2 Hebrews 2:14, 16-17; Hebrews 4:15.
3 Luke 1:27, 31, 35; Galatians 4:4.
4 Luke 1:35; Colossians 2:9; Romans 9:5; I Peter 3:18; I Timothy 3:16.
5 Romans 1:3-4; I Timothy 2:5.

paragraph (8.2). There is one person who has two natures that *were inseparably joined together*. This means that the union is permanent. Christ was not just God–man during his life on earth but he continues to be very God and very man today and will always be so. The two natures remain distinct, yet there is one person. There is no 'conversion' of the natures, that is God does not become a mere human nor is the human made God. They are not *mixed together* as if a part of each nature was taken to make a third thing.

The answer of the Shorter Catechism is superb:

> "The only Redeemer of God's elect is the Lord Jesus Christ, who, being the eternal Son of God became man, and so was, and continues to be God and man, in two distinct natures and one person for ever" (WSC 21).

Confession 8.3

> His human nature being thus united to the divine, the Lord Jesus was sanctified and anointed with the Holy Spirit beyond all measure.[1] He had in him all the treasures of wisdom and knowledge,[2] and in him it pleased the Father that all fulness should dwell.[3] God's purpose was that Jesus, being holy, harmless, undefiled, and full of grace and truth,[4] should be completely equipped to execute the office of mediator and guarantor.[5] Jesus did not take this office himself but was called to it by his Father,[6] who gave and commanded him to use all power and judgment.[7]

The third paragraph (8.3) discusses the gifts which the Father gave through the Holy Spirit to the incarnate Son. It is not the Son as the second person of the Trinity who is being spoken about here but the Son as Mediator carrying out the plan of the Father. He is set apart to the office of Mediator and God equips him to fulfil that function. All the fullness of the Father dwells in the incarnate Son (Colossians 1:19). He was the guarantee of the New Covenant. 'The first Adam' failed. Those born into the Sinai covenant failed, but he would not. He was the *mediator and guarantor*.

> *For in him all the fullness of God was pleased to dwell, and through him to reconcile to himself all things, whether on earth or in heaven,*

---

1 Psalm 45:7; John 3:34.
2 Colossians 2:3.
3 Colossians 1:19.
4 Hebrews 7:26; John 1:14.
5 Acts 10:38; Hebrews 12:24, 7:22.
6 Hebrews 5:4-5.
7 John 5:22, 27; Matthew 28:18; Acts 2:36.

making peace by the blood of his cross" (Colossians 1:19-20).

He did not usurp this office, but it was given to him by the Father as a part of the eternal plan of salvation. God gave him all power and judgement and the authority to perform all that was required of him as Mediator.

The fact that he is the only mediator between God and man is underlined.

The work of the Mediator

Confession 8.4

> The Lord Jesus undertook this office completely voluntarily.[1] In order to discharge it, he was made under[2] and perfectly fulfilled the law.[3] He endured extremely severe torment in his soul[4] and extremely painful suffering in his body.[5] He was crucified and died.[6] He was buried and remained under the power of death, but his body did not decay.[7] On the third day he arose from the dead[8] with the same body in which he had suffered[9] and with which he also ascended into heaven. There he sits at the right hand of his Father,[10] interceding for believers.[11] He will return to judge men and angels at the end of the world.[12]

In this paragraph the work of the Mediator is expounded and a number of important points should be noted:

1. The Son acted as Mediator willingly. It was not forced upon him. It was out of love for his people that he came to act on their behalf.
2. He lived under the old covenant and *fulfilled* all its requirements, unlike the rest of the human race who broke *the law* of God. He also died the cruel death at Golgotha. The Confession correctly mentions not only the bodily suffering but also the *torment in his soul* both prior to the crucifixion (Gethsemane is in mind here) and

---

1 Psalm 40:7-8 with Hebrews 10:5-10; John 10:18; Philippians 2:8.
2 Galatians 4:4.
3 Matthew 3:15, 5:17.
4 Matthew 26:37-38; Luke 22:44; Matthew 27:46.
5 Matthew chapters 26 and 27.
6 Philippians 2:8.
7 Acts 2: 23, 24, 27, 13:37; Romans 6:9.
8 I Corinthians 15:3, 4.
9 John 20:25, 27.
10 Mark 16:19.
11 Romans 8:34; Hebrews 9:24; Hebrews 7:25.
12 Romans 14:9,10; Acts 1:11; Acts 10:42; Matthew 13:40-42; Jude 6; II Peter 2:4.

on the cross. He was forsaken of the Father, and this was hell to him. That was the apex of his suffering.

3. When he was buried, his body saw no decay and *he arose from the dead with the same body in which he suffered, with which also he ascended to heaven*. The important thing to note here is the certain affirmation of the bodily resurrection and ascension. No one should sign the Confession who does not believe these truths.

Presently Christ is making intercession in heaven and will return at the end of the world.

Confession 8.5

> By his perfect obedience and sacrifice, offered up to God once and for all through the eternal Spirit, the Lord Jesus has completely satisfied the justice of his Father[1] and purchased not only reconciliation but also an everlasting inheritance in the kingdom of heaven for everyone whom the Father has given to him.[2]

While the fourth paragraph (8.4) explains what Jesus did, the fifth (8.5) explains what he achieved. His obedience, which included the keeping of the law and going to the cross, *satisfied the justice of* the *Father*. Both his *obedience and sacrifice* were *perfect* and were achieved *through* the help of *the Spirit*. He fulfilled all that his Holy Father required.

This double work of Christ (law keeping and sacrifice) ensures that fellowship is restored with the Father and that heaven is made certain. This work of Christ was for the elect, *for everyone whom the Father has given to him*.

Confession 8.6

> Although the work of redemption was not actually done by Christ until after his incarnation, yet the power, effectiveness, and benefits of it were given to the elect in all ages from the beginning of the world by means of those promises, types, and sacrifices which revealed him and indicated that he would be the seed of the woman, would bruise the serpent's head, and was the lamb slain from the beginning of the world. Jesus Christ is yesterday and today and forever the same.[3]

The sixth paragraph (8.6) teaches that while *redemption was not actually done by Christ until after his incarnation, yet the power,*

---

[1] Romans 5:19; Hebrews 9:14, 16, 10:14; Ephesians 5:2; Romans 3:25-26.
[2] Daniel 9:24, 26; Colossians 1: 19, 20; Ephesians 1:11, 14; John 17:2; Hebrews 9:12, 15.
[3] Galatians 4:4-5; Genesis 3:15; Revelation 13:8; Hebrews 13:8.

effectiveness, and benefits of it were given to the elect in all ages. The Old Testament sacrificial system and the various prophecies pointed forward to the coming Redeemer. His work as the Messiah was certain. He was *"the Lamb who was slain from the creation of the world"* (Revelations 13:8 NIV).

Confession 8.7

> In the work of mediation Christ acts according to both his natures, each nature doing what is proper to each.[1] However, because of the unity of his person Scripture sometimes attributes what is proper to one nature to the person indicated by the other nature.[2]

This paragraph (8.7) explains the meaning of scriptural phrases like; *"be shepherds of the church of God which he bought with his own blood"* (Acts 20:28 NIV). Some people thought that this meant that the divine nature of Christ had become humanized with flesh and blood but this is an error. The Confession teaches that because Christ is one person, the characteristics which belong to one nature are sometimes spoken of as if they belong to the other nature. Suffering, weakness and limited knowledge, which belong to the human nature and all-knowledge and power, which belong to the divine nature are both ascribed to the person who is God-man.

The work of the Mediator is effective

Confession 8.8

> Christ insures with absolute certainty that everyone for whom he purchased redemption actually accepts and receives it.[3] He makes intercession for them,[4] reveals the mysteries of salvation to them in and by the word,[5] and effectively persuades them to believe and obey by his Spirit. He governs their hearts by his word and Spirit[6] and overcomes all their enemies by his almighty power and wisdom in such ways as are most in agreement with his wonderful and un-knowable administration of things.[7]

The Confession teaches with great clarity that Jesus did not come just to make salvation possible for those who may wish to come to

---

1 Hebrews 9:14; I Peter 3:18.
2 Acts 20:28; John 3:13; I John 3:16.
3 John 6:37, 39, 10:15, 16.
4 I John 2:1, 2; Romans 8:34.
5 John 15: 13, 15; Ephesians 1: 7-8, 9; John 17:6.
6 John 14:16; Hebrews 12:2; II Corinthians 4:13; Romans 8:9, 14, 15:18-19; John17:17.
7 Psalm 110:1; I Corinthians 15:25-26; Malachi 4:2-3; Colossians 2:15.

gladly to put their trust in the Saviour.

Confession 10.2

> This effectual call is freely made by God and is entirely an act of his special grace. It does not depend on anything God foresaw about the person called,[1] who is completely passive. God himself gives life and renewal by the Holy Spirit.[2] He thereby enables each person to answer his call and to accept the grace he offers and actually gives.[3]

The order of salvation inferred here is that regeneration/new birth is prior to faith. Conversion is the result of the new nature not the cause of it. Conversion is understood to be the response of the person in faith and repentance. The fact that this call is all of God is emphasized in this second paragraph (10.2). *It does not depend on anything God foresaw about the person called, who is completely passive. God himself gives life and renewal by the Holy Spirit.* The phrase, *'accept the grace'* refers to the salvation in Christ. Note also that grace goes along with the call, this is why it is effectual.

This statement on salvation is foundational to the teaching of the Confession and no one can accept the Confession if they deny the priority of regeneration to saving faith.

A word of warning should be entered here. We are not to think that the new birth occurs a long time before conversion. The teaching of the Confession is that the response to the call (faith and repentance) is immediate. The regenerate sinner always exercises faith.

A note on infant salvation

Confession 10.3

> Elect infants, dying in infancy, are regenerated and saved by Christ through the Spirit,[4] who works when, where, and how he pleases.[5] The same is true of all other elect persons who are incapable of being outwardly called by the ministry of the word.[6]

The subject of infant salvation is one that is a great concern pastorally. The Confession does not teach that all infants will be saved nor does it deny it. It seeks to reflect the silence of Scripture on the subject. We note:

---

1 II Timothy 1:9; Titus 3:4-5; Ephesians 2:4-5, 8-9; Romans 9:11.
2 I Corinthians 2:14; Romans 8:7; Ephesians 2:5.
3 John 6:37; Ezekiel 36:27; John 5:25.
4 Luke 18:15-16 and Acts 2: 38-39 and John 3:3, 5 and I John 5:12 and Romans 8:9 cp.
5 John 3:8.
6 I John 5:12; Acts 4:12.

1. It is assumed that there are *Elect infants* and as a result that there will be infants saved. It does not teach that all infants are elect.
2. These infants are *saved by Christ.* They too *are regenerated.* If we deny the priority of the new birth and say that faith occurs first then we deny the salvation of infants and others who are incapable of intelligent faith.
3. Others such as those who are seriously mentally impaired are included here.
4. The Confession does not theorize about the so-called 'age of responsibility' since this is a non-biblical idea.

The way in which the Confession deals with this delicate subject teaches us that we too must claim the lack of knowledge where Scripture is silent.

The position of the non-elect

Confession 10.4

> Others, not elect, may be called by the ministry of the word,[1] and the Spirit[2] may work in them in some of the same ways he works in the elect. However, they never truly come to Christ and therefore cannot be saved.[3] And, of course, people not professing the Christian religion cannot be saved in any other way at all,[4] no matter how hard they try to live a moral life according to their own understanding or try to obey the rules of some other religion. To say they can be saved is extremely harmful and should be considered a horrible suggestion.[5]

This final paragraph (10.4) discusses the position of the non-elect. Two categories are mentioned, those who have heard the gospel but have not responded and those who are members of other religions.

It is admitted that many hear the Word but never come to faith. They hear and to an extent understand that they need salvation but do not seek it. The Holy Spirit may indeed bless them in common grace and they may experience some of the spin-offs of saving grace. This

1 Matthew 22:14.
2 Matthew 7:22, 13:20-21; Hebrews 6:4-5.
3 John 6:64-66, 8:24.
4 Acts 4:12; John 14:6; Ephesians 2:12; John 4:22, 17:3.
5 II John 9-11; I Corinthians 16:22; Galatians 1: 6-8.

often happens in times of revival when people are carried along with the crowd but do not come to faith themselves. Such people *never come to Christ and therefore cannot be saved* because of their own refusal to come to the Saviour who is the only way of salvation.

In the case of those who are members of other religions, the Confession teaches that it is impossible for them to be saved apart from the gospel. The final sentence of this paragraph is important in light of much contemporary teaching, *To say they can be saved is extremely harmful and should be considered a horrible suggestion*.

Cross references with the Catechisms:

Shorter: 31, 32; Larger: 67-69

To think over and discuss:

1. How should this teaching on effectual calling affect our evangelism? (The making of public appeals and so forth).
2. According to the teaching in this chapter, no person can be saved apart from the gospel. What are you doing in world outreach?

JUSTIFICATION

Ref. Confession Chapter 11 – Justification

In this study you will discover:

- The meaning of Justification
- How Justification fits into the Plan of God
- The relationship between Justification and Forgiveness in believers

The doctrine of justification is crucial to our understanding of the biblical faith and its demise today has thrown the church into woolly thinking. The Confession and the Catechisms speak with the clarity of the noonday sun on this subject and a careful study of this chapter will enable Church leaders and members to have a correct understanding of this central doctrine.

The meaning of Justification

To be justified means to be in a right relationship with God, to be accepted by him. This implies that the sinner is forgiven.

Confession 11.1

> Those whom God effectually calls he also freely justifies.[1] He does not pour righteousness into them but pardons their sins and looks on them and accepts them as if they were righteous – not because of anything worked in them or done by them, but for Christ's sake alone. He does not consider their faith itself, the act of believing, as their righteousness or any other obedient response to the gospel on their part. Rather, he imputes to them the obedience and judicial satisfaction earned by Christ.[2] For their part, they receive and rest on Christ and his righteousness by faith (and this faith is not their own but is itself a gift of God).[3]

This section (11.1) opens by linking effectual calling with justification, that is, those who are called are justified,

> *"And those whom he predestined he also called, and those whom he called he also justified, and those whom he justified he also glorified"* (Romans 8:30).

The all-important distinction between imparted and imputed righteousness is then stated. A person is not put right with God by a change of nature, *he does not pour righteousness into them* this is

1 Romans 8:30, 3:24.
2 Romans 4:5-8; II Corinthians 5:19, 21; Romans 3:22, 24-25, 27-28; Titus 3:5,7; Ephesians 1:7; Jeremiah 23:6; I Corinthians 1:30-31; Romans 5:17-19.
3 Acts 10:44; Galatians 2:16; Philippians 3:9; Acts 13:38-39; Ephesians 2:7, 8.

known as 'imparted righteousness'. This is not acceptable because they are being made righteous through either a gift of righteousness or the work of the Holy Spirit in them in regeneration and sanctification. The implication of imparted righteousness is that their good deeds make them acceptable to God. This is the teaching of Roman Catholicism.

In contrast, the Reformed Faith teaches that God accepts a person because the righteousness of Christ has been credited, or accounted to him. This is known as 'imputed righteousness'. It is because of the righteousness of Christ that has been imputed to the sinner, so the sinner is declared 'not guilty'. Justification is a legal term. A judge cannot change the nature of a person by declaring him not guilty. God, in declaring the sinner not guilty, does not change the sinner's nature, rather the penalty of the law is removed. A person's nature is changed in salvation, but that is not the reason for their acceptance by God. That aspect of salvation, namely sanctification, will be discussed in a following chapter (Confession Chapter 13).

The reason a person is accepted is due to the activity of Christ alone, his work not theirs. It is vital to note the phrase, *'He imputes to them the obedience and judicial satisfaction earned by Christ'*. It was both his life, in his keeping of the law, and the death of Christ that earned salvation for the elect. He did good works on their behalf, he died to take the punishment of a holy God against sin. In doing so he satisfied the divine requirements.

It is this righteousness that is credited to the sinner, so that God can declare him not guilty because of the Messiah's work. This is not a piece of legal fiction, it is true because those in Christ are counted righteous because of him. It is not faith that is imputed (faith is only the instrument or means) or any other work that a person might perform, it is the work of Christ which is imputed.

Confession 11.2

> Faith, thus receiving and resting on Christ and his righteousness, is the only means of justification.[1] In the person justified, however, it is always accompanied by all the other saving graces and is not a dead faith, but works by love.[2]

"Faith does not justify a sinner in the sight of God because of those other graces which always accompany it, or because of good works which are its fruit, nor is the grace of faith or any act of faith credited to him for his

1 John 1:12; Romans 3:28, 5:1.
2 James 2:17, 22, 26; Galatians 5:6.

justification. But **faith justifies only in that it is an instrument** by which the sinner receives and applies Christ and his righteousness" (WLC 73 emphasis added).

In these first two paragraphs the relationship of faith to justification is discussed. The following is taught:

- It is not faith which saves, it is Christ.
- Faith is a gift of God, it is not earned.
- It is faith in Christ alone and the gift of *his righteousness, is the only* way the sinner receives *justification*.
- Faith is an instrument or means, just as a thirsty person quenches his thirst with water, it is his hand that takes the glass to his mouth, it is not the hand that quenches his thirst, but the water, faith is only the means by which we receive Christ.
- *In the person* who is truly *justified*, this faith is not alone but is accompanied by good works. These works follow faith and justification but they are not the cause of them.

The subject of saving faith will be further explored in a later chapter.

How Justification fits into the Plan of God

There is always the danger of regarding Christ as stepping between an angry Father and sinners, the third paragraph guards against this false idea.

Confession 11.3

> By his obedience and death Christ completely discharged the debt of all those who are so justified, and he made the correct, real, and full satisfaction to his Father's justice on their behalf.[1] Since Christ was voluntarily given by the Father for them,[2] and since his obedience and satisfaction were accepted in their place[3] and not for anything in them, their justification is the result only of his free grace[4] – so that both the perfect justice and the rich grace of God might be glorified in the justification of sinners.[5]

The paragraph opens with a clear statement that Christ satisfied the justice of the Father on behalf of the elect. God is holy, he could not ignore sin, so Christ took the punishment due to sinners and hence

---

1 Romans 5:8-9, 10, 19; I Timothy 2:5-6; Hebrews 10:10, 14; Daniel 9:24, 26; Isaiah 53:4-6, 10-12.
2 Romans 8:32.
3 II Corinthians 5:21; Matthew 3:17; Ephesians 5:2.
4 Romans 3:24; Ephesians 1:7.
5 Romans 3:26; Ephesians 2:7.

satisfied the justice of God. But it was the Father who gave the Son. This was out of love and it demonstrates the grace of God. So the act of the Father and the Son in *justification is the result only of his free grace so that both the perfect justice and the rich grace of God might be glorified in the justification of sinners.*

It is worth noting in this section, the emphasis on the fact that the exact justice of God was satisfied, so that sinners have nothing to add. Their justification is all of free grace.

Confession 11.4

> From all eternity God decreed the justification of all the elect,[1] and in the fullness of time Christ died for their sins and rose again for their justification.[2] Nevertheless, the elect are not justified until the Holy Spirit in due time does actually apply Christ to them.[3]

In this paragraph (11:4), the teaching that the elect are justified from all eternity is opposed. While it is part of the plan of God to justify the elect and the death and resurrection of Christ are the means to bring this about. The actual fact of justification in the individual, does not take place *until the Holy Spirit in due time does actually apply Christ to them.*

The relationship between justification and forgiveness in believers

Confession 11.5

> God continues to forgive the sins of those who are justified.[4] Although they can never fall from the state of justification,[5] they may by their sins come under God's fatherly displeasure and not have a sense of his presence with them until they humble themselves, confess their sins, ask for forgiveness, and renew their faith in repentance.[6]

The old question, what happens if a believer sins is answered in this paragraph.

Those who are justified continue to receive forgiveness, they cannot lose their justification. This is because it depends on Christ and

1 Galatians 3:8; I Peter 1:2, 19-20; Romans 8:30.
2 Galatians 4:4; I Timothy 2:6; Romans 4:25.
3 Colossians 1:21-22; Galatians 2:16; Titus 3:4-7.
4 Matthew 6:12; I John 1: 7, 9, 2:1-2.
5 Luke 22:32; John 10:28; Hebrews 10:14.
6 Psalms 89: 31-33, 51:7-12, 32:5; Matthew 26:75; I Corinthians 11:30, 32; Luke 1:20.

part, and the erroneous belief of 'let go and let God'.

Confession 13.3

> Although the old nature temporarily wins battles in this warfare,[1] the continual strengthening of the sanctifying Spirit of Christ enables the regenerate nature in each believer to overcome.[2] And so believers grow in grace,[3] perfecting holiness in the fear of God.[4]

While the whole man is influenced in sanctification it will never be perfect in this life. There is a war between the old nature, the flesh, and the new nature, and this will continue until the day we die.

At times it will appear that the sinful nature is getting the upper hand, but God will supply the grace so that the new nature will have the ultimate victory. The Confession does not teach the theory of a constant victorious life. It is realistic and recognizes that there will be times when believers are defeated. The defeat however in the true believer is never final.

Cross references with the Catechisms:

Shorter: 35; Larger: 75, 77-78. ***WLC 77 is important as it clearly defines the difference between justification and sanctification.***

> "Although sanctification is inseparably connected to justification, yet they differ. In justification God credits the righteousness of Christ whereas in sanctification he infuses grace and enables its exercise; in justification sin is pardoned while in sanctification it is subdued. Justification frees all believers equally and perfectly in this life from the avenging wrath of God so that they will never fall into condemnation, whereas sanctification is not equal in everyone nor is it perfect in any one in this life, but grows up to perfection" (WLC 77).

To think over and discuss:

1. In what way could a lack of emphasis in the initial act of sanctification lead people to hunt for a second blessing?
2. Explain the vital differences between sanctification and justification.

---

1 Romans 7:23.
2 Romans 6:14; I John 5:4; Ephesians 4:15, 16.
3 II Peter 3:18; II Corinthians 3:18.
4 II Corinthians 7:1.

FAITH AND REPENTANCE

Ref. Confession Chapter 14 - Saving Faith,
Ref. Confession Chapter 15 - Repentance unto Life

In this study you will discover:

- The origin of Saving Faith
- The true nature of Saving Faith
- The necessity of Repentance
- The true nature of Repentance

The Holy Scripture speaks of true or saving faith and of deluded or false faith,

> *"Not everyone who says to me, 'Lord, Lord,' will enter the kingdom of heaven, but the one who does the will of my Father who is in heaven"* (Matthew 7:21ff),

> *"What good is it, my brothers, if someone says he has faith but does not have works? Can that faith save him?"* (James 2:14ff).

The Confession is well aware that it is possible to be deluded, so in this chapter the true nature of saving faith is explained.

The origin of Saving Faith

Confession 14.1

> The gift of faith makes it possible for the souls of the elect to be saved by believing in Jesus Christ.[1] This gift is the work of the Spirit of Christ in the hearts of the elect[2] and is ordinarily accomplished by the ministry of the word.[3] It is also increased and strengthened by the word, by prayer, and by the administration of the sacraments.[4]

Many people think faith is something they work up to until they can believe, but the Confession teaches that faith is a gift, this is why it refers to *the gift of faith*. This is saving faith and the elect exercise it

> *"For by grace you have been saved through faith. And this is not your own doing; it is the gift of God,"* (Ephesians 2:8ff).

Faith is planted in the heart by the Holy Spirit. It is he who enables us to believe. In this action the Holy Spirit uses the ministry of the Word, especially preaching. This reflects the reformed conviction of the importance of preaching, considered in the Shorter and Larger Catechisms.

---

1. Hebrews 10:39.
2. II Corinthians 4:13; Ephesians 1:17-19, 2:8.
3. Romans 10:14, 17.
4. I Peter 2:2; Acts 20:32; Romans 4:11; Luke 17:5; Romans 1:16-17.

> "The spirit of God maketh the reading, but especially the preaching of the word, an effectual means of convincing and converting sinners, and of building them up in holiness and comfort, through faith, unto salvation" (WSC 89).
>
> "This spirit of God maketh the reading, but especially the preaching of the word, an effectual means of enlightening, convincing, and humbling sinners; of driving them out of themselves, and drawing them unto Christ; of conforming them to his image, and subduing them to his will; of strengthening them against temptations and corruptions; of building them up in grace, and establishing their hearts in holiness and comfort through faith unto salvation" (WLC 155).
>
> As adopted by the Church of Scotland in the Act of 1647

Through the Word, the mind is informed of the truth and by the Spirit it is able to accept and act on it. This is the normal way in which God works. It is the way we should expect him to work. The Word *ordinarily* leaves room for the freedom of God to work in some other way on rare occasions. In doing so it guards against tying the hand of God but also prevents people seeking after novelty.

Faith *is also increased* through the *sacraments* and *prayer*. The important word here *is increased*, *the sacraments* are not "converting ordinances", but a means to strengthen the *faith* which has been created by the Holy Spirit through *the ministry of the word*.

The true nature of Saving Faith

Confession 14.2

> By this faith a Christian believes whatever is revealed in the word to be the true, authentic, authoritative statement of God himself.[1] By this faith the believer also acts according to what particular passages in the word say. By faith the believer humbly submits to and obeys God's various commands.[2] He trembles at God's awesome threats[3] and eagerly embraces his promises about this life and the life to come.[4] But the chief actions of saving faith are accepting, receiving, and resting on Christ alone for justification, sanctification, and eternal life, in the power of the covenant of grace.[5]

This saving faith has two parts to it, the acceptance of Holy Scripture as true and trust in Christ. The latter is impossible without the former.

---

1 John 4:42; I Thessalonians 2:13; I John 5:10; Acts 24:14.
2 Romans 16:26.
3 Isaiah 66:2.
4 Hebrews 11:13; I Timothy 4:8.
5 John 1:12; Acts 16:31; Galatians 2:20; Acts 15:11.

The Christian accepts as true what Scripture teaches and recognizes the authority of God in its words. The response of the believer depends on the content of the passage. If it is a command, then obedience. If it is warning, we tremble before it. If it is a promise, we embrace it and act upon it. If anyone does not believe that Scripture is true and carries the authority of God, then it is ignored, but if a person has true faith it is impossible for him or her to reject the authority of Scripture.

It is on this foundation that we can trust in Christ, for if we believe the Bible is mistaken, then we cannot accept what it says about Christ. This means we know nothing about him and to have faith in one we know nothing about is either foolish or impossible. Once the Spirit enables us to accept as true what Scripture records about Jesus Christ then it is possible to trust the One we know about. Faith is concerned with the object. We will put our money into a bank that we know, rather than give it to a stranger at the door to look after.

When we know about Christ's person and work, then we can trust him alone for salvation. Saving faith does not stop at believing the truth of what is said about Jesus, but it goes on to trust him, to rely on him *alone for justification, sanctification and eternal life*. Faith must never be reduced to the mere acceptance of facts. It is trust in the person who is revealed by those facts.

Confession 14.3

> This faith has different degrees of strength and weakness.[1] It may be attacked and weakened often and in many ways, but it gets the victory.[2] In many believers it matures and becomes completely assured through Christ,[3] who both creates and perfects our faith.[4]

The third paragraph in this chapter (14.3) makes it clear that faith is not constant. At times it is weak, but it will never die. It will have *the victory through Christ* who is its author and sustainer.

The necessity of Repentance

Confession 15.1

> Repentance which leads to life is the blessed product of the gospel working in believers' lives.[5] Along with the doctrine of faith in Christ it is a doctrine to be preached by every minister of the gospel.[6]

---

1 Hebrews 5:13-14; Romans 4:19-20; Matthew 6:30, 8:10.
2 Luke 22:31-32; Ephesians 6:16; I John 5:4-5.
3 Hebrews 6:11-12, 10:22; Colossians 2:2.
4 Hebrews 12:2.
5 Zechariah 12:10; Acts 11:18.
6 Luke 24:47; Mark 1:15; Acts 20:21.

Repentance is the other side of faith. True faith is always coupled with repentance and the reverse is also true. Repentance is the change of mind which results in turning and accepting the new life in Christ. It should be noted that repentance *is the blessed product of the gospel*, that is, it is produced by the Gospel, not our own efforts.

Confession 15.3

> Although repentance is not any satisfaction for sin and does not cause the forgiveness of sins[1] (since forgiveness is an act of God's voluntary grace in Christ[2]), yet it is necessary to all sinners, and no one may expect to be forgiven without it.[3]

In the third paragraph (15.3) the absolute necessity of repentance is stated; *yet it is necessary to all sinners, and no one may expect to be forgiven without* repentance. This statement is carefully guarded in case it is thought that repentance earns salvation. In this paragraph a warning is also given that repentance is not to be trusted for salvation *since forgiveness is an act of God's voluntary grace in Christ.* In the first paragraph (15.1) it is taught that repentance is the product *of the gospel working in believers' lives*, and not something which man works up by his own determination. Penance therefore, is ruled out since the Doctrine of Penance wrongly teaches that it is the people's self-effort which atones for sin.

This doctrine is to be proclaimed by every minister of the gospel, it is basic in all witnessing, for without it there can be no salvation. This refers back to 15.1.

The true nature of Repentance

Confession 15.2

> In this repentance the sinner is able to see his sins as God sees them, as filthy and hateful, and as involving great danger to the sinner, because they are completely contrary to the holy nature and righteous law of God. Understanding that God in Christ is merciful to those who repent, the sinner suffers deep sorrow for and hates his sins, and so he determines to turn away from all of them. And turning to God,[4] he tries to walk with him according to all his commandments.[5]

The reason the sinner repents is not merely due to the fear of eternal damnation, but also because he has begun to recognize the true

1 Ezekiel 36: 31-32, 16: 61-63.
2 Hosea 14:2, 4; Romans 3:24; Ephesians 1:7.
3 Luke 13:3, 5; Acts 17:30, 31.
4 Ezekiel 18:30, 31, 36:31; Isaiah 30:22; Psalm 51:4; Jeremiah 31:18-19; Joel 2:12-13; Amos 5:15; Psalm 119:128; II Corinthians 7:11.
5 Psalm 119: 6, 59, 106; Luke 1:6; II Kings 23:25.

nature of sin as a contradiction of the *holy nature* of God (15.2). Sin has become odious to him. At the same time he sees the mercy of God in Christ for those who are penitent, that is, sorry for their sin and willing to forsake it, and so the sinner *hates his sins*, and turns from them *all* to God. His future desire is to walk in the way of God's law.

Confession 15.4

> Just as there is no sin so small that it does not deserve damnation,[1] so there is no sin so great that it can bring damnation upon those who truly repent.[2]

Confession 15.5

> Believers should not be satisfied with general repentance. Rather it is everyone's duty to try to repent of every individual sin individually.[3]

It is not just a matter of being sorry, but of leaving all sin. In the fourth and fifth paragraphs the serious nature of 'small sins' is underlined, as is the duty to forsake particular sins. It is not a general "I am sorry", but "I am sorry for x, y, and z", and "I forsake x, y, and z". The sinner will make compensation if required.

> *"And Zacchaeus stood and said to the Lord, 'Behold, Lord, the half of my goods I give to the poor. And if I have defrauded anyone of anything, I restore it fourfold'"* (Luke 19:8ff).

Confession 15.6

> Everyone is also bound to confess privately his sins to God and to pray for forgiveness for them.[4] Confession, prayer for forgiveness, and the forsaking of sins which have been forgiven will find God's mercy.[5] Similarly, anyone who sins against his spiritual brother or the church should be willing to confess, privately or publicly, to demonstrate sorrow for his sin, and openly to state his repentance to those whom he has hurt.[6] They in turn are to be reconciled to him and to receive him in love.[7]

The final part of this chapter (15.6) covers the relationship between

---

1 Romans 6:23, 5:12; Matthew 12:36.
2 Isaiah 55:7; Romans 8:1; Isaiah 1:16, 18.
3 Psalm 19:13; Luke 19:8; I Timothy 1:13, 15.
4 Psalms 51:4-5, 7, 9, 14, 32:5-6.
5 Proverbs 28:13; I John 1:9.
6 James 5:16; Luke 17:3-4; Joshua 7:19; [Psalm 51].
7 II Corinthians 2:8.

confession and repentance. The primary confession is to God, to seek his forgiveness and grace to forsake sin. However, if someone has offended another, or scandalized the church of Christ, he must declare his repentance to the parties he has offended. It is their duty to be reconciled to him and receive him. If it is a private offence then it is to be a private act, but if it is public then the person is to make a public confession and the other party is to declare publicly the reconciliation.

Cross references with Catechisms:

Shorter: 86-89; Larger: 72, 73, 76 cf. 149-153, 155

To think over and discuss:

1. Discuss the relationship between faith and repentance.
2. Why must regeneration be prior to faith and repentance?
3. In what ways could your evangelism be defective due to a lack of balance or a neglect of either faith or repentance?

neglect the things that God has commanded.

Cross references with the Catechisms:

There are no direct references in the catechisms to good works as the Confession discusses them. The impossibility of keeping God's law is dealt with in the Shorter: 82-84 and Larger: 149-152.

To think over and discuss:

1. Why is it so important to emphasize the need of the Holy Spirit to enable us to do good works?
2. "It is sinful for an unregenerate person to pray and attend church, but not to do so is even a greater sin". Discuss the truth and implications of this statement.

GOING ON

Ref. Confession Chapter 17 – The Perseverance of Christians

In this study you will discover:

- True believers will never lose their salvation
- It is possible for believers to fall into sin

Christians have often debated the possibility of a believer losing salvation. On the one side there are those who teach that if a believer backslides he is lost until he repents. On the other extreme there are those who teach that a believer can fall into the worst of sins, and continue unrepentant and still be saved. The Confession avoids both of these extremes, teaching that true believers may fall, but they will be restored and go on to the end.

True believers will never lose their salvation

Confession 17.1

> Those whom God has accepted in his Son and has effectually called and sanctified by his Spirit can never completely or finally fall out of their state of grace. Rather, they shall definitely continue in that state to the end and are eternally saved.[1]

It is important to understand that the Confession is not speaking about anyone who has made a profession, but about true believers, those who have been really converted. Note how they are described: *accepted in his Son, effectually called, and sanctified by his Spirit . . .* This is quite different from saying that they signed a card or made a decision.

It is they who cannot *completely or finally fall out of their state of grace*. They will be saved. The Confession does not say that they cannot fall, nor does it say that if they fall they will be lost.

Confession 17.2

> This endurance of Christians does not depend on their own free will but on God's unchangeable decree of election, flowing from his voluntary, unchangeable love.[2] It also depends on the effectiveness of the merit and intercession of Jesus Christ,[3] on the indwelling Spirit and indwelling seed of God in believers,[4] and on the nature of the covenant of grace.[5] All these establish the certainty and infallibility of their preservation.[6]

The reasons for their perseverance are given in the second

1 Philippians 1:6; II Peter 1:10; John 10:28-29; I John 3:9; I Peter 5, 9.
2 II Timothy 2: 18, 19; Jeremiah 31:3.
3 Hebrews 10:10,14, 13:20-21, Hebrews 9:12-15; Romans 8: 33-39; John 17:11, 24; Luke 22:32; Hebrews 7:25.
4 John 14:16-17; I John 2:27; I John 3:9.
5 Jeremiah 32:40.
6 John 10:28; II Thessalonians 3:3; I John 2:19.

paragraph (17.2). The source is God, not their own ability. A number of reasons are given:

- God's love and election, (he does not choose to lose)
- The work of Christ, (he lived, died and lives to save - not to try to save).
- The Holy Spirit indwelling each believer and the possession of a new nature, *indwelling seed of God in believers*.

Keep in mind the Covenant of Grace. If we did not earn salvation by works, we cannot forfeit it because of our failure. The Covenant graciously promises that God will be our God forever. He does not break his Word.

> *"Behold, the days are coming, declares the LORD, when I will make a new covenant with the house of Israel and the house of Judah, not like the covenant that I made with their fathers on the day when I took them by the hand to bring them out of the land of Egypt, my covenant that they broke, though I was their husband, declares the LORD.*
> *But this is the covenant that I will make with the house of Israel after those days, declares the LORD: I will put my law within them, and I will write it on their hearts. And I will be their God, and they shall be my people.*
> *And no longer shall each one teach his neighbour and each his brother, saying, 'Know the LORD', for they shall all know me, from the least of them to the greatest, declares the LORD. For I will forgive their iniquity, and I will remember their sin no more"* (Jeremiah 31:31-34ff).

It is possible for true believers to fall into sin

Confession 17.3

Nevertheless, the temptations of Satan, the world, and their old carnal natures, along with neglect of the means of their preservation, may lead believers to commit serious sins[1] and to continue in them for a time.[2] They consequently displease God[3] and grieve his Holy Spirit,[4] have some of the fruit of God's grace and his comforts taken away from them,[5] have their hearts hardened[6] and their consciences wounded,[7] hurt and offend others,[8] and bring temporal judgments on themselves.[9]

1 Matthew 26:70, 72, 74.
2 Psalm 51: Title and verse 14.
3 Isaiah 64: 5, 7, 9; II Samuel 11:27.
4 Ephesians 4:30.
5 Psalm 51:8, 10, 12; Revelation 2:4; Song of Solomon 5:2-4, 6.
6 Isaiah 63:17; Mark 6:52, 16:14.
7 Psalms 32:3-4, 51:8.
8 II Samuel 12:14.
9 Psalm 89:31-32; I Corinthians 11:32.

Believers are not perfect and they may not only fall into sin but into 'serious' sin. King David's adultery with Bathsheba is a typical example. The third paragraph lists a number of reasons for this:

- *the temptations of Satan* and *the world*,
- the remaining corruption of our nature

and significantly the Confession adds,

- the *neglect of the means of their preservation*; the Word, Prayer, Fellowship and Sacrament (cf. WLC 154).

> "The outward and ordinary means by which Christ gives to his church the benefits of his mediation are all his ordinances, especially the word, sacraments and prayer, and all these are made effective in the salvation of the elect" (WLC 154).

This fall into serious sin will not be permanent. Believers will only continue in them for a time. God cannot ignore it and his people suffer for their disobedience. They are under the displeasure of God as David was after his serious fall,

> *"And when the mourning was over, David sent and brought her to his house, and she became his wife and bore him a son. But the thing that David had done displeased the LORD"* (II Samuel 11:27).

The Confession lists a number of ways the displeasure of God is displayed. God cannot ignore sin, not even in his child, but this is his chastening hand and they will return to him and experience his smile forever.

Cross references with the Catechisms:

Shorter: no direct questions; Larger: 77-79.

To think over and discuss

1. Why is it important to distinguish between the true believer and the mere professor in the Doctrine of Perseverance?
2. What is wrong with the common expression "once saved, always saved"?
3. Meditate on signs of God's displeasure in confession 17.3, and think of biblical examples and examples from your own experience.

ASSURANCE

Ref. Confession Chapter 18 – The Assurance of Grace and Salvation

In this study you will discover:

- Assurance of salvation is possible
- The basis and nature of assurance
- Assurance, though not necessary for salvation, is to be sought

The theme of this chapter may seem strange to many who are used to the idea that a person has assurance the moment they make a 'decision'. This was not always and is not always the case. Often assurance was difficult to obtain and its possibility was denied by Roman Catholic teaching. It is against this background that the chapter should be read.

Assurance of salvation is possible

Confession 18.1

> Hypocrites and other unregenerate men may deceive themselves with false hopes and carnal presumptions about their being in God's favor and about their being saved.[1] Their presumptions will die with them.[2] However, those who truly believe in the Lord Jesus, who honestly love him and try to walk in good conscience before him, may in this life be assured with certainty that they are in a state of grace.[3] They may also rejoice in the hope of the glory of God, and they will never be ashamed of that hope.[4]

In this first paragraph we are taught that while there are those who will delude themselves with *false hopes* of salvation genuine believers can have assurance.

> *"On that day many will say to me, 'Lord, Lord, did we not prophesy in your name, and cast out demons in your name, and do many mighty works in your name?'"* (Matthew 7:22).

This assurance is for this life, that is, we can know with certainty that we are in a state of grace. We do not have to wait until after we

1 Job 8:13-14; Micah 3:11; Deuteronomy 29:19; John 8:41.
2 Matthew 7:22-23.
3 I John 2:3, 3:14, 18-19, 21, 24, 5:13.
4 Romans 5:2, 5.

die. This assurance is not for the careless professor, he has no right to conclude that he has salvation. It is for *those who truly believe in the Lord Jesus, who honestly love him and try to walk in good conscience before him, may in this life be assured with certainty that they are in a state of grace.*

Assurance increases the joy of the believer, but the one who lives in a world of doubt with regard to the certainty of his salvation cannot have much joy. The man who has the certainty of salvation can look forward to a great future with the Lord and rejoice in it.

The basis and nature of assurance

Confession 18.2

> This certainty is not based on the fallible hope of guesswork or probabilities. Rather, it is the infallible assurance of faith,[1] established on the divine truth of the promises of salvation.[2] There is also the inner evidence of spiritual insight, given to us by God, to which these promises are directed.[3] And there is the testimony of the Spirit of adoption, witnessing with our spirits that we are the children of God.[4] This Spirit is the pledge of our inheritance. By him we are sealed until the day of redemption.[5]

It is not merely a guessing matter, nor is it a hope built on unsure foundation *probabilities*. There is certainty because the foundation on which we build our assurance is secure. In this paragraph (18.2) the Confession gives three biblical reasons on which we build our assurance.

1. Holy Scripture is given by God (Confession Chapter 1) and is therefore true and can be trusted. In Scripture God *promises salvation* to those who believe,

   "For God so loved the world, that he gave his only Son, that whoever believes in him should not perish but have eternal life" (John 3:16),

   "And they said, 'Believe in the Lord Jesus, and you will be saved, you and your household'" (Acts 16:31),

   and since God does not lie, a true believer can say they are

1 Hebrews 6:11,19.
2 Hebrews 6:17-18.
3 II Peter 1:4-5,10-11; I John 2:3, 3:14; II Corinthians 1:12.
4 Romans 8:15-16.
5 Ephesians 1:13-14, 4:30; II Corinthians 1:21-22.

saved. The assurance of salvation is founded on the belief of the truth of Scripture. If we have doubts about it's reliability, assurance of salvation is impossible.

2. The second pillar is what the Confession calls: *the inner evidence of spiritual insight, given to us by God, to which these promises are directed.* This refers to the changed life that results from conversion.
   The major questions are:
   a. How is a person to know that their faith is real and not counterfeit? The answer lies in examining the life in light of the scripture references quoted below.
   b. Do we desire to keep the law of God?

      "If you love me, you will keep my commandments" (John 14:15),

      "And by this we know that we have come to know him, if we keep his commandments" (I John 2:3),

      "We know that we have passed out of death into life, because we love the brothers. Whoever does not love abides in death" (I John 3:14),

      "Little children, let us not love in word or talk but in deed and in truth" (I John 3:18).
   c. Do we hunger and thirst after righteousness?

      "Blessed are those who hunger and thirst for righteousness, for they shall be satisfied" (Matthew 5:6).
   d. Are we in some measure bearing the fruit of the Spirit?

      "But the fruit of the Spirit is love, joy, peace, patience, kindness, goodness, faithfulness . . ." (Galatians 5:22ff).
   e. Do we hate the world?

      "Do not love the world or the things in the world. If anyone loves the world, the love of the Father is not in him" (I John 2:15ff).

3. The third pillar *is the testimony of the Spirit of adoption, witnessing with our spirits that we are the children of God.* This teaching is based on Romans 8:16.

> *"The Spirit himself bears witness with our spirit that we are children of God, and if children, then heirs—heirs of God and fellow heirs with Christ, provided we suffer with him in order that we may also be glorified with him"* (Romans 8:16-17).

It does not say that the Spirit speaks directly to us that we are God's children, rather the Holy Spirit bears witness *with* (not to) *our* spirit. He enables us to discern the evidence, he guides and leads us through the Word.

The Holy Spirit is the guarantee given to every believer that they are God's, this is the meaning of the last phrase in this paragraph. He is the earnest, the deposit, he is the seal (himself, not merely his work) that is the mark of God's ownership, and *This Spirit is the pledge of our inheritance. By him we are sealed until the day of redemption.*

> *"and who has also put his seal on us and given us his Spirit in our hearts as a guarantee (or down payment)"* (II Corinthians 1:22).

The Holy Spirit dwelling within the believer is the foretaste of heaven. This is the privilege of every true believer.

Assurance, though not necessary for salvation, is to be sought

Confession 18.3

> This infallible assurance is not so essential to faith that a true believer may not have doubts and conflicts about it, possibly wait some time for it, and grow into it.[1] But since the Spirit enables believers to know the things which are freely given to them by God, every believer may come to a full assurance of salvation by the ordinary working of the Spirit without unusual revelation.[2] Therefore it is every believer's duty to establish the certainty of his calling and election[3] so that his heart may be filled with peace and joy in the Holy Spirit, with love and thankfulness to God, and with strength and cheerfulness of obedience. These are the true products of assurance,[4] which is never conducive to an undisciplined life.[5]

It is possible to be a Christian and not have assurance of salvation. A true believer may have to wait a long time before he is granted this

---

1 I John 5:13; Isaiah 50:10; Mark 9:24; [Psalms 88, 77:1-12].
2 I Corinthians 2:12; I John 4:13; Hebrews 6:11-12; Ephesians 3:17-19.
3 II Peter 1:10.
4 Romans 5:1-2, 5, 14:17, 15:13; Ephesians 1:3-4; Psalms 4:6-7, 119:32.
5 I John 2:1-2; Romans 6:1-2; Titus 2:11-12, 14; II Corinthians 7:1; Romans 8:1, 12; I John 3:2-3; Psalm 130:4; I John 1:6-7.

assurance which is not necessary for salvation but for the joy of salvation. The Confession knows nothing of a preacher telling a person they are saved after they have made some kind of profession. It is God who grants assurance, but he does this through the ordinary means of grace and not some special direct revelation. Every *believer may come to a full assurance of salvation by the ordinary working of the Spirit without unusual revelation.* This implies that a person is not to expect some voice from heaven telling them they are saved, but a growing conviction that all is well with their soul, as they examine themselves for the evidence of grace outlined above. It is the duty of everyone *to establish the certainty of his calling and election,* as this will increase their joy and usefulness as believers. A person who is unsure will not have the same joy or zeal in the service of God.

In reply to those who would say that this teaching on assurance only causes a person to be careless in how they live, the Confession teaches that it encourages obedience rather than looseness. The reason is that when a person lives as God intends, he has greater assurance and greater joy. If the true believer falls into sin, he is convicted and loses the joy of salvation,

> *"Restore to me the joy of your salvation, and uphold me with a willing spirit"* (cf. Psalm 51:12).

Confession 18.4

> The assurance true believers have of their salvation may be shaken, lessened, or interrupted for various reasons: from neglecting to preserve it; from committing some particular sin, which wounds the conscience and grieves the Spirit; from some sudden or strong temptation; or from God's withdrawing the sense of his presence and allowing them to walk in darkness.[1] Nevertheless, they are never completely without God's seed, the life of faith, the love of Christ and of other believers, and the sincere heart and obedient conscience, out of which the Spirit may revive this assurance in due time[2] and by which they are in the meantime kept from complete despair.[3]

The final paragraph (18.4) teaches that the strength of assurance may vary and indeed may be lost altogether. It is often lost due to the sin of the believer, but this is not always the case. The Christian may

1 Song of Solomon 5:2-3, 6; Psalm 51:8, 12, 14; Ephesians 4:30, 31; Psalm 77:1-10; Matthew 26:69-72; Psalm 31:22; [Psalm 88]; Isaiah 50:10.
2 I John 3:9; Luke 22:32; Job 13:15; Psalms 73:15, 51:8, 12; Isaiah 50:10.
3 Micah 7: 7-9; Jeremiah 32:40; Isaiah 54:7-10; Psalm 22:1; [Psalm 88].

pass through a great time of trial or temptation (like Bunyan's pilgrim in the valley of the shadow of death) and so doubt their salvation and lose assurance. Or in the plan of God a person, who is living a godly life with no known sin, can pass through an extreme time of doubt, this is described as *God's withdrawing the sense of his presence and allowing them to walk in darkness* (cf. book of Job).

> *"Who among you fears the LORD and obeys the voice of his servant? – Let him who walks in darkness and has no light – trust in the name of the LORD and rely on his God"* (Isaiah 50:10).

The true believer, however, always has the seed of God within. He is never destitute of the grace of God, though he may find it impossible to discern its marks in his soul. It is because of this fact he is prevented from lapsing into utter despair. Assurance may in due time return, but the Confession does not say that it will always return before death. It is possible for a true believer to pass into eternity doubting his salvation. Mr Fearing in Pilgrim's Progress was in many ways a brave pilgrim, but his great fear was that he would not be accepted at the last.

Cross references with the Catechisms:

Shorter: 36; Larger: 80-81.

To think over and discuss:

1. Is the practice in evangelism that instructs a person not to depend on feelings or doubt his salvation correct?
2. How would you help a person who lacks assurance?
3. I John 5:13 states that the letter was written so that a person may know they have eternal life. Study I John and list the marks of grace that are given in it.

CHAPTER IV

LIVING THE CHRISTIAN LIFE

THE IMPORTANCE OF GOD'S LAW

Ref. Confession Chapter 19 – The Law of God

In this study you will discover:

- The origin of law
- Three types of law
- The purpose of law

The origin of law

Confession 19.1

> God gave Adam a law as a covenant of works. He required Adam and all his descendants to obey this law, individually, completely, perpetually, and in precise accordance with its provisions. God promised life for keeping it and threatened death for disobeying it, and he gave man the power and ability to keep it.[1]

The first paragraph informs us that the origin of law is God, it was he who gave it to Adam. Adam had the requirements of the law of God inscribed on his conscience,

> *"For when Gentiles, who do not have the law, by nature do what the law requires, they are a law to themselves, even though they do not have the law.*
>
> *They show that the work of the law is written on their hearts, while their conscience also bears witness, and their conflicting thoughts accuse or even excuse them on that day when, according to my gospel, God judges the secrets of men by Christ Jesus"*
> (Romans 2:14-16).

After the fall this was distorted but not lost. Even today the most evil of men have a sense of right and wrong, though their standards are wrong. As we discovered earlier in Confession Chapter 7, God entered into a covenant of life or works with his child Adam. A part of a

[1] Genesis 1:26, 27, 2:17; Romans 2:14-15, 10:5, 5:12, 19; Galatians 3:10, 12; Ecclesiastes 7:29; Job 28:28.

covenant is always the call to obedience expressed in terms of law. In Adam's pre-fall condition this would have been a joy to him, the loving, joyful obedience to his Creator. Provided he obeyed, Adam had life and fellowship with God. But it was the failure to obey which caused his downfall and ruptured fellowship with the Creator. He had no need to rebel since God had given him the power to obey.

Adam was the head of the race and the covenant of life was not only for him but also for all generations after him. This bound him and all who descended from him *to obey this law, individually, completely,* and *perpetually*. The law was not suspended when Adam fell, rather his relationship to the law changed. Before it was joy to obey, promising life and glory, now it condemned and pointed to God's wrath upon those who disobeyed – and no man could keep it fully.

Confession 19.2

> After the fall this law continued to be a perfect rule of righteousness and was given, as such, by God on Mount Sinai in the Ten Commandments, written on two tablets.[1] The first four commandments establish our obligations to God and the remaining six our obligations to human beings.[2]

The second paragraph (19.2) states what is implied in the first, namely that the law which was given to Adam continued to be God's requirement for man and was republished at Sinai as the Ten Commandments.

Three types of law

The Confession teaches the traditional idea that the two stone tablets contained four laws on the first and six on the second expounding our duty to God and man respectively. Apart from this questionable division into duty to man and God, (all is to God – even the man-ward commandments) research into the Ancient Near Eastern covenant treaties explain why there were two tablets. At that time when a king captured another ruler's territory, they drew up a covenant treaty, this had laws with curses and blessings for disobedience and obedience. Duplicate copies of the laws were made, one was placed in the sanctuary of the victor and the other in the sanctuary of the conquered. God was the great King on this occasion, duplicate copies

[1] James 1:25, 2:8, 10-12; Romans 13:8-9; Deuteronomy 5:32, 10:4; Exodus 34:1.
[2] Matthew 22:37-40.

Old Testament believers.

The freedom of conscience

Confession 20.2

> God alone is Lord of the conscience[1] and has left it free from the doctrines and commandments of men which are in any way contrary to or different from his word in matters of faith or worship.[2] And so, believing any such teachings or obeying any such commandments of men for conscience's sake actually betrays true freedom of conscience.[3] Requiring implicit or absolute, blind obedience also destroys freedom of conscience as well as the free use of reason.[4]

This section (20.2) expounds the great Christian charter of freedom. A number of points are worthy of note:

1. *God alone is Lord of the conscience*. We are responsible to God alone and not to men.
2. The conscience is not bound to obey and, indeed, must not obey laws and rules of men that are *contrary to* the *Word* of God. This applies to all areas of life whether civil or in connection with the faith. No human authority can demand obedience on matters that contradict God's law. They cannot bind conscience.
3. In matters of faith and worship (doctrine, church rules and so forth.) no church can demand any member to accept anything which is not taught in the Word of God or can be deduced from it (see Confession Chapter 11). A church cannot tell people to remain single or make regulations about clerical dress or forbid people to abstain from certain drinks or foods. The only demands, which can be required of people are those that the Word of God demands and nothing else. It should be noted that this discussion is limited to matters of faith and worship. It does not remove the right of civil government to introduce rules which are in addition to God's Word but not contrary to it. For example rules about

---

1 James 4:12; Romans 14:4.

2 Acts 4:19, 5:29; I Corinthians 7:23; Matthew 23:8-10; II Corinthians 1:24; Matthew 15:9.

3 Colossians 2:20-23; Galatians 1:10, 2:4-5, 5:1.

4 Romans 10:17; Romans 14:23; Isaiah 8:20; Acts 17:11; John 4:22; Hosea 5:11; Revelation 13:12, 16-17; Jeremiah 8:9.

wearing seat belts when driving a car are additional to the Word of God, but allowed by the Confession. A law to require everyone in a general election to vote on the Sabbath would go against the fourth commandment and should not be obeyed by the believer.

4. To obey such man-made requirements out of conscience is to betray true liberty of conscience. Conscience must always be obeyed, a person must always do what they believe to be right, yet to have conscience programmed by matters which God does not require is to deny a person liberty. Their freedom is destroyed.
5. If a church requires blind acceptance of its rules, then this not only destroys conscience but also destroys reason. God has given to every believer the right to be a Berean, that is, to examine the Scripture to see if what men teach is true.

> *"Now these Jews were more noble than those in Thessalonica; they received the word with all eagerness, examining the Scriptures daily to see if these things were so"* (Acts 17:11).

No church can remove this right and demand obedience to things which are not taught in God's Word. Neither can members or elders bind each other.

This is the true freedom which Christ gives, and no man must remove it whether it be Pope, Preacher, General Assembly, Session, Member or Lodge.

Freedom does not imply licence to practice evil

Confession 20.3

> Those who practice any sin or nourish any sinful desire on the pretext of Christian freedom destroy the whole purpose of Christian freedom, which is, that, having been rescued out of the hands of our enemies, we might serve the Lord without fear and in holiness and righteousness before him all the days of our lives.[1]

The third paragraph (20.3) teaches that no person has the freedom to practice sin because Christ has made them free. This paragraph is aimed at those who would teach that the believer is free from the moral law: a 'let us sin that grace may abound' notion! Throughout the

[1] Galatians 5:13; I Peter 2:16; II Peter 2:19; John 8:34; Luke 1:74-75.

history of the church there have been those who taught freedom from the law in this sense. They are known as Antinomians. The Confession then steers the biblical middle course of those who would bind believers with man-made rules and those who would reject the fact that the believer is still to obey God's law.

Confession 20.4 – Kelly

> God intends that the authorities he has ordained on earth and the freedom Christ has purchased should not destroy but mutually uphold and preserve each other. And so, those who oppose any lawful power or the lawful exercise of power, whether civil or ecclesiastical, on the pretext of Christian freedom are actually resisting God. The support, promotion, or practice of such opposition, which contradicts natural understanding or the known principles of Christianity on matters of faith, worship, and associations, which denies the power of godliness, or which disrupts the peace and unity among believers, may lawfully be called to account and proceeded against by the church.

Confession 20.4 – as adopted by the Church of Scotland in the Act of 1647

> *And because the powers which God has ordained, and the liberty which Christ has purchased, are not intended by God to destroy, but mutually to uphold and preserve one another; they who, upon pretence of Christian liberty, shall oppose any lawful power, or the lawful exercise of it, whether it be civil or ecclesiastical, resist the ordinance of God.*[1] *And for their publishing of such opinions, or maintaining of such practices, as are contrary to the light of nature, or to the known principles of Christianity, whether concerning faith, worship, or conversation; or to the power of godliness; or such erroneous opinions or practices, as either in their own nature, or in the manner of publishing or maintaining them, are destructive to the external peace and order which Christ hath established in the church; they may lawfully be called to account, and proceeded against by the censures of the church,*[2] ***and by the power of the civil magistrate***.[3] (emphasis added)

---

1 Matthew 12:25; I Peter 2:13-14, 16 [Romans 13:1-8] Hebrews 13:17.

2 Romans 1:32 with I Corinthians 5:1, 5, 11, 13; II John verses 10-11 and II Thessalonians 3:14 and I Timothy 6:3-5 and Titus 1:10-11, 13 and Titus 3:10 with Matthew:18:15-17; I Timothy 1:19-20; Revelation 2:2, 14-15, 20, 3:9.

3 [Deuteronomy 13:6-12]; Romans 13:3-4 with II John 10-11; Ezra 7:23-28; Revelation 17:12, 16-17; Nehemiah 13:15, 17, 21-22, 25, 30; II Kings 23:5-6, 9, 20-21; II Chronicles 34:33, 15:12-13, 16; Daniel 3:29; I Timothy 2:2; Isaiah 49:23; Zechariah 13:2-3.

The final paragraph (20.4) considers the relationship between lawful authority (Church and State) and Christian freedom. The following points should be noted:

(i) It is the purpose of *God* that *ordained* authority and Christian *freedom* should both *uphold each other*. The State, for example, must protect liberty and the Christian must not oppose any lawful action of the State.

(ii) No Christian has the right under the guise of Christian freedom to oppose lawful rule by Church or State. He must not rebel against the correct use of discipline by the Church nor can he refuse to obey State law **which is not contrary to God's law**. He may not like paying VAT or giving a breath test to the police but he cannot refuse on the grounds of liberty.

(iii) They may not take actions which destroy the peace of the Church or the order of the Church. In other words they must not start or encourage practices which will cause rows within the church. If this is the case the Church must censure them. (The official version of the Confession – that is, the version accepted by PCI – also adds, *and by the power of the civil magistrate* 'that the civil power may also act'. This will be discussed in a later section when we consider the relation between Church and State in Chapter 23).

Cross references with the Catechisms:

The main reference in the catechism is WLC 105 where in its exposition of the first commandment it refers to *making men lords of faith and conscience*. cf. Shorter: 36; Larger 83.

To think over and discuss:

1. "Conscience must always be obeyed even if it is wrong." Discuss this statement.
2. What are the ways in which the Church or other believers could bind your conscience?

THE STATE

Ref. Confession Chapter 23 – Civil Authorities

A few parts of this chapter in the original (1647 version) in the author's view are unbiblical, coloured no doubt by the politics of the era in which they were written, so that they are not accepted by the Presbyterian Church in Ireland (Code Chapter 1 Paragraph 13 see appendix I to this chapter). Other churches (for example USA) that accept the Confession have rewritten this chapter. The majority of this chapter is however biblical and we must be careful not to reject it all. Civil magistrate refers to civil authorities, namely the State rather than a chairman of a court as in our day. In this chapter two modern versions are given: Kelly, McClure, III and Rollinson use the USA version and Ward generally follows the original.

In this study you will discover:

- The origin and duties of civil authority
- The duties of people to the State
- The relationship between Church and State

The origin and duties of civil authority

In the first and second paragraphs, the Confession expounds the basic doctrine of civil government.

Confession 23.1 – Kelly

> God, the supreme Lord and King of the whole world, has ordained civil authorities to be over people under him for his own glory and the public good. For this purpose he has armed civil authorities with the power of the sword to defend and encourage those who are good and to punish wrongdoers.[1]

Confession 23.1 – Ward

> With a view to his glory and the public good, God, the world's supreme Lord and King, has ordained civil authorities answerable to himself to be over the people. To accomplish his aims, God has armed them with the power of the sword to defend and encourage those who are good and to punish wrongdoers.

---

[1] Romans 13: 1-4; I Peter 2:13-14.

Note the following points:

1. God who is king over all has appointed civil government under him and over the people. Civil rulers are his vice-regents. They rule by his authority. Even in a democracy they do not get their authority from the people but from God.
2. They rule for the glory of God and for the public good. In the thinking of the Confession and Scripture, *good* is defined by God's Word. Civil government actions are meant to reflect the law of God.
3. They have the authority to punish evildoers and to defend good people. The *sword* implies the ultimate of capital punishment.

Confession 23.2 – Kelly

> It is lawful for Christians to accept and execute offices of civil authority when that is their calling.[1] In the administration of such offices they should take care to support true religion, justice, and peace, according to the beneficial laws of each government,[2] and in so doing they may lawfully under the New Testament wage war on just and necessary occasions.[3]

Confession 23.2 – Ward

> It is lawful for Christians to accept and carry out the duties of public office when called to do so. In carrying out such tasks they ought to take care to uphold piety, justice and peace in accordance with the sound laws of each commonwealth they serve, and in so doing the New Testament permits them to engage in war if there is just and necessary cause.

4. A Christian may take on civil office. It is not forbidden for a Christian to be a politician.
5. The Christian ruler is to seek to maintain true religion, justice and peace. He does not do this by making the State a body for evangelizing, rather by his influence he gives the church room to do its work. The laws of the land are to protect the church rather than hinder it. At the same time he is to seek to get the

---

1 Proverbs 8:15-16; Romans 13:1-2, 4.
2 Psalm 2:10-12; I Timothy 2:2; Psalm 82:3-4; II Samuel 23:3; I Peter 2:13.
3 Luke 3:14; Romans 13:4; Matthew 8:9-10; Acts 10:1-2; Revelation 17:14, 16.

laws of the State in line with Scripture. He may be the only Christian in government and while he can exert influence, it will be within the scope of the laws of that particular State.

6. The final statement at the end of the second paragraph (23.2) teaches the Doctrine of the Just War. The Confession is not a pacifist document.

The duties of people to the State

Confession 23.4 – Kelly

> It is people's duty to pray for those in authority,[1] to honor them,[2] to pay them taxes and whatever is owed them,[3] to obey their lawful commands, and to be subject to them for conscience's sake. Unbelief or different religious views on the part of civil authorities does not mean that they are to be disobeyed by believers,[4] including clergymen,[5] in the legitimate pursuit of their duties. The pope, of course, has no power or jurisdiction over civil authorities or the people under them in secular affairs. The pope never has any right to usurp secular authority, particularly capital punishment in cases of what is judged to be heresy or any other fault.[6]

Confession 23.4 – Ward

> It is the duty of people to pray for those in authority in the state, to honour their persons, to pay them taxes or other dues, to obey their lawful commands, and to be subject to their authority, for the sake of conscience. The civil power's just and legal authority is not made void by reason of him being an unbeliever or of different religious beliefs, nor are the people freed from their due obedience to such. Church office-bearers are not exempt from the obedience due to the civil authorities. Still less has the pope any power and jurisdiction over civil rulers in their dominions or over any of their people, and, least of all, has he any power to deprive them of their dominions or their lives, if he considers them to be heretics or chargeable with any other fault at all.

---

1 I Timothy 2:1-2.
2 I Peter 2:17.
3 Romans 13:6-7.
4 Romans 13:5; Titus 3:1.
5 I Peter 2:13-14,16.
6 Romans 13:1; I Kings 2:35; Acts 25:9-11; II Peter 2:1,10-11; Jude 8-11.

It is because government carries divine authority that people have a duty to it. A number of very important ideas are expressed in this paragraph.

1. Believers are to pray for civil rulers. Paul said this, even for the pagan rulers in his day,

   > *"First of all, then, I urge that supplications, prayers, intercessions, and thanksgivings be made for all people, for kings and all who are in high positions, that we may lead a peaceful and quiet life, godly and dignified in every way. This is good, and it is pleasing in the sight of God our Saviour, who desires all people to be saved and to come to the knowledge of the truth"* (I Timothy 2:1-4ff).

2. They are to be respected. Our age does not respect civil government but this is not biblical. We must respect and honour those the Lord has placed over us.

3. Their lawful commands are to be obeyed. They cannot be obeyed when they ask the citizen to do anything contrary to Scripture. Otherwise their authority is to be accepted for conscience sake, that is, so that we can have a clear conscience. Obedience includes paying taxes. It is hoped that those who refuse to pay taxes will not have a clear conscience!

4. Even if the civil ruler is an atheist that does not make void his authority or remove from us the need to obey.

5. Those who hold office in the Church, such as a minister, are bound to obey civil law just like the ordinary citizen, for they too are members of the State. The minister and the Church as a body must obey normal civil rules about tax, planning regulations and so forth.

6. The final section of this paragraph is directed against Roman Catholicism which regarded itself as above the State and sought to usurp civil authority for its own ends. This could have included taking the lives of people. The Confession is clear that the Church cannot take over the Affairs of State.

The relationship between Church and State

Confession 23.3 – Kelly

> Civil authorities may not take on themselves the ministering of God's word and the sacraments, the administration of spiritual power, or any interference with matters of faith. Nevertheless it is the duty of civil authorities to protect the church of our Lord, without giving preference to any denomination of Christians, so that every person with church affiliations or duties will be able to function with complete and unquestioned freedom. Since Jesus Christ has directed the establishment of regular government and discipline in his church, no law of any civil government should interfere with, abridge, or hinder the proper exercise of church government among the voluntary members of Christian denominations, acting in accordance with their own professed beliefs. It is the duty of civil authorities to protect the person and good name of all people so that none are abused, injured, or insulted on account of his religious faith or lack of it. It is also their duty to see to it that all religious and ecclesiastical assemblies are held without disturbance.

Confession 23.3 – Ward

> The civil authorities may not take to themselves the administration of the word and sacraments, or interfere in the spiritual government of the church, yet they have authority, and it is their duty, to see to it that unity and peace is preserved in the church, the truth of God is kept pure and complete, all blasphemies and heresies are suppressed, all corruptions and abuses in worship and discipline prevented or reformed, and all the ordinances of God duly established, administered and observed. To carry out these ends more effectively in circumstances where the church is disorganised or corrupt, the civil authorities have power to call synods, to be present at them, and to insist that whatsoever is transacted in them be according to the mind of God.

Confession 23.3 – as adopted by the Church of Scotland in the Act of 1647

> *III. The civil magistrate may not assume to himself the administration of the Word and sacraments, or the power of the keys of the kingdom of heaven:[1] yet he hath authority, and it is his duty, to take order, that unity and peace be preserved in the Church, that the truth of God be kept pure and entire, that all blasphemies and heresies be suppressed, all corruptions and abuses in worship and discipline prevented or reformed, and all the ordinances of God duly settled, administered, and observed.[2] For the better effecting whereof, he hath power to call synods, to be present at them, and to provide that whatsoever is transacted in them be according to the mind of God.[3]*

This is the paragraph which causes problems. There are several views on the relationship between Church and State. On one extreme there are those who say that the Church is supreme and she is over the State (traditional Roman Catholic teaching). At the other extreme there are those who contend that the State is over the Church and can interfere in her affairs.

Then in the middle there are those who teach the separation of Church and State. This has several degrees to it. In one corner there are those who say that the Church must take nothing to do with the State. She is a city set on a hill. Some will not allow members to take civil office or vote, because their kingdom is not of this world. Others within this group would teach that while the State cannot interfere in the affairs of the Church, that is, it cannot make laws for the Church or perform spiritual functions like preaching, and baptizing, it has a duty to help the Church perform her task. This is the basic position of the Confession. With this background we are in a position to examine the teaching of the Confession.

1. Civil authorities cannot preach or celebrate the sacraments. Nor can they interfere in affairs of discipline. The Church rules supreme here. No king or politician has the right to tell the Church what to do in this area. This teaching is biblical and no one should have any argument with it.
2. It is the duty of the State according to the original chapter in the Confession to ensure that *the truth of God be kept pure and entire, that all blasphemies and heresies be suppressed, all corruptions and abuses in worship and*

[1] II Chronicles 26:18 with Matthew 18:17 and 16:19; I Corinthians 12:28-29; Ephesians 4: 11-12; I Corinthians 4:1-2; Romans 10:15; Hebrews 5:4.

[2] Isaiah 49:23; Psalm 122:9; Ezra 7:23, 25-28; Leviticus 24:16; Deuteronomy 13:5-6, 12; II Kings 18:4; [I Chronicles 13:1-9; II Kings 23:1-26]; II Chronicles 34:33, 15:12-13.

[3] II Chronicles 19:8-11; [Chapters 29, 30] Matthew 2:4-5.

discipline prevented or reformed[1] . . . *For* some, at the time the Confession was written, this meant that while the Church condemned the person, the State could carry out the sentence, such as capital punishment. One way that the State could help is indicated here, *to call synods and to be present at them, and to provide that whatsoever is transacted in them be according to the mind of God.*[2]

The biblical basis quoted for this teaching is Isaiah 49:23,

> *"Kings shall be your foster fathers, and their queens your nursing mothers.*
> *With their faces to the ground they shall bow down to you, and lick the dust of your feet.*
> *Then you will know that I am the* LORD*; those who wait for me shall not be put to shame"* (Isaiah 49:23).

This passage is a prophecy and it cannot be regarded as commanding a nation to do this. It will not sustain the meaning, which the Confession puts on it.

The most we can expect from the State is moral support, so that the Church is not hindered in its God-given task. No State can be neutral with regard to religion. They either, to a greater or lesser extent, support the teaching of God's Word or oppose it. The Church cannot control the State, but she can evangelize so that there are more Christians who will get involved in public affairs and hence change State law. It is also the duty of the Church to proclaim the teaching of the Word of God to the nation.

In the author's view, the Confession goes too far in this paragraph with respect to the duties of the State, but we must be careful not to go to the other extreme and allow the State to be wholly pagan. In this respect the changes made by the church in USA as expressed in Kelly are correct.

Cross references with the Catechisms:

Shorter: 64 & 65; Larger: 124-130

To think over and discuss:

1. In the light of the Confession's teaching, list the ways in which you are failing in your duties to the State and how you can change this?
2. Discuss the role of Church and State in our secular society. Are we correct in thinking that the State is neutral, or should be, as far as religion is concerned?

---

[1] Confession as adopted by the Church of Scotland in the Act of 1647
[2] Confession as adopted by the Church of Scotland in the Act of 1647

APPENDIX I

Chapter one, Section three, Paragraph thirteen, of the Code of the Presbyterian Church in Ireland, has the caveat with respect to civil rulers:

CHAPTER 1 – GENERAL PRINCIPLES

SECTION III – THE STANDARDS OF THE CHURCH

10. **The Word of God** as set forth in the Scriptures of the Old and New Testaments is the only infallible rule of faith and practice, and the supreme standard of the Church.
11. **It is the privilege, right and duty of everyone** to examine the Scriptures personally, and each individual is bound to submit to their authority. Having formed a definite conviction as to what the will of God is upon any subject, it is the duty of everyone to accept and obey it. In exercising the inalienable right of private judgement, individual Christians are not to set their reason above the Word of God, or to refuse light from any quarter. Guided by the Holy Spirit, they are to use their reason to ascertain the divine will as revealed in Scripture, and are to refuse to subject conscience to any authority but that of the Word of God. In the words of the Westminster Confession "God alone is Lord of the conscience, and has left it free from the doctrines and commandments of men which are in anything contrary to His Word, or beside it, in matters of faith or worship."[1]
12. **The Presbyterian Church in Ireland,** as a witness for Christ, has adopted subordinate standards in which is set forth what she understands the Word of God to teach on certain important points of doctrine and worship. These subordinate standards are a testimony for truth and against error, and serve as a bond of union for members of the Church.
13. **The Confession of Faith** (as approved by the Church of Scotland in her Act of 1647), and the Larger and Shorter Catechisms, prepared by the Westminster Assembly of Divines, are the subordinate standards of the Presbyterian Church in Ireland. Accepting these subordinate standards, the Church holds that, although civil rulers are bound to render obedience to Christ in their own province, yet they ought not to attempt in any way to constrain anyone's religious beliefs, or invade the rights of conscience.
14. **In the Church** resides the right to interpret and explain her standards under the guidance of the Spirit of God.

---

[1] Confession Chapter XX – Paragraph II, as adopted by the Church of Scotland in the Act of 1647.

Confession on divorce. The Confession, unlike Roman Catholicism[1], recognised that in a fallen world provision had to be made for divorce. The rules governing divorce were not to be of any human invention, but only those taught in the Scriptures (see Confession Chapter 24.6 below).

An engagement, in those days, had a much stronger bond than now, but if a couple are engaged and a partner had a sexual relationship with someone else, then the innocent party could terminate the engagement.

In the case of a sexual relationship with someone else after marriage, the innocent party could request a divorce,

> *"It was also said, 'Whoever divorces his wife, let him give her a certificate of divorce'"* (Matthew 5:31);
>
> *"And I say to you: whoever divorces his wife, except for sexual immorality, and marries another, commits adultery"* (Matthew 19:9).

It should be noted that neither the Confession nor Scripture teach that divorce should be automatic in the case of adultery. If possible, reconciliation should take place. This depends on the repentance of the guilty party.

After divorce on the grounds of adultery, the innocent party may remarry since effectively the marriage has been dissolved and the offending party is regarded as dead.

Confession 24.6

> Although the corrupt nature of man is inclined to support arguments for the wrong separation of those whom God has joined together in marriage, yet the only causes which warrant dissolving the bond of marriage are adultery or deliberate desertion which cannot be remedied in any way by the church or civil authority.[2] Proceedings for divorce must be public and orderly, and the persons involved must not be allowed to manage their cases according to their own desires and judgment.[3]

In the final paragraph (24.6) we read: '*deliberate desertion which cannot be remedied in any way by the church or civil authority*', is a sufficient cause of dissolving the bond of marriage. It would seem that the Confession here allows any wilful desertion, yet the Scripture passage on which this is based teaches that it only applies in the case when an unsaved partner deserts a saved partner.

---

1 Catholicism of Catholic Church Para (1647-1650).
2 Matthew 19:6, 8-9; I Corinthians 7:15.
3 Deuteronomy 24:1-4.

> *"But if the unbelieving partner separates, let it be so. In such cases the brother or sister is not enslaved. God has called you to peace"* (I Corinthians 7:15).

The Christian partner is not allowed to desert and sue for divorce. There is an obligation on the believing partner to remain with the non-Christian in marriage,

> *"If any woman has a husband who is an unbeliever, and he consents to live with her, she should not divorce him. For the unbelieving husband is made holy because of his wife, and the unbelieving wife is made holy because of her husband. Otherwise your children would be unclean, but as it is, they are holy"* (I Corinthians 7:13-14ff).

In the author's opinion, the Confession has applied this passage too widely and thus caused misunderstanding in this area. Interestingly enough, there is no mention of remarriage in this case and even the word divorce is avoided, though it seems to be implied.

The Confession also teaches that divorce is not a private affair but a *public and orderly* course of proceedings must be observed.

We live in an age when the civil law allows grounds for divorce other than these two that are taught in Scripture, (adultery and wilful desertion by the unsaved partner). This means the Church must recognise, that many people are still married whom the State regard as divorced.

Cross references with the Catechisms:

Shorter: 71 & 72; Larger: 138 & 139.

To think over and discuss:

1. Should the church refuse to marry or ask a blessing on any marriage between single people?
2. Why should the church only marry those who profess to be believers?
3. How can the church be faithful to the biblical standards on marriage/divorce in these days of easy divorce?
4. What would you advise a person to do whose husband is sexually faithful but is cruel in other ways (for example wife beating)?

CHAPTER V

THE CHURCH OF CHRIST

THE TRUE CHURCH

Ref. Confession Chapter 25 – The Church

In this study you will discover:

- The Church's identity
- The Church's task
- The Church's purity
- The Church's Head

The Church's identity

What is the Church? This is a basic question, yet many people confuse the Church with a building or a denomination. Many groups, churches and sects all claim to be the true Church. The clarity of the Confession in its teaching on the Church enables us to avoid serious pitfalls. The Confession, in common with Reformation teaching, makes a useful distinction between the invisible and visible Church. Correctly understood this distinction is very helpful.

Confession 25.1

> The catholic or universal church is invisible and consists of all the elect who have been, are, or ever will be gathered into one under Christ, the head. The church is his body and spouse, the fullness of God, who fills all in all.[1]

The *universal church* (25.1), which consists of all the elect of all ages, from the time of Adam until the close of the age, *is invisible*. This is clearly so, for no human being has ever seen the whole Church, nor does any man know infallibly who belongs to the true Church. A person belongs to the true Church because he is or will be 'in Christ', that is, he is in union with Christ. He has been regenerated, justified and adopted. He is a member of his body, he is under his rule, having through grace left the rule of the first Adam and come under the authority of the last Adam, Jesus Christ. We can never see these things, let alone see all the elect, who are known to God alone. We can

[1] Ephesians 1:10, 22-23, 5:23, 27, 32; Colossians 1:18.

seek to discern the evidence of true conversion, but we will err on occasions. Think how hypocrites who have many disguises, often appear to be genuine.

Confession 25.2

> The visible church is also catholic or universal under the gospel, i.e., it is not confined to one nation as previously under the Mosaic Law. It consists of all the people in the world who profess the true religion[1] together with their children.[2] The visible church is the kingdom of the Lord Jesus Christ[3] and the house and family of God,[4] outside of which people cannot ordinarily be saved.[5]

The visible church is the Church that we observe, this is the professing Church, and in it the invisible Church is manifest. We must never think that the invisible Church is completely hidden, in totality it is, but it comes to expression in *the visible church*.

Membership of the visible Church is from all nations. In the Old Testament it was restricted in the main to Israel, but since the coming of Christ the Church has been international. The day of Pentecost bears witness to this fact (Acts 2).

Membership of the visible Church is by profession of the true religion that is a profession of faith in Christ. This must not be understood as a mere affirmation of some creed, but as profession of saving faith (cf. WSC 86).[6]

This profession is to be credible, that is it can be believed. It may not be true, but there ought to be nothing in the outward life, from a biblical standpoint, which would raise serious questions as to its reality.

When a person applies for membership of a local church this is all that can be required. We have no right to deny membership to anyone who can make a credible profession. We cannot add conditions for membership of the professing Church which God does not demand for salvation. No mere human rules must be added. If later a person denies that profession by word or life they are to be disciplined and this may involve excommunication (see Confession Chapter 30). No man can

1 I Corinthians 1:2, 12:12-13; Psalm 2:8; Revelation 7:9; Romans 15:9-12.
2 I Corinthians 7:14; Acts 2:39; Ezekiel 16:20-21; Romans 11:16; Genesis 3:15, 17:7.
3 Matthew 13:47; Isaiah 9:7.
4 Ephesians 2:19; Ephesians 3:15.
5 Acts 2:47.
6 "Faith in Jesus Christ is a saving grace by which we receive and rest upon him alone for salvation as he is freely offered to us in the gospel" (WSC 86).

judge the heart, so God has made membership of the professing or visible Church dependent on that which can charitably be judged by men. The phrase which teaches that *'The visible church'* also consists of the *children* of those who profess faith will be discussed in the chapter on baptism.

The Church is the kingdom of the Lord Jesus Christ, in the sense that he rules it. Indeed Christ rules all things for the good of the Church,

> *"And he put all things under his feet and gave him as head over all things to the church . . ."* (Ephesians 1:22).

It is because he rules the Church that its members must be subject to his Word, the Holy Scriptures. The Church is also described here as the house and family of God.

Some people have questioned the statement, *'outside of which people cannot ordinarily be saved'*. It does not refer to the invisible Church, outside of which a person could not be saved, but to the visible Church. It does not say 'cannot be saved' but ordinary possibility of salvation. In the normal course of events those who are converted make a public profession and identify with a local church. To refuse to do so is to be disobedient to Scripture and to ignore a means God has appointed for Christian growth. The Confession would question the sincerity of those who refuse to join a local church when one is available. It is possible to be an isolated believer, and not belong to a local congregation where none exists. A modern example would be someone converted in a remote part of the world through the message they heard through a radio broadcast.

The Church's task

Confession 25.3

> In order to gather and perfect God's people in this life until the end of the world Christ has given the ministry, Scriptures, and ordinances of God to this universal visible church, and by his own presence and Spirit he enables the church to function in this way according to his promise.[1]

God has given the Church a task to perform and in doing so has equipped his Church. God has given to his Church *the ministry*. This is to be understood as the special ministry of the Word and Sacraments

[1] I Corinthians 12:28; Ephesians 4:11-13; Matthew 28:19-20; Isaiah 59:21.

to which God calls people. It does not refer to the ministry or service of every member, which is also true, but is not taught here. The Scriptures teach that there is special ministry,

> *"But we will devote ourselves to prayer and to the ministry of the word"* (Acts 6:4),

> *"I thank him who has given me strength, Christ Jesus our Lord, because he judged me faithful, appointing me to his service,"* (I Timothy 1:12),

Paul has been appointed to service or ministry, cf. II Timothy 4:11[1]. This is in keeping with the Larger Catechism which refers to 'the ministry of the Gospel' (WLC 63). In our current emphasis that everybody in the Church has a ministry or a job to do, we must not neglect or deny that there is *the ministry*.

God has also given to the Church the Scriptures and ordinances (preaching, prayer and sacraments). Many today lack confidence in the ordained ministry as being an effective means of extending the kingdom and building up the Church. The Confession teaches that God has promised to make this means effectual. It is not of course, that the Confession is advocating a hierarchical church, but rather that we give due emphasis to the teaching eldership.

The Church's purity

Confession 25.4

> This universal church has been sometimes more and sometimes less visible.[2] Particular churches, which are members of it, are also more or less pure, depending on how the gospel is accepted and taught, how the ordinances of God are administered, and how public worship is performed.[3]

There have always been those who are looking for the perfect church. This is impossible when the church is composed of fallible people.

The Confession reminds us that at times the Church has not been very visible due to apostasy, for example in the time of Elijah (I Kings chapters 17–21) and at the time prior to the Reformation.

The Confession lists three factors which characterise the purity of

1 "Luke alone is with me. Get Mark and bring him with you, for he is very useful to me for ministry" (II Timothy 4:11).
2 Romans 11:3-4; Revelation 12:6, 14.
3 [Revelation 2 and 3]; I Corinthians 5:6-7.

the Church.

1. The Doctrine of the Gospel taught and accepted. It is possible for correct doctrine to be preached but rejected by the people. If that is the case no church exists. The people, on the other hand, may believe and live out the gospel although it is not preached in purity. If that is the case the Church is not pure.

2. The way the sacraments are administered is an indication of the purity of the Church. If error is taught with reference to baptism or the Lord's Supper then the degree of this error is indicative of the purity of the Church. For example, to believe that a person is saved through water baptism is a greater error than to advocate that all babies should be baptised. While both are wrong the former misunderstands the way of salvation while the latter is error over the extent of the Covenant.

3. The way public worship is performed. If any unbiblical elements are introduced which emphasise the sensual rather than the spiritual, then the Church is moving further away from purity.

Examples include the emphasis on dress and music rather than the spiritual state of the worshipper.

Confession 25.5

> The purest churches under heaven are subject both to impurity and error.[1] Some churches have so degenerated that they are not churches of Christ, but synagogues of Satan.[2] Nevertheless, there will always be a church on earth to worship God according to his will.[3]

In the fifth paragraph the necessary warning is given, that no church is perfect, all have a mixture of truth and error (yes, even your congregation!) so there is no point in looking for the perfect church.

The error can become so great that the Church ceases to be a church and is just *synagogues of Satan*. This should make all, but especially elders, vigilant to ensure purity in their own congregations and in the denomination as a whole.

---

1 I Corinthians 13:12; [Revelation 2 and 3]; Matthew 13:24-30, 47.
2 Revelation 18:2; Romans 11:18-22.
3 Matthew 16:18; Psalms 72:17, 102:28; Matthew 28:19-20.

The Confession affirms no matter how dark and corrupt things may become that there shall always be a Church on earth to worship God according to his will.

The Church's Head

Confession 25.6

> There is no other head of the church than the Lord Jesus Christ.[1] In no sense can the pope in Rome be the head of it. Rather, he is that antichrist, the man of sin and son of damnation, who glorifies himself as opposed to Christ and everything related to God.[2]

The Confession, in common with all Christians, teaches that the Head of the Church is Jesus Christ. He alone is the Head of the Church

> *"Rather, speaking the truth in love, we are to grow up in every way into him who is the head, into Christ, from whom the whole body, joined and held together by every joint with which it is equipped, when each part is working properly, makes the body grow so that it builds itself up in love"* (Ephesians 4:15-16).

The problem arises when the question is asked, 'Who is the visible head of the Church of Christ on earth?' To this, Roman Catholicism would answer, " *. . . the Roman Pontiff, by reason of his Office as Vicar of Christ and pastor of the entire church has full supreme and universal power over the whole church, a power which he can always exercise unhindered"*. (Paragraph 882 Catechism of the Catholic Church 1994). Article 37 of the "Thirty Nine Articles" of the Church of England would recognise that the civil power has a certain authority over the Church. The Confession not only understands Christ as Head of the invisible Church, but also of the Church on earth; **there can be no other Head of the Church but the Lord Jesus Christ**. He has appointed government for that Church on earth which is chosen from its membership and does not allow any one person to be a leader. This is the system of elders in the local congregation and presbytery for groupings of congregations. This biblical system of Church government is discussed in chapters 31 and in more detail in "The Form of Church Government" produced by the Westminster Assembly.

The question that has vexed many people over the last number of years is the sentences of the sixth paragraph (25.6). *In no sense can the*

---

1 Colossians 1:18; Ephesians 1:22.
2 Matthew 23:8-10; II Thessalonians 2:3-4, 8-9; Revelation 13:6.

pope in Rome be the head of it. Rather, he is that antichrist, the man of sin and son of damnation, who glorifies himself as opposed to Christ and everything related to God.

The discussion on this has created more 'heat than light'. No one who is concerned about biblical religion can object to the statement that the Pope cannot be Head of the Church. It is the phrase about the Pope being Antichrist which irritates some people, while a few regard it as being the most important statement in the Confession!

The basic question is, "Is the statement manifestly biblical so that it warrants inclusion in a confessional document"? The following points should be considered.

1. The word antichrist only occurs in the books of 1st & 2nd John and it refers there to the heresy of denying the incarnation[1].

   > *"Children, it is the last hour, and as you have heard that antichrist is coming, so now many antichrists have come. Therefore we know that it is the last hour. They went out from us, but they were not of us; for if they had been of us, they would have continued with us. But they went out, that it might become plain that they all are not of us. But you have been anointed by the Holy One, and you all have knowledge. I write to you, not because you do not know the truth, but because you know it, and because no lie is of the truth. Who is the liar but he who denies that Jesus is the Christ? This is the antichrist, he who denies the Father and the Son. No one who denies the Son has the Father. Whoever confesses the Son has the Father also"* (I John 2:18-23ff) cf. II John 7.

   It is a matter of fact that Roman Catholic teaching does not deny the incarnation. Also it should be noted that the Confession does not refer to the verses in John's letters in its proof texts. Clearly it is using the word 'antichrist' in a different sense than the Bible.

2. Historically the word 'antichrist' has been used to refer to the *man of sin*[2] or *"lawlessness"*,[3] or the beast out of the sea in

---

1 "By this you know the Spirit of God: every spirit that confesses that Jesus Christ has come in the flesh is from God, and every spirit that does not confess Jesus is not from God. This is the spirit of the antichrist, which you heard was coming and now is in the world already" (I John 4:2-3ff).

2 Confession Chapter 25.6.

3 "Let no one deceive you in any way. For that day will not come, unless the rebellion comes first, and the man of lawlessness is revealed, the son of destruction, who opposes and exalts himself against every so-called god or object of worship, so that he takes his seat in the temple of God, proclaiming himself to be God" (II Thessalonians 2:3-4ff).

Revelation 13. This is how the Confession is using the word as the proof texts show. Note it refers to the Pope as that Antichrist, not the Antichrist.

3. Reformed theology has been divided in its understanding of these verses. Some have regarded it as a future figure, others as the Papacy, while yet others claim the man of sin had already come in the person of a Roman emperor. The interpretation depends to a large extent on the person's overall view of the second coming and the last things.

   It is for these reasons that this statement should not have confessional status and be made binding on the conscience of those who sign the Confession. There may be a few who can accept it due to their understanding of the last things but many cannot.

4. In a resolution the 1988 Assembly of the Presbyterian Church in Ireland, expressed its opinion that the acceptance of the clause was non-obligatory. In the opinion of that Assembly a person should be left free to accept or reject the view that the Pope is the Antichrist. A copy of the resolution is reproduced in the appendix.

In conclusion it has to be admitted that no doctrine of the Confession has to be altered if this phrase is omitted.

Cross references with the Catechisms:

Shorter: None - it does not discuss the Church.
Larger: 61-65 cf. 156-160.

To think over and discuss:

1. In what way is the distinction between the visible church and the invisible Church useful?
2. While acknowledging the part every member of the body of Christ has to duty to serve, how can we emphasise the importance of the distinctive roles of Ruling and Teaching elders in the church?
3. What can you do to promote the purity of the Church?
4. Discuss paragraph 25.6 in the light of the resolution of the Assembly (re. Appendix 1).

THE COMMUNION OF SAINTS

Ref. Confession Chapter 26 – The Fellowship of God's People

In this study you will discover:

- All true believers are united to Christ
- Believers are united to each other and are to help each other
- The union with Christ and each other is not to be misunderstood

All true believers are united to Christ

Confession 26.1

> All believers are united to Jesus Christ, their head, by his Spirit and by faith, and have fellowship with him in his grace, suffering, death, resurrection, and glory.[1] United to one another in love, God's people have fellowship in each other's gifts and grace[2] and are obliged to perform those public and private duties which nourish their mutual good, both spiritually and physically.[3]

In this first paragraph the fact that *All* true *believers are united to Christ* is taught. United to or union with Christ is often expressed in Scripture by the phrase 'in Christ' and is a central theme of the New Testament.

> *"There is therefore now no condemnation for those who are in Christ Jesus"* (Romans 8:1),
>
> *"But I, brothers, could not address you as spiritual people, but as people of the flesh, as infants in Christ"* (I Corinthians 3:1),
>
> *"For as in Adam all die, so also in Christ shall all be made alive"* (I Corinthians 15:22),
>
> *"Therefore, if anyone is in Christ, he is a new creation. The old has passed away; behold, the new has come"* (II Corinthians 5:17), cf. (Ephesians 1:4, 4:15; Philippians 3:9; I Thessalonians 4:16).

While it is 'in Christ' that believers are chosen, this is not experienced

[1] I John 1:3; Ephesians 3:16-19; John 1:16; Ephesians 2:5-6; Philippians 3:10; Romans 6:5-6; II Timothy 2:12.
[2] Ephesians 4:15-16; I Corinthians 12:7, 3:21-23; Colossians 2:19.
[3] I Thessalonians 5:11, 14; Romans 1:11-12, 14; I John 3:16-18; Galatians 6:10.

until conversion.

> *"In him we have obtained an inheritance, having been predestined according to the purpose of him who works all things according to the counsel of his will, so that we who were the first to hope in Christ might be to the praise of his glory"* (Ephesians 1:11-12).

This union is not the same as that between the persons of the Trinity, nor the union of the human and divine natures in the Redeemer. Nor is it like a leader and his followers, nor merely social, as it is between good friends. It is a spiritual union, that is, the Holy Spirit brings it about. It is he who regenerates[1] and dwells in the believer[2]

> *"And I will ask the Father, and he will give you another Helper, to be with you forever, even the Spirit of truth, whom the world cannot receive, because it neither sees him nor knows him. You know him, for he dwells with you and will be in you"* (John 14:16-17).

This is a vital, living fellowship with Christ which is experienced by faith

> *" . . . that according to the riches of his glory he may grant you to be strengthened with power through his Spirit in your inner being, so that Christ may dwell in your hearts through faith — that you, being rooted and grounded in love, may have strength to comprehend with all the saints what is the breadth and length and height and depth, and to know the love of Christ that surpasses knowledge, that you may be filled with all the fullness of God"* (Ephesians 3:16-19ff).

This is possible because Christ is the head of the new race. He is the one who lived, died and rose again so that sinners might leave the old race of Adam and come under his rule,

> *"Therefore, just as sin came into the world through one man, and death through sin, and so death spread to all men because all sinned . . ."* (Romans 5:12ff).

The richness of this union with Christ is illustrated in Scripture in

---

[1] "Jesus answered him, 'Truly, truly, I say to you, unless one is born again he cannot see the kingdom of God'" (John 3:3).
"But God, being rich in mercy, because of the great love with which he loved us, even when we were dead in our trespasses, made us alive together with Christ — by grace you have been saved . . ." (Ephesians 2:4-5).

[2] "You, however, are not in the flesh but in the Spirit, if in fact the Spirit of God dwells in you. Anyone who does not have the Spirit of Christ does not belong to him. But if Christ is in you, although the body is dead because of sin, the Spirit is life because of righteousness" (Romans 8:9-10ff).
"And because you are sons, God has sent the Spirit of his Son into our hearts, crying, 'Abba! Father!'" (Galatians 4:6).

THE SACRAMENTS

Ref. Confession Chapter 27 – The Sacraments

In this study you will discover:

- What the sacraments are
- What the sacraments do

What the Sacraments are

There is always a great deal of confusion over the Doctrine of the Sacraments. The Confession is a great help in clearing the air.

The word 'sacrament' does not occur in the Bible, but it has been used by the Church to refer to certain ordinances. This should not disturb us, since the words 'trinity' or 'incarnation' do not occur either. However, it is important that we understand these words biblically.

Confession 27.4 – (see Author's clarification p191)

> There are only two sacraments ordained by Christ our Lord in the gospel: baptism and the Lord's supper. Neither of these may be administered by anyone but a lawfully ordained minister of the word.[1]

The sacraments of the Old Testament were Circumcision and the Passover. The sacraments of the New Testament are Baptism and the Lord's Supper (27.4). These only have been appointed by Christ as *signs and seals* (27.1). This is in opposition to the Roman Catholic teaching of seven sacraments (Baptism, Confirmation, Eucharist, Penance, Marriage, Extreme Unction and Orders).

Confession 27.1

> Sacraments are holy signs and seals of the covenant of grace.[2] They were instituted by God along with that covenant[3] to represent Christ and his benefits, to confirm our position with and in him,[4] to demonstrate a visible difference between those who belong to the church and the rest of the world,[5] and solemnly to engage believers in the service of God in Christ according to his word.[6]

---

1 Matthew 28:19; I Corinthians 11:20, 23, 4:1; Hebrews 5:4.
2 Romans 4:11; Genesis 17:2, 10.
3 Matthew 28:19; I Corinthians 11:23.
4 I Corinthians 10:16, 11:25-26; Galatians 3:27.
5 Romans 15:8; Exodus 12:48; Genesis 34:14.
6 Romans 6:3-4; I Corinthians 10:16, 21.

The first paragraph (27.1) considers the sacraments in general and it can apply to Old or New Testament. *Sacraments* are divinely appointed, they are not something which man invents and puts into the Church. Rather God has given them to the Church. This corresponds to what we discovered in the regulative principle as it applies to worship (see Confession Chapter 21).

They *are holy signs and seals of the covenant of grace*. They are given to believers and not to the world. A sign represents and points to the real thing. A seal is a mark of ownership, it confirms and states something is genuine. The seal is given for the benefit of the receiver, not the giver. A friend may send you a typed letter, he knows it is genuine, but you may take it as a hoax unless his signature (seal) appears on it. A wedding ring is both sign and seal, representing and confirming real love. The sacraments may be regarded as visual aids, appealing to the eye as the word appeals to the ear.

The Confession lists four truths about the sacraments:

1. Sacraments represent Christ and his benefits. Baptism speaks of the new birth; the Lord's Supper of Christ's death and nourishment to the believer (see also Confession Chapters 28 & 29).

2. Sacraments confirm our interest in him. In the sacraments, God has pledged himself to us. In the Old Testament the rainbow reminded Noah that God had pledged not to destroy the earth by another flood. A person may be interviewed for work and told after the interview that he had been successful. He may have found this hard to believe, but when the letter of confirmation comes, he looks at it and it confirms what he was told. A person may doubt the love of God for him, the fact that they are his, but the Lord's Supper reminds him in a visual way of Christ's love for him.

3. Sacraments put a visible difference between those that belong to the Church and the rest of the world. In the Old Testament, the practice of circumcision and the celebration of the Passover marked out the people of Israel from other nations. They were signs to them that they were special – they belonged to God. It was the same in the apostolic church. To be baptised was a sign to the Church that this person had left their false religion and joined the Church. It was costly, and may have cost them

employment, or being cast out of their family. The same is true in many cultures today, for example, in the Muslim world. The fact of the matter is that in our situation, where the sacraments mean little, they no longer serve this function of marking out God's people as they should.

4. Sacraments solemnly engage believers in the service of God in Christ, according to his Word. When a person was converted, he belonged to Christ and not to the world. The sacraments confirmed this, so it was impossible, for example, to partake of the Lord's Supper and idol feasts. Those who partake of the sacraments are saying 'we serve Christ'. To partake of the Lord's Supper and serve the world and the devil is hypocrisy.

> *"You cannot drink the cup of the Lord and the cup of demons. You cannot partake of the table of the Lord and the table of demons. Shall we provoke the Lord to jealousy? Are we stronger than he?"*
> (I Corinthians 10:21-22).

Confession 27.2

> In every sacrament there is a spiritual relationship or sacramental union between the sign and the thing signified. And so the names and effects of the one are attributed to the other.[1]

The second paragraph discusses the relationship between the sign and what it represents. In the Lord's Supper, the sign is bread and the fruit of the vine which represent the body and blood of Christ. In the teaching of Roman Catholicism, the connection between the sign and what it represented or signified is a real connection: the bread and wine are said to become the actual body and blood of Christ. In Reformed teaching the connection is described as a *sacramental union*. This is a phrase coined to define the close, but not literal relationship between the sign and what it represents. This fact is borne out in Scripture when there is attributed to the sign what it represents and effects. In Genesis 17:10, the covenant is described in terms of circumcision,

> *"This is my covenant, which you shall keep, between me and you and your offspring after you: Every male among you shall be circumcised. You shall be circumcised in the flesh of your foreskins,*

---

[1] Genesis 17:10; Matthew 26:27-28; Titus 3:5.

and it shall be a sign of the covenant between me and you" (Genesis 17:10-11).

The following verse makes it clear that circumcision is the sign of the covenant and represents the circumcision of the heart[1]

> *"And the Lord your God will circumcise your heart and the heart of your offspring, so that you will love the LORD your God with all your heart and with all your soul, that you may live"* (Deuteronomy 30:6).

Peter refers to 'Baptism which now saves you' but says the water symbolises this,

> *"Baptism, which corresponds to this, now saves you, not as a removal of dirt from the body but as an appeal to God for a good conscience, through the resurrection of Jesus Christ, who has gone into heaven and is at the right hand of God, with angels, authorities, and powers having been subjected to him"* (I Peter 3:21-22).

Water baptism, of course, only represents salvation, the cleansing of the new birth and the forgiveness of justification,

> *". . . he saved us, not because of works done by us in righteousness, but according to his own mercy, by the washing of regeneration and renewal of the Holy Spirit"* (Titus 3:5).

The same idea can be seen at the institution of the Lord's Supper, when Christ refers to the fruit of the vine and says *" . . . for this is my blood of the covenant . . ."* (Matthew 26:28). In no case does it mean that the one is actually the other, that is, wine becomes blood, but the relationship is so close that on occasions one is called the other, hence the name sacramental union. The Confession also calls it a spiritual relation, since the symbols have been appointed by God, and so named in Scripture by the Holy Spirit.

---

1 "'You stiff-necked people, uncircumcised in heart and ears, you always resist the Holy Spirit. As your fathers did, so do you. Which of the prophets did your fathers not persecute? And they killed those who announced beforehand the coming of the Righteous One, whom you have now betrayed and murdered, you who received the law as delivered by angels and did not keep it'" (Acts 7:51-53ff).

"For no one is a Jew who is merely one outwardly, nor is circumcision outward and physical. But a Jew is one inwardly, and circumcision is a matter of the heart, by the Spirit, not by the letter. His praise is not from man but from God" (Romans 2:28-29ff).

What the sacraments do

Confession 27.3

> The grace revealed in or by the sacraments in their right use does not come from any power in them. Neither does the effectiveness of a sacrament depend on the devoutness or the intention of whoever administers it.[1] Rather the power and effectiveness of the sacraments are the result of the work of the Spirit[2] and rest on God's word instituting them since his word authorizes their use and promises benefits to worthy receivers of them.[3]

There has been much controversy in Christendom over what the sacraments actually do.

At one extreme there are those who believe that the sacraments are channels of grace and that God always works through them, provided that they are performed with the right intention and no obstacle is put in the way. Thus for example, in the case of baptism, the teaching of Roman Catholics, Anglo-Catholics and others is that regeneration always occurs and a mark is put on the soul which cannot be removed. This system of belief is often called Sacerdotalism.

At the other extreme there are those who virtually deny that the sacraments are a means of grace. This group would regard the Lord's Supper as a mere memorial and nothing more.

The Westminster standards do teach that the sacraments are a means of grace, and not just bare signs. (WSC 88, 92; WLC 154, 162 Confession 27.3 & 27.5) The sense in which they are a means of grace is explained in this section of the Confession. *The grace, revealed in or by the sacraments in their right use does not come from any power in them . . . Rather the power and effectiveness of the sacraments are the result of* ***the work of the Spirit*** *and rest on* ***God's word instituting them*** *. . . and promises benefits to worthy receivers of them.* (emphasis added). This rendering by Kelly is much clearer than the 1647 version, where, over time, the word "exhibit" used has changed in meaning.

The Shorter Catechism uses the word 'applied' in this context

> "A sacrament is a holy ordinance appointed by Christ by which, by visible signs, Christ, and benefits of the new covenant, are represented, sealed and **applied** to believers"
> (WSC 92 emphasis added).

---

[1] Romans 2:28-29; I Peter 3:21.
[2] Matthew 3:11; I Corinthians 12:13.
[3] Matthew 26:27-28, 28:19-20.

How then do the sacraments apply grace? The basic requirement is that the sacraments must be 'rightly used' (*in their right use*). Any superstitious use or glib approach would negate them being a means of grace.

There are two negatives.

- **First**, grace *does not come from any power in them*. There is nothing in the water, or bread and wine which automatically confer grace.
- **Secondly**, nor does grace depend on the piety or the intention of the administrator of the sacraments. He is not a miracle worker who has to be in a special frame of mind. This is set against the teaching of Roman Catholicism which regards the priesthood as central to the efficacy of the sacraments (apart from baptism).

There are three positives.

- **First**, it depends on *the work of the* Holy *Spirit*. It is not the sacraments themselves, but the *Spirit* who works along with the symbols who grants grace (cf. WLC 161 & 162).

  > "A sacrament is an holy ordinance appointed by Christ in his church to signify, seal and set forth to those who are within the covenant of grace," (WLC 162).

- **Secondly**, *God's word instituting them*. The reason that the sacraments confer grace through the work of the Holy Spirit is that they have been appointed by Christ. They are instruments given by the Lord himself for this end.
- **Thirdly**, the final aspect is *worthy receivers*. This does not mean that the *receivers* have to be worthy so as to merit grace, but that they look to Christ in faith for his *worthy* blessing,

  > "The sacraments become effective means of salvation not because of any power in them or in him who administers them," (WSC 91).

The biblical rationale for all this is rooted in the Covenant of Grace and the fact that sacraments operate within the Covenant. Even in a secular context a covenant had some visual means of ratifying it. It may have been by the dismembering of an animal, or the exchange of treaty documents. With Abraham the Covenant was ratified by circumcision (Genesis 17) and with the children of Israel by shed blood

(Exodus 24). In the New Testament the outward signs are baptism and the Lord's Supper.

In the covenant of grace there are two parties, Christ and the believer. In the sacrament, Christ and his benefits are offered to the believer. The believer in return surrenders himself to Christ and thus receives Christ and his blessings. There is covenantal fellowship. If Christ is not present, then the sacrament is just a mere sign, conveying no spiritual blessing apart from a moral effect. If the believer does not respond to the offer, then the sacrament becomes a type of magic action, in which blessing is conveyed without a response on his part. The biblical teaching on the covenant implies that for the sacrament to be valid there must be Christ and the act of faith on the part of the receiver.

Confession 27.5

> The sacraments of the Old Testament signify and reveal in substance the same spiritual things as those of the New.[1]

The final paragraph teaches that the two sacraments of the Old Testament are parallel in what they signify and apply to the sacraments of the New Testament. Circumcision in the Old, for example, signified the new birth, as does Baptism in the New Testament

> *"And the Lord your God will circumcise your heart and the heart of your offspring, so that you will love the LORD your God with all your heart and with all your soul, that you may live"* (Deuteronomy 30:6),
>
> *"For in him the whole fullness of deity dwells bodily, and you have been filled in him, who is the head of all rule and authority. In him also you were circumcised with a circumcision made without hands, by putting off the body of the flesh, by the circumcision of Christ, having been buried with him in baptism, in which you were also raised with him through faith in the powerful working of God, who raised him from the dead"* (Colossians 2:9-12ff).

(Author's clarification on Confession 27.4)

> . . . baptism and the Lord's supper. Neither of these may be administered by anyone but a lawfully ordained minister of the word.[2]

The statement that the sacraments may not be dispensed by any, but by a *minister of the Word* lawfully *ordained*, jars on the modern free mind. The reason behind this does not lie in any unbiblical theory of a

[1] I Corinthians 10:1-4.
[2] Matthew 28:19; I Corinthians 11:20, 23, 4:1; Hebrews 5:4.

special priesthood but on two biblical principles.

- **First**, that everything in the Church

  > *"should be done decently and in order",*
  > (I Corinthians 14:40).

  If every elder, or indeed layperson, could baptise, how could any discipline be maintained?

- **Secondly**, verses such as: I Corinthians 4:1[1] and Hebrews 5:4

  > *"And no one takes this honour for himself, but only when called by God, just as Aaron was . . ."*
  > (Hebrews 5:4)

  would seem to infer that God calls men to the task of handling the holy things of God in the New Testament as he did in the Old. This does not just include the sacraments but preaching as well. Some think that this is reading too much into these verses.

- **Finally**, if we believe preaching is only to be performed by those called and lawfully ordained to that office, then the sacraments can only be celebrated by the teaching elder since they are a visual extension of preaching.

Cross references with the Catechisms:

Shorter: 88, 91-93; Larger: 154, 161-164.

To think over and discuss:

1. What are the common misunderstandings about the sacraments among the people you meet? Who should participate in the Lord's Supper? What can you do to help them gain a correct understanding?
2. Do you think that others, as well as the minister, should have the right to celebrate the sacraments? If so, who and on what biblical grounds do you argue it? How could discipline be maintained?

---

[1] "This is how one should regard us, as servants of Christ and stewards of the mysteries of God" (I Corinthians 4:1).

BAPTISM

Ref. Confession Chapter 28 – Baptism

In this study you will discover:

- What baptism is
- To whom and how baptism is to be administered
- What baptism does

What Baptism is

Confession 28.1

> Baptism is a sacrament of the New Testament, ordained by Jesus Christ.[1] By baptism a person is solemnly admitted into the visible church.[2] Baptism is also a sign and seal of the covenant of grace,[3] of ingrafting into Christ,[4] of rebirth,[5] of remission of sins,[6] and of yielding to God through Jesus Christ to walk in newness of life.[7] By Christ's own direction this sacrament is to be continued in his church until the end of the world.[8]

Baptism is a permanent appointment by Christ (28.1), and any group which fails to practice it, is living in disobedience to Christ and cannot be recognised as a church.

Baptism is a *New Testament sacrament* appointed by Christ,

> *"Go therefore and make disciples of all nations, baptizing them in the name of the Father and of the Son and of the Holy Spirit, teaching them to observe all that I have commanded you. And behold, I am with you always, to the end of the age"* (Matthew 28:19-20ff).

It is the ceremony which admits a person into the visible or professing Church. Water baptism is the outward symbol of Spirit-baptism,

> *"For in one Spirit we were all baptized into one body – Jews or Greeks, slaves or free – and all were made to drink of one Spirit"* (I Corinthians 12:13).

The Confession describes it as solemn admission, hence pointing to the seriousness of baptism.

Baptism is not just something that is merely administrative but as a sacrament, it is also a sign and a seal. (Refer to Confession Chapter 27

---

1 Matthew 28:19.
2 I Corinthians chapters 12 and 13.
3 Romans 4:11 with Colossians 2:11-12.
4 Galatians 3:27; Romans 6:5.
5 Titus 3:5.
6 Mark 1:4.
7 Romans 6:3-4.
8 Matthew 28:19-20.

The Sacraments for a discussion on these terms). As a sign it is symbolic of a number of aspects of salvation, it is a visual aid pointing to the richness of God's salvation. The text teaches:

1. *the covenant of grace*

   This is the covenant which God has made with his elect in Christ (cf. Confession Chapter 7). They come to experience it at the time of conversion[1]. Baptism is a sign and seal of entering into this covenant, as circumcision was in the Old Testament[2].

2. *ingrafting into Christ*

   The believer is united to Christ,[3] this is connected with baptism but not necessarily water baptism.[4]

3. *rebirth*

   As circumcision did in the Old Testament, so baptism symbolises the new birth[5]. The phrase, 'washing *of rebirth*'/regeneration[6] may have a baptism background.

4. *remission of sins.*

   This was the theme of John the Baptist,[7] as it was of Peter on the Day of Pentecost[1].

---

1 "He received the sign of circumcision as a seal of the righteousness that he had by faith while he was still uncircumcised. The purpose was to make him the father of all who believe without being circumcised, so that righteousness would be counted to them as well, and to make him the father of the circumcised who are not merely circumcised but who also walk in the footsteps of the faith that our father Abraham had before he was circumcised" (Romans 4:11-12).

2 "For in him the whole fullness of deity dwells bodily, and you have been filled in him, who is the head of all rule and authority. In him also you were circumcised with a circumcision made without hands, by putting off the body of the flesh, by the circumcision of Christ, having been buried with him in baptism, in which you were also raised with him through faith in the powerful working of God, who raised him from the dead. And you, who were dead in your trespasses and the uncircumcision of your flesh, God made alive together with him, having forgiven us all our trespasses, by cancelling the record of debt that stood against us with its legal demands" (Colossians 2:9-14ff).

3 "For one who has died has been set free from sin" (Romans 6:7).

4 "We were buried therefore with him by baptism into death, in order that, just as Christ was raised from the dead by the glory of the Father, we too might walk in newness of life" (Romans 6:4).

5 "Baptism, which corresponds to this, now saves you, not as a removal of dirt from the body but as an appeal to God for a good conscience, through the resurrection of Jesus Christ," (I Peter 3:21).

6 "he saved us, not because of works done by us in righteousness, but according to his own mercy, by the washing of regeneration and renewal of the Holy Spirit," (Titus 3:5).

7 "And he went into all the region around the Jordan, proclaiming a baptism of repentance for the forgiveness of sins" (Luke 3:3).

5. *and of yielding to God through Jesus Christ to walk in newness of life.*

    Like the covenant ceremonies of both the ancient world and Scripture, there is in baptism that pledge of both parties to each other. The believer consecrates himself to the service of his King to walk in a new way of life[2].

To whom and how is Baptism to be administered?

Confession 28.2

> The physical substance to be used in this sacrament is water. The person is to be baptized in the name of the Father, the Son, and the Holy Spirit by a lawfully called minister of the gospel.[3]

Baptism is to be in the Triune name. Water alone is to be used. The reason for this rather strange injunction is that occasionally prior to the Reformation all kinds of potions were used for baptism. The Triune Name rules out those who advocate we should baptise in the name of Jesus only as noted in the last chapter (27.4) only a minister is to baptise.

Confession 28.3

> Dipping the person into the water is not necessary. Baptism is correctly administered by pouring or sprinkling water on the person.[4]

There have been two questions which have divided the evangelical church since the time of the Reformation with regard to baptism. That is, how should it be administered, and who should be baptised? The Confession teaches that sprinkling is a valid mode of baptism and immersion in water is not necessary. It cannot be proved from the New Testament that all or even anybody was immersed, the likely mode being the person standing in a river and water being poured over them. As was shown above (28.1), baptism symbolises cleansing and in the Old Testament sprinkling was often associated with cleansing (Leviticus 16:14; Ezekiel 36:25 cf. Hebrews 9:10ff).

Confession 28.4

> Not only those who actually profess faith in and obedience to Christ are to be baptized[5] but also the infants of one or both believing parents.[1]

---

1 "And Peter said to them, 'Repent and be baptized every one of you in the name of Jesus Christ for the forgiveness of your sins, and you will receive the gift of the Holy Spirit'" (Acts 2:38), cf. "And now why do you wait? Rise and be baptised and wash away your sins, calling on his name" (Acts 22:16).

2 "Do you not know that all of us who have been baptized into Christ Jesus were baptized into his death?" (Romans 6:3).

3 Matthew 3:11; John 1:33; Matthew 28:19-20.

4 Hebrews 9:10, 19-22; Acts 2:41, 16:33; Mark 7:4.

5 Mark 16:15-16; Acts 8:37-38.

On the other question of who should be baptised, the Confession teaches that, *Not only those who actually profess faith in and obedience to Christ are to be baptized, but also the infants of one or both believing parents*. These believing parents must have the same profession as is required for Church membership. Only those who are members of the Church in good standing should have their children baptised. The Confession therefore rejects indiscriminate baptism of all infants, and the 'adult only' baptism of those churches which practise adult immersion only.

The reason why infants of believers are to be baptised is because infants were treated as members of the covenant people in the Old Testament. There is nothing in the New Testament to say that they have been excluded from the covenant blessings and as infants in the Old Testament were circumcised, so covenant infants in the New are to be baptised. This is the reason why in Confession Chapter 25, the Church's membership *consists of all the people in the world who profess the true religion together with their children* (25.2).

N.B. It is impossible in the space available to do justice to this aspect of the Confession's teaching, those interested in further study should refer to the books in the Further Reading section.

What Baptism does

The Confession strikes a balance between the necessity of baptism and its neglect.

Confession 28.5

> Although it is a great sin to condemn or neglect this sacrament,[2] baptism is not inseparably connected with God's grace and salvation. One can be saved and reborn without baptism,[3] and, on the other hand, everyone who is baptized is not therefore unquestionably reborn.[4]

Baptism is important because God has commanded it. There is a moral duty on every believer to ensure that he and his children have been baptised, to neglect it is a sin.

Baptism, although important, is not essential for salvation. Baptism

1 Genesis 17:7, 9 with Galatians 3:9, 14 and Colossians 2:11-12 and Acts 2:38-39; Romans 4:11-12; I Corinthians 7:14; Matthew 28:19; Mark 10:13-16; Luke 18:15.

2 Luke 7:30 with Exodus 4:24-26.

3 Romans 4:11; Acts 10:2 ,4, 22, 31, 45, 47.

4 Acts 8:13, 23.

does not automatically cause regeneration. This is the teaching of Roman Catholic and ritualistic denominations. The Confession rejects this as error.

Confession 28.6

> The effectiveness of baptism is not tied to that moment in time in which it is administered.[1] However, by the correct use of this sacrament the grace promised in it is not only offered but actually embodied and conferred by the Holy Spirit to everyone (adult or infant) to whom that grace is given, according to the purpose of God's own will and in his appointed time.[2]

At the same time the Confession has a high view of baptism and does not regard it as a mere ritual, *by the correct use of this sacrament the grace promised in it is not only offered but actually embodied and conferred by the Holy Spirit* . . . Baptism is a sign (27.1). The believer is taught by it and in this sense it is a means of grace. It is also a seal by which the believer is reminded of the wonderful pledge of God to him in his own baptism or when others are being baptised. Just as the godly Jew looked to his circumcision and recalled the promises of God, so the believer recalls the promise made to him in baptism.

Baptism is however more than this. According to our Confession it confers and conveys the grace of which it is a sign. This is true only of believers. Just as the Word conveys grace to those who believe, so does the visible word, 'baptism'. This is not magical, but the work of the Holy Spirit. Water baptism is the outward counter-part of Spirit-baptism[3]

While the connection is real, it does not mean that the moment a person is baptised they are saved, any more than the moment they hear the Word of God they are saved. A person who hears the Word of God may not come to faith for years or may never come to faith. So it is with the visible Word of baptism. Salvation may occur years after it is administered or it may never occur at all. In the Old Testament both Jacob and Esau were circumcised, Jacob came to faith years afterwards, but Esau never experienced salvation. The fact is that truth, either in verbal or visual Word, is only effective if believed. Baptism has no efficacy where there is no faith in the gospel it preaches.

---

1 John 3:5, 8.

2 Galatians 3:27; Titus 3:5; Ephesians 5:25-26; Acts 2:38, 41.

3 "For as many of you as were baptized into Christ have put on Christ. (Gal. 3:27) For in one Spirit we were all baptized into one body — Jews or Greeks, slaves [a] or free — and all were made to drink of one Spirit.
[a] Or servants; Greek bondservants" (I Corinthians 12:13).

Confession 28.7

> The sacrament of baptism should be administered only once to a person.[1]

The last paragraph (28.7) of this section makes it clear that re-baptism is wrong. Since baptism is the sacrament of entrance into the Church, this can only be administered once. A person is only regenerate once, united to Christ once, justified once. To repeat baptism is to say that these great once-for-all blessings symbolised in baptism must be repeated.

It has been the consistent teaching of the Reformed Church that provided baptism has been in the Triune Name and with water there is no need to repeat it. A person who has been baptised as an infant does not need to be immersed when he comes to faith, for all that was symbolised in his infant baptism, has come to pass. Rather than desiring to be immersed he should praise God for keeping his promises to him symbolised in his infant baptism.

Cross references with the Catechisms:

Shorter: 94, 95; Larger: 165-167.

To think over and discuss:

1. In what ways have we failed to see the full meaning of baptism?
2. How can the understanding and practice of infant baptism be improved in your congregation?
3. Should those who do not believe in the practice of the baptism of believing adults and their children be allowed to hold office in our denomination?
4. How can we teach our young people to fulfil their baptism?

---

[1] Titus 3:5. (There is no command, and no adequate example for the repetition of baptism.)

THE LORD'S SUPPER

Ref. Confession Chapter 29 – The Lord's Supper

In studying this chapter we should remember that it was written against the controversy between the Reformed Church and Roman Catholicism.

In this study you will discover:

- What the Lord's Supper is
- The main areas of controversy with Roman Catholicism
- The benefits of the Lord's Supper

What the Lord's Supper is

Confession 29.1

> The night Jesus was betrayed he instituted the sacrament of his body and blood, called the Lord's supper, to be observed in his church until the end of the world as a perpetual remembrance of his sacrifice in death and as the seal of all the benefits of that sacrifice for true believers. It also signifies the spiritual nourishment and growth of believers in Jesus and their additional commitment to perform all the duties they owe him. Finally it is a bond and pledge of believers' communion with Jesus and with each other as members of his mystical body.[1]

This paragraph teaches us a number of important things about the Lord's Supper:

1. It was appointed by Christ, and because of this we must treat it with great seriousness.
2. It is to be celebrated until Christ comes again. There is no direct command by the Lord or his apostles as to the frequency of celebration. The emphasis of Scripture would be frequent rather than occasional.
3. It is a memorial of his death. The bread and wine representing his body and blood. The gospels do not use the word wine in this connection[2], though fermented wine was used on occasions. This is clear from the account in

[1] I Corinthians 11:23-26, 10:16-17, 21, 12:13.

[2] "I tell you I will not drink again of this fruit of the vine until that day when I drink it new with you in my Father's kingdom" (Matthew 26:29).

Corinthians in which we are told some of the members got drunk![1]

4. It is a seal (cf. Confession Chapter 27) to the partaker and also provides for his growth in grace. In this it differs from baptism which illustrates the initial blessings of the Christian life. The Lord's Supper is the sacrament of growth. Just as food nourishes our body so the Lord's Supper nourishes our spiritual life. It should be noted that this refers to believers only. Neither the Confession nor Scripture regard the Lord's Supper as a converting ordinance. The partaker also pledges himself to Christ. It is an act of commitment to him. He is saying, "I belong to Christ and wish to serve him".
5. Since it is a covenantal meal, believers have fellowship with Christ and with each other.[2] They are members of the one family, called in the Confession *his mystical body*; it is a bond of unity.

The main areas of controversy with Roman Catholicism

Confession 29.2

> In this sacrament Christ is not offered up to his Father, nor is any actual sacrifice made for the remission of sins of the living or the dead.[3] Rather, this sacrament commemorates Christ's offering up of himself, by himself, on the cross once for all, and it spiritually offers up to God every possible praise for that sacrifice.[4] Consequently the so-called sacrifice of the Roman Catholic mass does detestable injustice to Christ's one sacrifice, which is the only propitiation for all the sins of the elect.[5]

In these paragraphs the main disagreements with Roman Catholicism are outlined.

---

1 "But in the following instructions . . . when you come together as a church . . . it is not the Lord's supper that you eat. For in eating, each one goes ahead with his own meal. One goes hungry, another gets drunk" (I Corinthians 11:17-21ff).

2 "The cup of blessing that we bless, is it not a participation in the blood of Christ? The bread that we break, is it not a participation in the body of Christ?" (I Corinthians 10:16).

3 Hebrews 9:22, 25-26, 28.

4 I Corinthians 11:24-26; Matthew 26:26-27.

5 Hebrews 7:23-24, 27, 10:11-12, 14, 18.

The Lord's Supper is not a re-offering of Christ's sacrifice

as taught in the Roman Catholic Mass (Confession 29.2).

The Roman Catholic Catechism of Catholic Church (1994 here after CCC) states:

> Para 1365f " . . . *In the Eucharist Christ gives us the very body he gave up for us on the cross, the very blood he 'poured out for many for the forgiveness of sins'. The Eucharist is thus a sacrifice, because it* ***re-presents*** *(makes present the sacrifice of the cross, because it is a memorial and because it applies its fruit . . .*"
> (emphasis original)

The Confession denies this teaching as unscriptural. Christ made only one sacrifice on the cross for his people. This sacrifice can never be repeated in any form.[1]

In the celebration of the Lord's Supper, the death of Christ is remembered and not re-enacted. In no way does it remit the sins of the living or the dead.

The celebration of the Lord's Supper is a spiritual thank offering to God. As it is celebrated, it is an act of praise to God for the sacrifice of Christ, rather than re-enacting his death.

The Lord's Supper is for public celebration only

Confession 29.3

> In the administration of the Lord's supper Jesus has directed his ministers to declare to the congregation his words instituting this sacrament, to pray, and to bless the bread and wine, which are thus set apart from their ordinary use and put to holy use. His ministers are to take and break the bread, to take the cup, and (communicating themselves, as well) to give both to the communicants[2] – but not to anyone else not present at that time in the congregation.[3]

It is questionable if the phrase, '*bless the bread and wine, which are thus*

[1] "And every priest stands daily at his service, offering repeatedly the same sacrifices, which can never take away sins. But when Christ had offered for all time a single sacrifice for sins, he sat down at the right hand of God, waiting from that time until his enemies should be made a footstool for his feet" (Hebrews 10:11-13ff).

[2] Matthew 26:26-28 and Mark 14:22-24 and Luke 22:19-20 with I Corinthians 11:23-26.

[3] Acts 20:7; I Corinthians 11:20.

set apart from their ordinary use and put to holy use', is biblically correct. In the minds of many people something happens to the bread and wine when they are 'blessed'. In the Gospel accounts it does not say that Jesus blessed the elements.[1] The *"it"* which occurs in many versions is not in the original. The word *"bless"* simply means to give thanks, Christ gave thanks to God, he praised him. The verse in I Corinthians 10 *"the cup of blessing that we bless"* v.16 should be understood as giving thanks for what the cup represents, rather than blessing the cup cf. NIV *"the cup of thanksgiving for which we give thanks"*. A minister in celebrating the sacrament gives praise to God for Christ and his sacrifice and for what the elements represent. It is only in this sense they are set apart. They are symbolically special during the service only.

The Minister is to give both the bread and wine to the people, (in normal Roman Catholic practice only the bread/wafer is given) but it is limited to those who are in the congregation. The idea of the minister carrying elements to those who are sick at home is not permitted. If this was practised it would imply in the minds of some that communion was necessary for salvation prior to death, or that there was something magical about the elements. The elements are only symbolic during the service, afterwards there is nothing special about them. The Lord's Supper is for public worship in a regular meeting of the congregation where the Word is preached. The Lord's Supper is an integral part of the service.

---

[1] "Now as they were eating, Jesus took bread, and after blessing it broke it and gave it to the disciples, and said, 'Take, eat; this is my body:' And he took a cup, and when he had given thanks he gave it to them, saying, 'drink of it, all of you, for this is my blood of the covenant, which is poured out for many for the forgiveness of sins'" (Matthew 26:26-28).

"And as they were eating, he took bread, and after blessing it broke it and gave it to them, and said, 'Take; this is my body.' And he took a cup, and when he had given thanks he gave it to them, and they all drank of it. And he said to them, 'This is my blood of the covenant, which is poured out for many'" (Mark 14:22-24ff).

"And he took a cup, and when he had given thanks he said, 'Take this, and divide it among yourselves. For I tell you that from now on I will not drink of the fruit of the vine until the kingdom of God comes.' And he took bread, and when he had given thanks, he broke it and gave it to them, saying, 'This is my body, which is given for you. Do this in remembrance of me.' And likewise the cup after they had eaten, saying, 'This cup that is poured out for you is the new covenant in my blood'" (Luke 22:17-20ff).

"For I received from the Lord what I also delivered to you, that the Lord Jesus on the night when he was betrayed took bread, and when he had given thanks, he broke it, and said, 'This is my body which is for you. Do this in remembrance of me.' In the same way also he took the cup, after supper, saying, 'This cup is the new covenant in my blood. Do this, as often as you drink it, in remembrance of me'. For as often as you eat this bread and drink the cup, you proclaim the Lord's death until he comes" (I Corinthians 11:23-26ff).

Confession 29.4

> Practices contrary to the nature of this sacrament and to the institution of it by Christ are private masses or receiving the sacrament alone from a priest or anyone else;[1] denying the cup to the congregation;[2] and worshiping the bread and wine themselves by lifting them up or carrying them around for adoration or reserving them for any counterfeit religious use.[3]

The fourth paragraph rules out private Masses and by implication private communion. The practice of a priest performing a Mass for himself is also condemned. Other practices condemned in this paragraph include the denial of the wine to the people; the worshipping of the elements and lifting them up in the service for adoration by the people; any adoration of them whatsoever; and the keeping of them for future religious use. All these false ideas come from the fact that people believe something happens to elements by the so-called prayer of blessing. The Confession now considers the Roman Catholic error on this point.

There is no change in the elements

Confession 29.5

> The bread and wine in this sacrament, properly set apart to the uses ordained by Christ, so relate to him crucified that truly and yet only sacramentally they are sometimes called by the name of what they represent, that is, the body and blood of Christ.[4] Even so, they still remain in substance and nature only bread and wine, as they were before their sacramental use.[5]

In traditional Roman Catholic teaching the elements of bread and wine become the actual body and blood of Christ.

> " . . . In the most blessed sacrament of the Eucharist 'the body and blood, together with the soul and divinity, of our Lord Jesus Christ and therefore, *the whole Christ is truly, really and substantially contained . . .*'" (CCC para. 1374 emphasis original).

---

1 I Corinthians 10:16.

2 Mark 14:23; I Corinthians 11:25-29.

3 Matthew 15:9; (there is not the least appearance of a warrant for any of these things, either in precept or example, in any part of the word of God; see all the places in which the ordinance is mentioned).

4 Matthew 26:26-28.

5 I Corinthians 11:26-28; Matthew 26:29.

> "It is by the *conversion* of bread and wine into Christ's body and blood that Christ becomes present in this sacrament . . ." (CCC para. 1375 emphasis original).

(For more details consult CCC para's 1377-1380).

This theory came from ancient belief about the make-up of matter. The theory suggests that matter consists of two parts, 'accidents' which we see, touch and so forth, and 'substance' which is invisible being underneath the 'accident'. In the Mass, the 'substance', Christ's body the invisible changes, but the outward form the 'accidents', the physical wafer remains the same. Hence this teaching of Roman Catholicism is often called *"transubstantiation"*.

Roman Catholic dogma teaches that each part of the bread and each drop of the wine contain the whole Christ. This is the reason why the wine is not given to the people, for there is the danger of it being spilt. Hence the common Roman Catholic practice of communion is in one kind (bread).

Confession 29.6

> The teaching that the substance of the bread and wine is changed into the substance of Christ's body and blood (usually called transubstantiation) by the consecration of a priest or any other means is objectionable not only to Scripture but even to common sense and reason. Such teaching overturns the nature of the sacrament and has been and is the cause of much superstition and indeed flagrant idolatry.[1]

This elaborate theory is denied in the Confession as a gross error – *flagrant idolatry* (29.6). It is unscriptural as well as being contrary to common sense and reason. This is even clearer today with our modern understanding of the make up of matter.

The Confession describes the relationship between the elements and Christ crucified as sacramental. By this it means that the elements are sometimes called by what they represent. When Jesus said *"this is my body"* (Matthew 26:26) clearly he meant that it represented his body, not that the bread had become his actual body. In just the same way as when Jesus said, *"I am the gate for the sheep"* (John 10:7), no one understands him to mean he was an actual gate. The Confession rightly condemns the Roman teaching on the sacrament.

---

[1] Acts 3:21; I Corinthians 11:24-26; Luke 24:6, 39.

and censure. The *word* is when they apply the Word of God to individuals (as distinct from public preaching) who come under their discipline. So the Kirk Session can say to a person, that if they continue to act in a certain manner they are under the frown of God which is due to their sin, but if they repent they will be forgiven. This is only declarative it is not absolute. It is Christ who makes it absolute. Consider the case where a person professes to repent but does not. Although the Session may believe he has repented, it carries no blessing for Christ has not confirmed it. If however it is genuine repentance, then Christ will bless.

Condemnation refers to the exclusion from certain privileges which Church members have. These are considered later when we study the final paragraph.

The purpose and limits of church discipline

Confession 30.3

> Condemnation by the church is necessary in order to reclaim and regain spiritual brothers who have committed some serious offense; to deter others from committing similar offenses; to purge that leaven which might contaminate the whole lump; to vindicate the honour of Christ and the holy profession of the gospel; and to avoid the wrath of God, which might justly fall on the church, should it allow his covenant and the sacraments to be profaned by notorious and obstinate offenders.[1]

The teaching of this third paragraph may be explained under a number of short statements.

1. Church discipline applies to professing members *(spiritual brothers)* in the Confession. It is not for outsiders, the Church can only discipline those who claim to be its members.
2. Its purpose is to reclaim those who err. It is pastoral rather than punitive.
3. It may act as a deterrent to others not to follow the same sinful path.
4. It prevents sin and error spreading through the Church. If nothing is done about these, soon the whole body will be corrupted,

---

1 [I Corinthians 5]; Timothy 5:20; Matthew 7:6; I Timothy 1:20; [I Corinthians 11:27-34] with Jude 23.

> *"Your boasting is not good. Do you not know that a little leaven leavens the whole lump? Cleanse out the old leaven that you may be a new lump, as you really are unleavened. For Christ, our Passover lamb has been sacrificed. Let us therefore celebrate the festival, not with the old leaven, the leaven of malice and evil, but with the unleavened bread of sincerity and truth"*
> (I Corinthians 5:6-8ff).

5. Sin in the Church brings disgrace to Christ and his gospel. It is to prevent such dishonour and to avoid making the cause of God a laughing stock that discipline is to be applied.
6. If the Church leaders refuse to act, and allow sin and error to grow, then it will bring the wrath of God on the Church as happened to Israel in exile. Such an action by God would be just.

Note that the Confession calls such disobedience the profaning of *his covenant and the sacraments*. The Covenant of Grace is God's way of salvation and the sacraments are baptism and the Lord's Supper. To abuse any of these is to bring God's wrath upon us.

For a Kirk Session to refuse to apply discipline is a very serious matter. It demonstrates both their lack of pastoral care for those under their charge and their lack of concern for the glory of God.

Confession 30.4

> The best way to accomplish these purposes is for the officers of the church to act in accordance with the severity of the offense and the guilt of the offender by warning the offender, excluding him from the sacrament of the Lord's supper for a time, or excommunicating him from the church.[1]

The final paragraph explains the censures which the Session can apply. It is a basic principle that they can only remove what they have the right to give. The censures are limited to the spiritual.

They are:

1. Warning (admonition) - the direct word of correction. It will include encouragement and warning.
2. Suspension from the Lord's Supper for a season. The

[1] I Thessalonians 5:12; II Thessalonians 3:6, 14-15; I Corinthians 5:4-5,13; Matthew 18:17; Titus 3:10.

sacrament is a great privilege given by Christ to his people. It is the Session who admits to the Lord's Table. They have the right to suspend a person who is not living a godly life. This takes place after they fail to respond to the admonition. At this point the person is still a Church member and must be treated as a brother.

3. The final stage is excommunication. They are now treated as outsiders,

> *"If he refuses to listen to them, tell it to the church. And if he refuses to listen even to the church, let him be to you as a Gentile and a tax collector"* (Matthew 18:17).

It is hoped that this will in time bring the offender to repentance as it did the immoral brother at the church in Corinth,

> *"It is actually reported that there is sexual immorality among you, and of a kind that is not tolerated even among pagans, for a man has his father's wife. And you are arrogant! Ought you not rather to mourn? Let him who has done this be removed from among you"* (I Corinthians 5:1-2ff),

> *"Now if anyone has caused pain, he has caused it not to me, but in some measure—not to put it too severely—to all of you. For such a one, this punishment by the majority is enough, so you should rather turn to forgive and comfort him, or he may be overwhelmed by excessive sorrow. So I beg you to reaffirm your love for him"* (II Corinthians 2:5-8ff).

Excommunication is the limit of Church censures. The Church cannot apply social or physical punishment as the Roman church often did.

Cross references with the Catechisms:

Shorter 50; Larger 45, 108, 118.

To think over and discuss:

1. Why do you think there is little emphasis on discipline in the Church today?
2. In what areas do you think discipline needs to be applied?
3. What steps would you take to introduce true, pastoral discipline into your local congregation?

CHURCH COURTS

Ref. Confession Chapter 31 – Synods and Councils

In this study you will discover:

- The necessity of Church courts
- The function of Church courts
- The limitations of Church courts

This chapter needs to be understood against the debates in the 17th century concerning the right of the Church to govern herself independent of the State and also the correct form of that government.

The latter is not discussed in detail in this chapter but is expounded in another document of the Westminster Assembly: "The Form of Presbyterian Church Government."

The necessity of church courts

Confession 31.1 – Kelly

> The assemblies which are generally called synods or councils ought to be held for the better government and continuing improvement of the church. By virtue of their office and the power Christ has given them to build up and not destroy, the leaders of particular churches should arrange for such assemblies and meet together in them as often as is judged necessary for the good of the church.[1]

The first paragraph outlines the need for some form of church council so that the Church as a whole might be better ruled. While the details, due to the times, are not specific, strict Independency and Episcopacy are by inference excluded.

The synod/council referred to would be courts above the local church and in our case above presbytery level. We should think of something akin to the General Assembly. The "Councils" of the PCI are just large committees and are **not** courts and are not referred to in the Confession.

1 Acts 15:2, 4, 6.

Confession 31.2 – Kelly

> As far as the ministry is concerned, it is the responsibility of synods and councils to settle controversies of faith and cases relating to matters of conscience, to set down rules and directions for the better administration of the public worship of God and of church government, and to hear complaints in cases of maladministration and authoritatively to settle them. If these decisions conform to the word of God, they are to be accepted reverently and submissively, not only because they agree with the word but also because they rest on authority ordained and arranged by God in his word.

The second paragraph (31.2) in the original version of 1647 states:

Confession 31.2 – as adopted by the Church of Scotland in the Act of 1647

> *II. As magistrates may lawfully call a synod of ministers, and other fit persons, to consult and advise with about matters of religion;*[1] *so if magistrates be open enemies to the Church, the ministers of Christ, of themselves, by virtue of their office, or they, with other fit persons upon delegation from their Churches, may meet together in such assemblies.*[2]

This second paragraph in the 1647 version has been questioned as giving too much power to the State. If we take it just to mean that the State may request consultation with the churches then few could object. But if it is regarded as mandatory upon the Church to obey the State, it is unbiblical. No State can order a Church Court to meet. It should be noted that all the Confession says is that the State may consult and advise with the Synod; inferring that it cannot dictate. Note also the Synod is not to be ministers only, but also other fit persons.

The second part of the paragraph teaches the independence of the Church from the State. It was argued by many in those days that the church courts could not meet without permission from the State. This was the position of the so-called 'Aberdeen Doctors' of divinity who were opposed to the National Covenant of 1638. They taught that it was illegal to have meetings without the king's consent.

In opposition to such a position the assembly followed the teaching of Samuel Rutherford (1600-1661) who said that it was lawful to hold

---

1 Isaiah 49:23; I Timothy 2:1-2 [II Chronicles 19:8-11 and chapters 29 and 30] Matthew 2:4-5; Proverbs 11:14.

2 Acts 15:2, 4, 22-23, 25.

meetings without the consent of the king. This paragraph strikes a mighty blow for the spiritual independence of the Church.

The function of church courts

In the third paragraph (31.3) the functions of these higher church courts and councils are outlined. It is noted that they act ministerially, that is as servants of Christ, not as dictators. They are under Christ in all they do.

Confession 31.3 – as adopted by the Church of Scotland in the Act of 1647

III. It belongeth to synods and councils ministerially to determine controversies of faith, and cases of conscience; to set down rules and directions for the better ordering of the publick worship of God, and government of his church; to receive complaints in cases of mal-administration, and authoritatively to determine the same: which decrees and determinations, if consonant to the word of God, are to be received with reverence and submission, not only for their agreement with the word, but also for the power whereby they are made, as being an ordinance of God, appointed thereunto in his word.[1]

Confession 31.3 – Kelly

Since apostolic times all synods and councils, whether general or local, may make mistakes, and many have. Consequently synods and councils are not to be made a final authority in questions of faith and living but are to be used as an aid to both.

Their authority is in a number of areas:

1. **Determine controversies of faith.** That is to settle matters of controversy in doctrine. The Church has the right to state what she believes and to settle disputed points of doctrine. This has been the case since the apostolic era (Acts 15), through the great early councils, and up to the assembly at Westminster.
2. **Determine cases of conscience.** Cases of conscience have been debated from biblical times. In the New Testament there is the matter of meat offered to idols (I Corinthians 8). During Puritan times many cases were discussed such as, 'Is going to plays and other theatrical performances consistent with the profession and practice

[1] Acts 15:15, 19, 24, 27-31, 16:4; Matthew 18:17-20.

of Christianity?' Many cases could be dealt with at the local church pastoral level. Some however demanded the decisions of church courts. These had to be balanced of course with the business of Christian liberty discussed earlier (Confession Chapter 20).

3. **Rules for public worship and government.** The public worship of God was not to be a free for all. The church councils had a right to set out guidelines and directions. The same was true of the government of the local church. While the principles were in Scripture, the detailed rules for the local church were to be hammered out by the higher courts. This would include rules for the discipline of the membership. The great advantage of this was that there would be a common pattern and consistency within each local church.

4. **To deal with wrong decisions and actions of local churches and lower courts.** This is the right of appeal which is built into the Presbyterian system and which Independency sadly lacks.

The rules and decisions of courts are to be accepted not only because they agree with the Word of God but also because the courts have been appointed by God as a means of rule in his Church. If however some decision is not in keeping with the Word of God, then a person is not bound to it.

The limitations of church courts

Confession 31.4 – as adopted by the Church of Scotland in the Act of 1647

> *IV. All synods or councils since the apostles' times, whether general or particular, may err, and many have erred; therefore they are not to be made the rule of faith or practice, but to be used as a help in both.*[1]

Confession 31.4 – Kelly

> Synods and councils should consider and settle only ecclesiastical questions. They are not to meddle in civil affairs which concern the state except in extraordinary cases of modest petitions or in an advisory capacity prompted by religious conscience, when requested by civil authorities.

[1] Ephesians 2:20; Acts 17:11; I Corinthians 2:5; II Corinthians 1:24.

Confession 31.5 – as adopted by the Church of Scotland in the Act of 1647

> *V. Synods and councils are to handle or conclude nothing but that which is ecclesiastical; and are not to intermeddle with civil affairs, which concern the commonwealth, unless by way of humble petition, in cases extraordinary; or by way of advice for satisfaction of conscience, if they be thereunto required by the civil magistrate.*[1]

The infallibility of church courts and councils is denied in the third paragraph (31.3 Kelly) (the fourth in the 1647 original version). It is only Scripture which is without error. The statement, *"they are not to be made the rule of faith or practice but to be used as a help in both"* (31.4 in 1647 original version) sets out the proper attitude to them. It is the Word of God which is to convince us of our belief and practice. The teaching of church councils may help us in understanding what Scripture teaches, but we must not base our faith on them.

Paragraphs 31.4 and 31.5 in the 1647 original version have been combined and teach that the synods are to be concerned with Church affairs and not to meddle in politics and the affairs of the State. They do not make State law. We do not live in a 'Churchocracy' where the Church rules the State as Rome has sought to do.

The Church may make appeal to the State in special circumstances or advise the State when asked to do so.

This paragraph is not to be understood as denying the right of the Church to the prophetic ministry of declaring to the State God's Word on certain issues. This the Church must do. It is being involved in government and attempting to run the State which is condemned here.

Kelly's and Ward's modern English versions used in these notes differ in minor detail from the original 1647 version. The original version should be read in conjunction with the comments above. It is the 1647 version that ministers and elders sign up to in the Presbyterian Church in Ireland.

Cross references with the Catechisms

There are no direct references in either catechism.

To think over and discuss:

1. Discuss why there seems to be little respect for church

[1] Luke 12:13-14; John 18:36.

courts among the membership of our denomination.

2. If a member disagrees with a decision of the Church Court what should he do?
3. Has the Church any authority to speak on matters of State if the Word of God is silent on the particular subject?

CHAPTER VI

OUR GREAT FUTURE

DEATH AND THE RESURRECTION

Ref. Confession Chapter 32 – The Condition of man after Death and the Resurrection of the Dead

In this study you will discover:

- The meaning of death
- After death man has a conscious existence
- The nature of the resurrection body

The final section of the Confession outlines the biblical teaching on the 'last things'. In contrast to much of the speculation in the past, as well as today, it is remarkably brief and refuses to speculate. It deals with the basic essentials and does not speak where Scripture is silent. In this it is a model for us to copy so that we emphasise the certainties and are not drawn into needless controversy.

The meaning of death

Confession 32.1

> After death the bodies of human beings decompose and return to dust,[1] but their souls, which do not die or sleep, have an immortal existence and immediately return to God who created them.[2] The souls of the righteous are then perfected in holiness and are received into the highest heavens, where they behold the face of God in light and glory and wait for the full redemption of their bodies.[3] The souls of the wicked are thrown into hell, where they remain in torment and complete darkness, set apart for the great day of Judgment.[4] Scripture recognizes only these two places, and no other, for souls separated from their bodies.

---

1 Genesis 3:19; Acts 13:36.
2 Luke 23:43; Ecclesiastes 12:7.
3 Hebrews 12:23; II Corinthians 5:1, 6, 8; Philippians 1:23 with Acts 3:21 and Ephesians 4:10.
4 Luke 16:23-24; Acts 1:25; Jude 6-7; I Peter 3:19.

Physical death is the consequence of the Fall,

> *"For the wages of sin is death, but the free gift of God is eternal life in Christ Jesus our Lord"* (Romans 6:23),

cf. (Confession Chapter 6.6; WLC 28).

What are the punishments of sin in this world?

> "The punishments of sin in this world are either inward, such as blindness of mind, a depraved sense, strong delusions, hardness of heart, horror of conscience and shameful lusts; or outward, such as the curse of God on the creatures for our sakes, and all other evils that befall us in our bodies, reputations, possessions, relationships and occupations, together with death itself" (WLC 28).

There is no escape, since it is appointed unto all men

> *"And just as it is appointed for man to die once, and after that comes judgement . . ."* (Hebrews 9:27).

In the first section of this chapter (32.1) the meaning of death and the existence after death is discussed.

Death itself is unnatural as it is a separation of human nature. Man is body-soul (Confession Chapter 4.2) and death separates the body and the soul.

The body then begins to decay, this in the Confession is called *decompose*, *and* finally *returns to dust*.

The soul however does not die, it has immortal existence, and therefore will live forever. This is not a natural power, it only lives forever because God grants it the ability to do so. God alone has an immortal nature,

> *". . . who alone has immortality, who dwells in unapproachable light, whom no one has ever seen or can see. To him be honour and eternal dominion. Amen"* (I Timothy 6:16).

At death the soul immediately returns to God. It is under the control of God. It is not floating about as master of its own destiny, but in the hand of God who consigns it at the moment of death to heaven or hell.

After death there is conscious existence

There is no soul sleep

The Confession by its statement, *'their souls, which do not die or sleep'* opposed the ancient heresy of soul sleep, which is believed by a number of groups to this day.

Orthodoxy has always taught that there is a conscious, intermediate state between death and the resurrection. It is not a matter of dying one moment and then in thousands of years awaking in a new universe with a new body as if it were the next moment. There is a period of conscious waiting between death and the resurrection. There is time in this intermediate state in the sense that things will happen in sequence. The experience of it may be different from time in this age. For the believer the period between his death and the resurrection of his body may seem short because he is being taken up with Christ. On the other hand for the unbeliever there is no relief and the period seems long.

The souls of believers are in glory

The souls of believers at death are made perfect, they are made perfectly holy,

> *" . . . and to the assembly [a] of the firstborn who are enrolled in heaven, and to God, the judge of all, and to the spirits of the righteous made perfect" [a] Or church"* (Hebrews 12:23).

They *are received into the highest heavens, where they behold the face of God* (Confession Chapter 32.1). The word *received* implies a welcome just like Christian in Pilgrim's Progress received when he entered the Celestial city. The Scripture proofs for this immediate passing into glory and of its enjoyment include II Corinthians 5:8 where Paul writes, *"Yes, we are of good courage, and we would rather be away from the body and at home with the Lord"*.[1]

The souls of believers during this period are waiting for the redemption of their new bodies. Although not yet complete as persons since they have no body, they are perfectly happy.

The souls of the unsaved are cast into hell. This stands in contrast with the saved that, as we noted, are received into glory. In hell the

---

1 "I am hard pressed between the two. My desire is to depart and be with Christ, for that is far better" (Philippians 1:23).

"'There was a rich man who was clothed in purple and fine linen and who feasted sumptuously every day. And at his gate was laid a poor man named Lazarus, covered with sores, who desired to be fed with what fell from the rich man's table. Moreover, even the dogs came and licked his sores. The poor man died and was carried by the angels to Abraham's side. The rich man also died and was buried, and in Hades, being in torment, he lifted up his eyes and saw Abraham far off and Lazarus at his side. And he called out, 'Father Abraham, have mercy on me, and send Lazarus to dip the end of his finger in water and cool my tongue, for I am in anguish in this flame'" (Luke 16:19-24ff).

"They cried out with a loud voice, 'O Sovereign Lord, holy and true, how long before you will judge and avenge our blood on those who dwell on the earth?' Then they were each given a white robe and told to rest a little longer, until the number of their fellow servants and their brothers should be complete, who were to be killed as they themselves had been" (Revelation 6:10-11ff).

ungodly are in torment, with no hope of escape.[1] While the believers are waiting for their new bodies, the Confession says the souls of the wicked are, *set apart for the great day of Judgment.* Believers wait in hope, but the unsaved are reserved in hopelessness.

The final statement in this first paragraph states besides *these two places,* heaven and hell, *for souls separated from their bodies*, the Scriptures acknowledge none (Confession Chapter 32:1). This is over against the teaching of Roman Catholicism, which teaches purgatory - a place of temporal punishment for purification of the souls of those who have been baptised. In addition there is according to Roman Catholic teaching the "Limbus" (fringe) doctrine. "Limbus Patrum" was the place where Old Testament believers were kept until the resurrection of Christ. "Limbus Infantum is the abode of unbaptized infants. (In recent years Roman Catholic teaching has been toning down on this teaching but not denying it see Catechism of Catholic Church Para 1261).

There is, however, according to Scripture and the Confession only heaven and hell after death. There can be no passing from one to the other either during this intermediate state or after it.

The nature of the Resurrection Body

Confession 32.2

> Those who are alive at the last day will not die but will be changed.[2] At that time all the dead will be raised with the very same bodies and no other than the same bodies they had before, although with different characteristics, which will be united again to their souls forever.[3]

The Confession, in keeping with Scripture, teaches one general resurrection of the just and unjust. It knows nothing of the popular theories of several comings of Christ.

1. In *the last day* Christ will return and *those who are alive will be changed.* This refers to the change of their bodies to suit the new conditions of the new universe or

---

[1] "And someone said to him, 'Lord, will those who are saved be few?' And he said to them, 'Strive to enter through the narrow door. For many, I tell you, will seek to enter and will not be able. When once the master of the house has risen and shut the door, and you begin to stand outside and to knock at the door, saying, 'Lord, open to us,' then he will answer you, 'I do not know where you come from.' Then you will begin to say, 'We ate and drank in your presence, and you taught in our streets.' But he will say, 'I tell you, I do not know where you come from. Depart from me, all you workers of evil!'" (Luke 13:23-27ff).

[2] I Thessalonians 4:17; I Corinthians 15:51-52.

[3] Job 19:26-27; I Corinthians 15:42-44.

everlasting punishment.

2. At the same time those who are *dead will be raised* and *their souls will be united to* their *bodies*.

Confession 32.3

> By the power of Christ the bodies of the unjust shall be raised to dishonor, but by his Spirit the bodies of the just will be raised to honor and be made according to the pattern of his own glorious body.[1]

3. In the case of the unsaved, Christ will do this by his power so that they can be judged and punished. This is an act of justice on his part as one who rules over all.

4. The bodies of the believers will be changed by the power of the Holy Spirit to be like Christ's resurrection body. Their experience of resurrection follows from the fact that they are united to Christ, they have the Holy Spirit and it is he who brings this work to completion under the authority of Christ (cf. WLC 87). They have a *"spiritual body"* (I Corinthians 15:44) meaning a body which the Holy Spirit empowers and indwells rather than an unreal ghost-like 'body'. The Confession underlines that it is a real body when it teaches that it is like Christ's glorious body which was no ghost but a literal body equipped to live in the new universe.

Cross references with the Catechisms:

Shorter: 19, 37 & 38; Larger: 28, 29, 84-87.

To think over and discuss:

1. In what ways does much current prophetic teaching go beyond Scripture?
2. How do we prevent our people being led astray by these theories?
3. How would you reply to the Roman Catholic teaching on purgatory?

---

1 Acts 24:15; John 5:28-29; I Corinthians 15:43; Philippians 3:21.

THE LAST JUDGEMENT

Ref. Confession Chapter 33 – The Last Judgement

In this study you will discover:

- There is a final day of judgement
- The reasons for the last judgement
- Contemporary lessons from the last judgement

There is a final day of judgement

Confession 33.1

> God the Father has ordained a day in which he will judge the world in righteousness by Jesus Christ,[1] to whom he[2] has given all power and judgment.[3] In that day not only will the apostate angels be judged, but all the people who have lived on earth will appear before the court of Christ to give an account of their thoughts, words, and actions, and be judged according to what they have done in the body, whether good or evil.[4]

The Confession states, with great clarity, the solemn truths about the final judgement. It speaks of one judgement, just as it spoke of one resurrection (32.2). There is none of the speculative complexity of several judgements advocated by some teaching on the Lord's return. The teaching of this paragraph can be summarized under a number of headings:

1. **It is a divine appointment.**
   God himself has appointed the day, it is part of his Divine Plan. The day, although unknown to man, is fixed by God and therefore certain.

2. **The judgement will be just.**
   The standard is God's righteousness, not man's standards.

3. **Christ will be the judge.**
   The Father in the plan of salvation has given him this task. He is Saviour, Lord and Judge in the Divine Plan of

---

1 Acts 17:31.
2 John 5:22, 27.
3 I Corinthians 6:3; Jude 6; II Peter 2:4.
4 II Corinthians 5:10; Ecclesiastes 12:14; Romans 2:16, 14:10, 12; Matthew 12:36-37.

redemption. The one who was cursed at Golgotha because of the sins of men, now stands in judgement of men. He came to save, but at the close of the day of mercy he is judge.

4. **At the final judgement fallen men and angels will be judged.**
The Confession underlines by its statement *all the people who have lived on earth*, the fact that no one will be omitted. People often escape the judgement of human courts, but they will not escape God's final judgement.

5. **This judgement on people will be comprehensive.**
It does not only include their overt acts, but also their words and thoughts,

> *"on that day when, according to my gospel, God judges the secrets of men by Christ Jesus"* (Romans 2:16),
>
> *"I tell you, on the day of judgement people will give account for every careless word they speak"* (Matthew 12:36).

It reminds us that Christianity is a heart religion, not a mere outward performance. No thought, word or deed will be omitted, it is total.

6. **It is for *what they have done in the body*.**
Hence it is restricted to their earthly actions. The idea of doing works after death to earn salvation is ruled out. Once a person dies their destiny is sealed.

The reason for the Last Judgement

Confession 33.2

God's purpose in arranging for this day is to show forth the glory of his mercy in the eternal salvation of his chosen people and the glory of his justice in the damnation of the reprobate, who are wicked and disobedient. At that time the righteous will go into everlasting life and receive that fulness of joy and refreshment which will come from the presence of the Lord. But the wicked, who do not know God and do not obey the gospel of Jesus Christ, will be thrown into eternal torment and punished with everlasting destruction away from the presence of the Lord and the glory of his power.[1]

---

[1] [Matthew 25:31-46]; Romans 2:5-6, 9:22-23; Matthew 25:21; Acts 3:19; II Thessalonians 1:7-10.

The question is often asked, "If people are already in heaven and hell, why are they brought out to give an account before the tribunal of Christ? Why a final judgement since they are already judged at death?"

This paragraph attempts to answer this. The reasons given are for the manifestation of the glory of his mercy and of his justice. In other words, the last judgement will be a public demonstration of the mercy and justice of God. No one will be able to accuse God of injustice after the final assize. It will show his great mercy to the elect. It will be plain for all to see that they do not deserve to be saved and it was only an act of his mercy that they are. At the same time, no one can complain of their everlasting damnation for it will be plain to them and others that they are wicked and disobedient. The final judgement will silence forever the lips of those who accuse God of injustice in election. They will discover that all deserved hell, but it was only his mercy which saved a multitude which no one could number.

The destiny of the righteous is **everlasting life**, that is, they will live in fellowship with God, know his refreshing, and his joy for ever. The destiny of the wicked is **everlasting punishment**, they are described as the ones who know not God and obey not the gospel of Jesus Christ. In other words the wicked are not in fellowship with God since they had no time for the gospel of grace.

The words used to describe the condition of the wicked are fearful:

1. **Cast into eternal torments,** there is no relief in hell, joy and happiness are impossible there.

2. **Punished with everlasting destruction.** It is punishment. When people do wrong there must be punishment. Those who escaped the judgement of men cannot escape divine retribution. There is nothing reformatory here, nor is there any hope, it is everlasting punishment.

3. **It is from the loving presence of the Lord.** He is only present in wrath, not mercy. Those in hell will experience no glory in his power, they will have his frown and not his smile.

The teaching of the Confession cannot be squared with modern theories of annihilation or limited punishment. All who sign acceptance of the Confession must accept the biblical doctrine of everlasting punishment in hell.

Contemporary lessons from the Final Judgement

Confession 33.3

> Christ wants us to be completely convinced that there is going to be a day of judgment, as a deterrent to sin for everyone and as an added consolation for the godly in their suffering.[1] He has also made sure that no one knows when that day will be, so that we may never rest secure in our worldly surroundings, but, not knowing what hour the Lord will come, we must always be alert and may always be ready to say, "Come Lord Jesus, come quickly".[2] Amen.

The final paragraph (33.3) of the last chapter of the Confession is a paragraph of application. This truth is not for mere academic knowledge, but like all doctrine is to be applied to our hearts.

1. Christ wants us all *to be completely convinced that there is going to be a day of judgment*. It is one thing to believe as a creedal statement and another to live by it. The Confession wants it to be a life changing reality for us.

2. To know that we will be judged, should cause us to seek to live godly lives, this should deter us from even what men would call the smallest of sins.

3. It also speaks to the believer, living in this earthly valley of tears, that on the last day, justice is certain, and in this knowledge he can live with the opposition and suffering.

4. It teaches us to be watchful, not to depend on ourselves but on Christ, to guard our own souls, for he is coming back and we must be ready.

The Confession ends with the great hope of the return of the Lord. Not only for the writers of the Confession but for us all, this should be our great hope. We should be prepared for his coming. *"Amen. "Come, Lord Jesus!"* (Revelation 22:20) should be our desire and prayer.

---

1 II Peter 3:11, 14; II Corinthians 5:10-11; II Thessalonians 1:5-7; Luke 21:27-28; Romans 8:23-25.
2 Matthew 24:36, 42-44; Mark 13:35-37; Luke 12:35-36; Revelation 22:20.

Cross references with the Catechisms:

Shorter: 19, 38; Larger: 56, 88-90.

To think over and discuss:

1. In the light of the final judgement what has to be changed in your life and in the life of your church?
2. How can we communicate to people today the realities of heaven?
3. Has the loss of belief in the Doctrine of Hell blunted the zeal of the Church in evangelism and world mission?
4. Should those who reject the Doctrine of Everlasting Punishment be allowed to hold office of elder or teaching elder in the Church?

APPENDIX II

Resolution of General Assembly 1988 re – Pope as Anti-Christ

In exercising the right to interpret and explain her standards the Church may set forth her understanding of the meaning of disputed passages.

Chapter 25.6 of the Westminster Confession of Faith steadfastly proclaims that the Lord Jesus Christ is the only King and Head of the Church. From this it follows that no mere man can be head thereof, and any claim to such headship is unbiblical. The General Assembly under God, reaffirm this teaching but declare further their understanding that the historical interpretation that the Pope of Rome as a personal and literal fulfilment of the Biblical figure of "the Anti-Christ" and "the Man of Sin" is not manifestly evident from the Scripture. A variety of views have been long held on this topic consistent with a loyal regard for the authority of Scripture and genuine acceptance of Reformation standards.

10. What are the personal properties of the three persons in the Godhead?

It belongs to the Father to beget the Son,[1] and to the Son to be begotten of the Father,[2] and to the Holy Spirit to proceed from the Father and the Son from all eternity.[3]

11. How does it appear that the Son and the Holy Spirit are God equal with the Father?

The Scriptures show that the Son and the Holy Spirit are God equal with the Father, giving to them such names,[4] attributes,[5] works[6] and worship[7] as belong to God alone.

God's Eternal Plan [WCF 3]

12. What are the decrees of God?

God's decrees are the wise, free and holy acts of the purpose of his will,[8] by which, from all eternity, he has, for his own glory, unchangeably foreordained whatever comes to pass in time,[9] especially what concerns angels and men.

13. What has God specially decreed concerning angels and men?

God, by an eternal and unchangeable decree, solely out of his love and with a view to the praise of his glorious grace to be shown in due time, has elected some angels to glory;[10] and in Christ has chosen some persons to eternal life and ordained all the means to this end.[11] He has also, according to his sovereign power and the unsearchable purpose of his own will according to which he extends or withholds favour as he pleases, passed by and foreordained the rest to dishonour and wrath, to be inflicted because of their sin, to the praise of the glory of his justice.[12]

14. How does God carry out his decrees?

God carries out his decrees in the works of creation and providence, according to his infallible foreknowledge, and the

---

1 Hebrews 1:5-6, 8.
2 John 1:14, 18.
3 John 15:26; Galatians. 4:6.
4 Isaiah 6:3, 5, 8; cf. John 12:41; and Acts 28:25; I John 5:20; Acts 5:3-4.
5 John 1:1; Isaiah 9:6; John 2:24-25; I Corinthians 2:10-11.
6 Colossians 1:16; Genesis 1:2.
7 Matthew 28:19; II Corinthians 13:14.
8 Ephesians 1:11; Romans 11:33; Romans 9:14-15, 18.
9 Ephesians 1:4, 11; Romans 9:22-23; Psalm 33:11.
10 I Timothy 5:21.
11 Ephesians 1:4-6; II Thessalonians 2:13-14.
12 Romans 9:17-18, 21-22; Matthew 11:25-26; II Timothy 2:20; Jude 4; I Peter 2:8.

free and unchangeable purpose of his own will.[1]

Creation [WCF 4]

15. What is the work of creation?

The work of creation is the work God did in the beginning by his powerful word and for himself, when he made of nothing the world and all things in it, within the space of six days, and all very good.[2]

16. How did God create angels?

God created all the angels[3] spirits,[4] immortal,[5] holy,[6] excelling in knowledge,[7] mighty in power,[8] to carry out his commandments and to praise his name,[9] yet with the possibility of change.[10]

17. How did God create man?

After God had made all other creatures, he created man, male and female.[11] He formed the body of the man from the dust of the ground[12] and the woman from the rib of the man[13] and endowed them with living, reasoning and immortal souls.[14] He made them in his own image,[15] in knowledge,[16] righteousness and holiness.[17] They had the law of God written in their hearts[18] and power to fulfil it,[19] and rule over the creatures,[20] yet with the possibility of transgression.[21]

---

1. Ephesians 1:11.
2. Genesis 1; Hebrews 11:3; Proverbs 16:4.
3. Colossians 1:16.
4. Psalm 104:4.
5. Matthew 22:30.
6. Matthew 25:31.
7. II Samuel 14:17; Matthew 24:36.
8. II Thessalonians 1:7.
9. Psalm 103:20-21.
10. II Peter 2:4.
11. Genesis 1:27.
12. Genesis 2:7.
13. Genesis 2:22.
14. Genesis 2:7; cf. Job 35:11; Ecclesiastes 12:7; Matthew 10:28; and Luke 23:43.
15. Genesis 1:27.
16. Colossians 3:10.
17. Ephesians 4:24.
18. Romans 2:14-15.
19. Ecclesiastes 7:29.
20. Genesis 1:28.
21. Genesis 3:6; Ecclesiastes 7:29.

Providence [WCF 5 & 7:1-2]

18. *What are God's works of providence?*

God's works of providence are his most holy,[1] wise[2] and powerful preservation[3] and control[4] of all his creatures, appointing them and all their actions[5] to his own glory.[6]

19. *What is God's providence towards the angels?*

God in his providence permitted some of the angels to fall deliberately and irretrievably into sin and damnation,[7] setting limits to and appointing this and all their sins to his own glory.[8] He established the rest in holiness and happiness,[9] employing them all,[10] at his pleasure, in the service of his power,[11] mercy and justice.[12]

20. *What was the providence of God toward man in the state in which he was created?*

The providence of God toward man in the state in which he was created was placing him in paradise, appointing him to work it and giving him liberty to eat of the produce of the earth;[13] putting the creatures under his rule[14] and ordaining marriage for his help;[15] granting him communion with himself;[16] instituting the Sabbath;[17] entering into a covenant of life with him on condition of personal, perfect and perpetual obedience,[18] of which the tree of life was a pledge;[19] and forbidding him to eat of the tree of the knowledge of good and evil on penalty of death.[20]

---

1 Psalm 145:17.
2 Psalm104:24; Isaiah 28:29.
3 Hebrews 1:3.
4 Psalm 103:19.
5 Matthew 10:29-31; Genesis 45:7.
6 Romans 11:36; Isaiah 63:14.
7 Jude 6; II Peter 2:4; Hebrews 2:16; John 8:44.
8 Job 1:12; Matthew 8:31.
9 I Timothy 5:21; Mark 8:38; Hebrews 12:22.
10 Psalm 104:4.
11 II Kings 19:35.
12 Hebrews 1:14.
13 Genesis 2:8, 15-16.
14 Genesis 1:28.
15 Genesis 2:18.
16 Genesis 1:26-29, 3:8.
17 Genesis 2:3.
18 Galatians 3:12; Romans 10:5.
19 Genesis 2:9.
20 Genesis 2:17.

Sin in the human race [WCF 6]

21. Did man continue in that state in which God at first created him? [WSC 13&15]

Our first parents, being left to the freedom of their own will, through the temptation of Satan transgressed the commandment of God by eating the fruit that God had forbidden. By this transgression they fell from the state of innocence in which they were created.[1]

22. Did all mankind fall in that first transgression? [WSC 16]

The covenant being made with Adam as a representative person for his descendants as well as for himself, all mankind descending from him in the ordinary manner,[2] sinned in him, and fell with him in that first transgression.[3]

23. Into what state did the fall bring mankind? [WSC 17]

The fall brought mankind into a state of sin and misery.[4]

24. What is sin? [WSC 14]

Sin is any failure to measure up to whatever God requires, or any disobedience to any of his commands given as a rule for creatures with reason.[5]

25. What is the sinfulness of that state into which man fell?

The sinfulness of the state into which man fell includes the guilt of Adam's first sin,[6] the lack of the righteousness which he had at first, and the corruption of his nature, by which he is utterly indisposed, disabled and opposed to all spiritual good and is wholly inclined to all evil, and that all the time.[7] This is commonly called Original Sin, and from it flow all actual sins.[8]

26. How is original sin conveyed from our first parents to their descendants?

Original sin is conveyed from our first parents as the human race reproduces itself, so that all who descend from them in the

---

1 Genesis 3:6-8, 13; Ecclesiastes 7:29; II Corinthians 11:3.
2 Acts 17 26.
3 Genesis 2:16-17; cf. Romans 5:12-20; and I Corinthians 15:21-22.
4 Romans 5:12, 3:23.
5 I John 3:4; Galatians 3:10, 12.
6 Romans 5:12, 19.
7 Romans 3:10-19; Ephesians 2:1-3; Romans 5:6, 8:7-8; Genesis 6:5.
8 James 1:14-15; Matthew 15:19.

ordinary manner are conceived and born in sin.[1]

27. What misery did the fall bring on mankind?

The fall brought upon mankind the loss of communion with God,[2] his displeasure and his curse, so that we are by nature children of wrath,[3] enslaved to Satan, [4] and justly liable to all punishments in this world and in that which is to come.[5]

28. What are the punishments of sin in this world?

The punishments of sin in this world are either inward, such as blindness of mind,[6] a depraved sense,[7] strong delusions,[8] hardness of heart,[9] horror of conscience[10] and shameful lusts;[11] or outward, such as the curse of God on the creatures for our sakes,[12] and all other evils that befall us in our bodies, reputations, possessions, relationships and occupations,[13] together with death itself.[14]

29. What are the punishments of sin in the world to come?

The punishments of sin in the world to come are everlasting separation from the enjoyment of God in his presence, and extremely severe torments in soul and body, without any break, in the fire of hell for ever.[15]

GOD'S COVENANT OF GRACE [WCF 7:3-6]

30. Does God leave all mankind to perish in the state of sin and misery?

God does not leave all men to perish in the state of sin and misery[16] into which they fell by breaking the first covenant, commonly called the covenant of works;[17] but solely of his love and mercy delivers his elect out of it, and brings them into a state

---

1 Psalm 51:5; Job 14:4, 15:14; John 3:6.
2 Genesis 3:8, 10, 24.
3 Ephesians 2:2-3.
4 II Timothy 2:26.
5 Genesis 2:17; Lamentations 3:39; Romans 6:23; Matthew 25:41, 46; Jude 7.
6 Ephesians 4:18.
7 Romans 1:28.
8 II Thessalonians 2:11.
9 Romans 2:5.
10 Isaiah 33:14; Genesis 4:13; Matthew 27:4.
11 Romans 1:26.
12 Genesis 3:17.
13 Deuteronomy 28:15-68.
14 Romans 6:21, 23.
15 II Thessalonians 1:9; Mark 9:43-44, 46, 48; Luke 16:24.
16 I Thessalonians 5:9.
17 Galatians 3:10, 12.

of salvation by the second covenant, commonly called the covenant of grace.[1]

31. With whom was the covenant of grace made?

The covenant of grace was made with Christ as the second Adam, and in him with all the elect as his seed.[2]

32. How is the grace of God shown in the second covenant?

The grace of God is shown in the second covenant by his freely providing and offering to sinners a Mediator,[3] and life and salvation by him.[4] God requires faith as the condition for a saving interest in the Mediator,[5] and therefore he promises and gives his Holy Spirit[6] to all his elect to work in them that faith[7] with all other saving graces.[8] Further, he enables them to all holy obedience,[9] and thus the truth of their faith[10] and thankfulness to God is evidenced,[11] and they progress in the way that he has appointed for their salvation.[12]

33. Was the covenant of grace always administered in the same way?

The covenant of grace was not always administered in the same way, but the administrations of it under the Old Testament were different from those under the New.[13]

34. How was the covenant of grace administered under the Old Testament?

The covenant of grace was administered under the Old Testament by promises,[14] prophecies,[15] sacrifices,[16] circumcision,[17] the Passover,[18] and other types and ordinances, all of which

---

1 Titus 3:4-7; Galatians 3:21; Romans 3:20-22.
2 Galatians 3:16; Romans 5:15-21; Isaiah 53:10-11.
3 Genesis 3:15; Isaiah 42:6; John 6:27.
4 I John 5:11-12.
5 John 3:16; John 1:12.
6 Proverbs 1:23.
7 II Corinthians 4:13.
8 Galatians 5:22-23.
9 Ezekiel 36:27.
10 James 2:18, 22.
11 II Corinthians 5:14-15.
12 Ephesians 2:10.
13 II Corinthians 3:6-9.
14 Romans 15:8.
15 Acts 3:20, 24.
16 Hebrews 10:1.
17 Romans 4:11.
18 I Corinthians 5:7.

foreshadowed Christ yet to come. They were for that time sufficient to build up the elect in faith in the promised Messiah,[1] by whom they had full remission of sin and eternal salvation.[2]

35. *How is the covenant of grace administered under the New Testament?*

Under the New Testament, when Christ the substance was revealed, the same covenant of grace was and still is to be administered in the preaching of the word,[3] and the administration of the sacraments of Baptism[4] and the Lord's Supper.[5] In these, grace and salvation are held forth in more fullness, clarity and spiritual power to all nations.[6]

CHRIST THE MEDIATOR [WCF 8]

The Person of Christ

36. *Who is the Mediator of the covenant of grace?*

The only Mediator of the covenant of grace is the Lord Jesus Christ,[7] the eternal Son of God, of one substance and equal with the Father.[8] When the time had fully come he became man,[9] and so was and continues to be God and man, in two entire distinct natures and one person, for ever.[10]

37. *How did Christ, the Son of God, become man?*

Christ the Son of God became man by taking to himself a body and a soul like ours,[11] being conceived by the power of the Holy Spirit in the womb of the Virgin Mary, of her substance, and born of her,[12] yet without sin.[13]

38. *Why was it necessary that the Mediator should be God?*

It was necessary that the Mediator should be God so that he might sustain and keep the human nature from sinking under the infinite

---

1 Hebrews chapters 8, 9 and 10, Hebrews 11:13.
2 Galatians 3:7-9, 14.
3 Mark 16:15.
4 Matthew 28:19-20.
5 I Corinthians 11:23-25.
6 II Corinthians 3:6-18; Hebrews 8:6, 10-11; Matthew 28:19.
7 I Timothy 2:5.
8 John 1:1, 14; John 10:30; Philippians 2:6.
9 Galatians 4:4.
10 Luke 1:35; Romans 9:5; Colossians 2:9; Hebrews 7:24-25.
11 John 1:14; Matthew 26:38.
12 Luke 1:27, 31, 35, 42; Galatians 4:4.
13 Hebrews 4:15, 7:26.

wrath of God and the power of death;[1] give value and effectiveness to his sufferings, obedience and intercession;[2] and satisfy God's justice,[3] obtain his favour,[4] purchase a people for his very own,[5] give his Spirit to them,[6] conquer all their enemies,[7] and bring them to everlasting salvation.[8]

39. Why was it necessary that the Mediator should be man?

It was necessary that the Mediator should be man so that he might advance our nature,[9] perform obedience to the law,[10] suffer and make intercession for us in our nature,[11] and sympathise with us in our weaknesses.[12] In this way we receive adoption as sons[13] and have comfort and access with boldness to the throne of grace.[14]

40. Why was it necessary that the Mediator should be God and man in one person?

It was necessary that the Mediator, who was to reconcile God and man, should himself be both God and man in one person, in order that the works appropriate to each nature might be accepted by God for us,[15] and relied on by us, as the works of the whole person.[16]

41. Why was our Mediator called Jesus?

Our Mediator was called Jesus because he saves his people from their sins.[17]

The Offices of Christ

42. Why was our Mediator called Christ?

Our Mediator was called Christ because he was anointed with the

---

1 Acts 2:24-25; Romans 1:4; cf. Romans 4:25; cf. Hebrews 9:14.
2 Acts 20:28; Hebrews 9:14, 7:25-28.
3 Romans 3:24-26.
4 Ephesians 1:6; Matthew 3:17.
5 Titus 2:13-14.
6 Galatians 4:6.
7 Luke 1:68-69, 71, 74.
8 Hebrews 5:8-9, 9:11-15.
9 Hebrews 2:16.
10 Galatians 4:4.
11 Hebrews 2:14, 7:24-25.
12 Hebrews 4:15.
13 Galatians 4:5.
14 Hebrews 4:16.
15 Matthew 1:21, 23, 3:17; Hebrews 9:14.
16 I Peter 2:6.
17 Matthew 1:21.

Holy Spirit to an unlimited extent.[1] Thus he was set apart and completely equipped with all authority and ability[2] to fill the offices of prophet,[3] priest[4] and king of his church[5] in his states both of humiliation and exaltation.

43. *How does Christ fill the office of a prophet?*

Christ fills the office of a prophet in revealing to the church[6] by his Spirit and word, both under the law and under the gospel[7] although in different ways,[8] the whole will of God,[9] in all things concerning the edification and salvation of his people.[10]

44. *How does Christ fill the office of a priest?*

Christ fills the office of a priest in his once offering of himself to God as a spotless sacrifice,[11] to be a reconciliation for the sins of his people;[12] and in making constant intercession for them.[13]

45. *How does Christ fill the office of a king?*

Christ fills the office of a king in calling out of the world a people for himself,[14] and giving them officers,[15] laws[16] and discipline by which he visibly governs them;[17] in bestowing saving grace on his elect,[18] rewarding their obedience[19] and correcting them for their sins,[20] preserving and supporting them during all their temptations and sufferings,[21] restraining and overcoming all their enemies,[22] and powerfully arranging all things for his own glory[23] and their

---

1 John 3:34; Psalm 45:7.
2 John 6:27; Matthew 28:18-20.
3 Acts 3:21-22; Luke 4:18-21.
4 Hebrews 5:5-7; Hebrews 4:14-15.
5 Psalm 2:6; Matthew 21:5; Isaiah 9:6-7; Philippians 2:8-11.
6 John 1:18.
7 I Peter 1:10-12. [The 1647 text has ‘in all ages’ for ‘both under the law and under the gospel’ but for the meaning see WCF 7.5].
8 Hebrews 1:1-2.
9 John 15:15.
10 Acts 20:32; Ephesians 4:11-13; John 20:31.
11 Hebrews 9:14, 28.
12 Hebrews 2:17.
13 Hebrews 7:25.
14 Acts 15:14-16; Isaiah 55:4-5; Genesis 49:10; Psalm 110:3.
15 Ephesians 4:11-12; I Corinthians 12:28.
16 Isaiah 33:22.
17 Matthew 18:17-18; I Corinthians 5:4-5.
18 Acts 5:31.
19 Revelation 22:12; Revelation 2:10.
20 Revelation 3:19.
21 Isaiah 63:9.
22 I Corinthians 15:25; Psalm 110:1-2ff.
23 Romans 14:10-11.

good;[1] and also in bringing punishment on the rest who do not know God and do not obey the gospel.[2]

Christ's State of Humiliation

46. What was the state of Christ's humiliation?

The state of Christ's humiliation was that low condition in which, for our sakes, he emptied himself of his glory, took upon himself the form of a servant in his conception and birth, life, death, and after his death until his resurrection.[3]

47. How did Christ humble himself in his conception and birth?

Christ humbled himself in his conception and birth in this way: although he was from all eternity the Son of God and at the Father's side, he was pleased, when the time had fully come, to become the son of man, made of a woman in humble circumstances, and to be born of her in conditions of more than ordinary lowliness.[4]

48. How did Christ humble himself in his life?

Christ humbled himself in his life by subjecting himself to God's law,[5] which he perfectly fulfilled;[6] and by confronting the contempt of the world,[7] the temptations of Satan,[8] and the frailties in his humanity, whether those common to human nature or those which accompanied his lowly state.[9]

49. How did Christ humble himself in his death?

Christ humbled himself in his death in this: having been betrayed by Judas,[10] forsaken by his disciples,[11] scorned and rejected by the world,[12] condemned by Pilate and tormented by his persecutors;[13] and having also confronted the terrors of death and the powers of darkness, and experienced and borne the weight of God's wrath,[14]

---

1 Romans 8:28.
2 II Thessalonians 1:8-9; Psalm 2:8-9.
3 Philippians 2:6-8; Luke 1:31; II Corinthians 8:9; Acts 2:24.
4 John 1:14, 18; Galatians 4:4; Luke 2:7.
5 Galatians 4:4.
6 Matthew 5:17; Romans 5:19.
7 Psalm 22:6; Hebrews 12:2-3.
8 Matthew 4:1-12; Luke 4:13.
9 Hebrews 2:17-18; Hebrews 4:15; Isaiah 52:13-14.
10 Matthew 27:4.
11 Matthew 26:56.
12 Isaiah 53:2-3.
13 Matthew 27:26-50; John 19:34.
14 Luke 22:44; Matthew 27:46.

he laid down his life as an offering for sin,[1] enduring the painful, shameful curse of death on the cross.[2]

50. *In what did Christ's humiliation after his death consist?*

Christ's humiliation after his death consisted in his being buried,[3] and continuing in the state of the dead and under the power of death until the third day,[4] which has been otherwise expressed in the words, 'He descended into hell'.

Christ's State of Exaltation

51. *What was the state of Christ's exaltation?*

The state of Christ's exaltation includes his resurrection,[5] ascension,[6] his sitting at the right hand of the Father,[7] and his coming again to judge the world.[8]

52. *How was Christ exalted in his resurrection?*

Christ was exalted in his resurrection in this way: since it was impossible for Christ to be held by death he experienced no decay in it.[9] He rose again from the dead the third day by his own power.[10] His body was the same body in which he suffered, possessed all its essential qualities[11] except mortality and other common weaknesses belonging to this life, and was truly united to his soul.[12] By his resurrection he declared himself to be the Son of God,[13] to have satisfied divine justice,[14] to have vanquished death and the one who had the power of death,[15] and to be the Lord of the living and the dead.[16] All this he did as a representative person,[17] the head of his church,[18] for the justification[19] and making alive in grace of his people,[1] for their

---

1 Isaiah 53:10.
2 Philippians 2:8; Hebrews 12:2; Galatians 3:13.
3 I Corinthians 15:3-4.
4 Psalm 16:10; cf. Acts 2:24-27, 31; Romans 6:9; Matthew 12:40.
5 I Corinthians 15:4.
6 Luke 24:51 [in lieu of Mark 16:19 in original].
7 Ephesians 1:20.
8 Acts 1:11; Acts 17:31.
9 Acts 2:24, 27.
10 John 10:18.
11 Luke 24:39.
12 Romans 6:9; Revelation 1:18.
13 Romans 1:4.
14 Romans 8:34.
15 Hebrews 2:14.
16 Romans 14:9.
17 I Corinthians 15:21-22.
18 Ephesians 1:20, 22-23; Colossians 1:18.
19 Romans 4:25.

support against their enemies,[2] and to assure them of their resurrection from the dead on the last day.[3]

53. *How was Christ exalted in his ascension?*

Christ was exalted in his ascension in this way: having during the forty days after his resurrection often appeared to and spoken with his apostles of the things belonging to the kingdom of God,[4] and commissioned them to preach the gospel to all nations,[5] he then in our nature, and as our head,[6] triumphing over enemies,[7] visibly ascended into the highest heavens. There he receives gifts for men,[8] raises our desires to things above,[9] and prepares a place for us[10] where he himself is, and where he shall continue until his second coming at the end of the world.[11]

54. *How is Christ exalted in his sitting at the right hand of God?*

Christ is exalted in his sitting at the right hand of God in this way: as the God-man he is advanced to the highest favour of God the Father,[12] with all fullness of joy,[13] glory[14] and power over all things in heaven and earth.[15] Thus he gathers and defends his church and subdues her enemies, equips his ministers and people with gifts and graces,[16] and makes intercession for them.[17]

55. *How does Christ make intercession?*

Christ makes intercession by his appearing in our nature continually before the Father in heaven[18] in the merit of his obedience and sacrifice on earth.[19] He declares his will to have his merit applied to all believers,[20] and answers all accusations against

---

1 Ephesians 2:1, 5-6; Colossians 2:12.
2 I Corinthians 15:25-27.
3 I Corinthians 15:20.
4 Acts 1:2-3.
5 Matthew 28:19-20.
6 Hebrews 6:20.
7 Ephesians 4:8.
8 Acts 1:9-11; Ephesians 4:10; Psalm 68:18.
9 Colossians 3:1-2.
10 John 14:3.
11 Acts 3:21.
12 Philippians 2:9.
13 Acts 2:28; cf. Psalm 16:11.
14 John 17:5.
15 Ephesians 1:22; I Peter 3:22.
16 Ephesians 4:10-12; Psalm 110:1ff.
17 Romans 8:34.
18 Hebrews 9:12, 24.
19 Hebrews 1:3.
20 John 3:16; John 17:9, 20, 24.

them.[1] Thus he secures for them peace of conscience (notwithstanding their daily failings),[2] access with boldness to the throne of grace,[3] and acceptance of their persons[4] and their service.[5]

56. ***How is Christ to be exalted in his coming again to judge the world?***

Christ is to be exalted in his coming again to judge the world in this way: he who was unjustly judged and condemned by wicked men,[6] shall come again at the last day in great power;[7] he shall come in the full revelation of his own glory and that of his Father with all his holy angels,[8] with a shout, with the voice of the archangel and with the trumpet of God,[9] to judge the world in righteousness.[10]

57. ***What benefits has Christ secured by his mediation?***

Christ by his mediation has secured redemption,[11] together with all other benefits of the covenant of grace.[12]

GOD'S EFFECTIVE CALL AND THE CHURCH [WCF 10:1-4; 25:1-6; 26:1]

58. ***How do we come to share in the benefits which Christ has secured?***

We are made to share in the benefits which Christ has secured by the application of them to us,[13] which is the work especially of God the Holy Spirit.[14]

59. ***Who are made to share redemption through Christ?*** [WCF 8:8]

Redemption infallibly reaches and is effectively received by all those for whom Christ purchased it,[15] and they are in time by the Holy Spirit enabled to believe in Christ according to the gospel.[16]

---

1 Romans 8:33-34.
2 Romans 5:1-2; I John 2:1-2.
3 Hebrews 4:16.
4 Ephesians 1:6.
5 I Peter 2:5.
6 Acts 3:14-15.
7 Matthew 24:30.
8 Luke 9:26; Matthew 25:31.
9 I Thessalonians 4:16.
10 Acts 17:31.
11 Hebrews 9:12.
12 II Corinthians 1:20.
13 John 1:11-12.
14 Titus 3:5-6.
15 Ephesians 1:13-14; John 6:37, 39; John 10:15-16.
16 Ephesians 2:8; II Corinthians 4:13.

60. Can those who have never heard the gospel and so do not know Jesus Christ, nor believe in him, be saved by living according to their conscience? [WCF 10:4b]

Those who have never heard the gospel,[1] and so do not know Jesus Christ[2] nor believe in him cannot be saved,[3] no matter how diligent they are in living their lives according to their conscience[4] and the teachings of the religion they profess;[5] nor is there salvation in any other but in Christ alone,[6] who is the Saviour only of his body the church.[7]

61. Are all those saved who hear the gospel and live in the church?

Not all who hear the gospel and live in the visible church are saved, but only those who are true members of the church invisible.[8]

62. What is the visible church? [WCF 25:2]

The visible church is a society made up of all those who in all ages and all places in the world profess the true religion,[9] together with their children.[10]

63. What are the special privileges of the visible church? [WCF 25:3-6]

The visible church has the privilege of being under God's special care and government;[11] of being protected and preserved in all ages despite the opposition of all enemies;[12] and of enjoying the communion of saints, the ordinary means of salvation,[13] and offers of grace by Christ to all the members of it in the ministry of the gospel, which bears witness that whoever believes in him shall be saved[14] and none who come to him shall be excluded.[15]

---

1 Romans 10:14.
2 II Thessalonians 1:8-9; Ephesians 2:12; John 1:10-12.
3 John 8:24; [Mark 16:16].
4 I Corinthians 1:20-24.
5 John 4:22; Romans 9:31-32; Philippians 3:4-9.
6 Acts 4:12.
7 Ephesians 5:23.
8 John 12:38-40; Romans 9:6; Matthew 22:14; Matthew 7:21; Romans 11:7; [WCF 10:4a].
9 I Corinthians 1:2; I Corinthians 12:13; Romans 15:9-12; Revelation 7:9; Psalms 2:8, 22:27-31, 45:17; Matthew 28:19-20; Isaiah 59:21.
10 I Corinthians 7:14; Acts 2:39; Romans 11:16; Genesis 17:7.
11 Isaiah 4:5-6; I Timothy 4:10.
12 Psalm 115:1-2, 9; and throughout, Isaiah 31:4-5; Zechariah 12:2-4, 8-9.
13 Acts 2:39, 42.
14 Psalm 147:19-20; Romans 9:4; Ephesians 4:11-12; [Mark 16:15-16].
15 John 6:37.

64. What is the invisible church? [WCF 25:1]

The invisible church is the whole number of the elect that have been, are, or shall be gathered into one under Christ the head.[1]

65. What special benefits do the members of the invisible church enjoy through Christ? [WCF 26:1]

Through Christ the members of the invisible church enjoy union and communion with him in grace [see WLC 69] and glory [see WLC 82].[2]

66. What is that union which the elect have with Christ?

The union which the elect have with Christ is the work of God's grace,[3] by which they are spiritually and mystically, yet truly and inseparably, joined to Christ as their head and husband[4] in their effective calling.[5]

67. What is effective calling? [WCF 10:1,2]

Effective calling is the work of God's almighty power and grace[6] by which, entirely as the outcome of his free and special love to his elect and not from anything in them moving him to it,[7] he invites and draws them in the time of his favour to Jesus Christ by his word and Spirit.[8] He savingly enlightens their minds,[9] renewing and powerfully directing their wills,[10] so that, although in themselves dead in sin, they are made willing and able freely to answer his call, and to accept and embrace the grace offered and conveyed in it.[11]

68. Are only the elect effectively called? [WCF 10:4]

All the elect, and they only are effectively called.[12] Although others may be, and often are, outwardly called by the ministry of the word[13] and have some common operations of the Spirit,[14] they wilfully neglect and hold in contempt the grace offered to them and so are justly left in their unbelief and never truly come to Jesus Christ.[15]

---

1 Ephesians 1:10, 22-23; John 10:16; John 11:52.
2 John 17:21; Ephesians 2:5-6; John 17:24.
3 Ephesians 1:22; Ephesians 2:6-8.
4 I Corinthians 6:17; John 10:28; Ephesians 5:23, 30.
5 I Peter 5:10; I Corinthians 1:9.
6 John 5:25; Ephesians 1:18-20; II Timothy 1:8-9.
7 Titus 3:4-5; Ephesians 2:4-5, 7-9; Romans 9:11.
8 II Corinthians 5:20; cf. II Corinthians 6:1-2; John 6:44; II Thessalonians 2:13-14.
9 Acts 26:18; I Corinthians 2:10, 12.
10 Ezekiel 11:19; Ezekiel 36:26-27; John 6:45.
11 Ephesians 2:5; Philippians 2:13; Deuteronomy 30:6.
12 Acts 13:48.
13 Matthew 22:14.
14 Matthew 7:22; Matthew 13:20-21; Hebrews 6:4-6.
15 John 12:38-40; Acts 28:25-27; John 6:64-65; Psalm 81:11-12.

69. *What is the communion in grace which the members of the invisible church have with Christ?* [WCF 26:1]

The communion in grace which the members of the invisible church have with Christ is their sharing in the virtue of his mediation, and thus in their justification,[1] adoption,[2] sanctification and whatever else in this life reveals their union with him.[3]

Justification and Faith [WCF 11 & 14]

70. *What is justification?* [WCF 11:1]

Justification is an act of God's free grace to sinners[4] in which he pardons all their sins, and accepts and accounts their persons to be righteous in his sight,[5] not because of anything worked in them or done by them,[6] but for the sake of the perfect obedience and full satisfaction of Christ alone, which is credited to them by God[7] and received by faith alone.[8]

71. *How is justification an act of God's free grace?* [WCF 11:3]

Christ by his obedience and death made a proper, real and full satisfaction to God's justice on behalf of all those who are justified.[9] Since God accepts the satisfaction of this guarantor, his one and only Son whom he provided, when he might have demanded satisfaction from his people,[10] and thus credits Christ's righteousness to them[11] requiring nothing for their justification but faith in him,[12] which faith is also his gift,[13] their justification is to them an act of God's free grace.[14]

72. *What is justifying faith?* [WCF14]

Justifying faith is a saving grace,[15] worked in the heart of a sinner

---

1 Romans 8:30.
2 Ephesians 1:5.
3 I Corinthians 1:30.
4 Romans 3:22, 24-25; Romans 4:5.
5 II Corinthians 5:19, 21; Romans 3:22, 24-25, 27-28.
6 Titus 3:5,7; Ephesians 1:7.
7 Romans 5:17-19; Romans 4:6-8.
8 Acts 10:43; Galatians 2:16; Philippians 3:9.
9 Romans 5:8-10, 19.
10 I Timothy 2:5-6; Hebrews 10:10; Matthew 20:28; Daniel 9:24, 26; Isaiah 53:4-6, 10-12; Hebrews 7:22; Romans 8:32; I Peter 1:18-19.
11 II Corinthians 5:21.
12 Romans 3:24-25.
13 Ephesians 2:8.
14 Ephesians 1:7.
15 Hebrews 10:39.

by the Spirit[1] and word of God.[2] By this grace he is convinced of his sin and misery and of the inability in himself and all other creatures to deliver himself from his lost condition.[3] He not only assents to the truth of the promise of the gospel[4] but receives and rests on Christ and his righteousness held forth in the gospel, for pardon of sin[5] and for the accepting and reckoning of himself as righteous in the sight of God for salvation.[6]

73. *How does faith justify a sinner in the sight of God?*

Faith does not justify a sinner in the sight of God because of those other graces which always accompany it, or because of good works which are its fruit,[7] nor is the grace of faith or any act of faith credited to him for his justification.[8] But faith justifies only in that it is an instrument by which the sinner receives and applies Christ and his righteousness.[9]

Adoption [WCF 12]

74. *What is adoption?*

Adoption is an act of the free grace of God[10] in and for his only Son Jesus Christ.[11] By this act those who are justified are received into the number of his children,[12] have his name put upon them,[13] the Spirit of his Son given to them,[14] are under his fatherly care and provision,[15] are admitted to all the liberties and privileges of the sons of God, and are made heirs of all the promises and fellow-heirs with Christ in glory.[16]

Sanctification [WCF 13]

75. *What is sanctification?*

Sanctification is a work of God's grace. By this work those

---

1 II Corinthians 4:13; Ephesians 1:17-19.
2 Romans 10:14, 17.
3 Acts 2:37; Acts 16:30; John 16:8-9; Romans 5:6; Ephesians 2:1; Acts 4:12.
4 Ephesians 1:13.
5 John 1:12; Acts 16:31; Acts 10:43.
6 Philippians 3:9; Acts 15:11.
7 Galatians 3:11; Romans 3:28.
8 Romans 4:5; cf. Romans 10:10.
9 John 1:12; Philippians 3:9; Galatians 2:16.
10 I John 3:1.
11 Ephesians 1:5; Galatians 4:4-5.
12 John 1:12.
13 II Corinthians 6:18; Revelation 3:12.
14 Galatians 4:6.
15 Psalm 103:13; Proverbs 14:26; Matthew 6:32.
16 Hebrews 6:12; Romans 8:17.

whom God has chosen before the foundation of the world to be holy are, in time, through the powerful operation of his Spirit[1] applying the death and resurrection of Christ to them,[2] renewed in the whole person in the image of God.[3] The seeds of repentance leading to life and all other saving graces are put in their hearts[4] and those graces so activated, increased and strengthened[5] that they more and more die to sin and rise to newness of life.[6]

Repentance leading to Life [WCF 15 & WSC 87]

76. What is repentance leading to life?

Repentance leading to life is a saving grace[7] worked in the heart of a sinner by the Spirit[8] and word of God.[9] By this grace he sees and feels the danger[10] and also the filthiness and odiousness of his sins.[11] Upon grasping God's mercy in Christ to those who are penitent,[12] he so grieves for[13] and hates his sins[14] that he turns from them all to God,[15] with resolution and constant effort to walk with him in all the ways of new obedience.[16]

Justification and Sanctification compared

77. How do justification and sanctification differ?

Although sanctification is inseparably connected to justification,[17] yet they differ. In justification God credits the righteousness of Christ[18] whereas in sanctification he infuses grace and enables its exercise;[19] in justification sin is pardoned[20] while in sanctification it is subdued.[21] Justification frees all believers equally and perfectly in this life from the avenging

---

1 Ephesians 1:4; I Corinthians 6:11; II Thessalonians 2:13.
2 Romans 6:4-6.
3 Ephesians 4:23-24.
4 Acts 11:18; I John 3:9.
5 Jude 20; Hebrews 6:11-12; Ephesians 3:16-19; Colossians 1:10-11.
6 Romans 6:4, 6, 14; Galatians 5:24.
7 II Timothy 2:25.
8 Zechariah 12:10.
9 Acts 11:18, 20-21.
10 Ezekiel 18:28, 30, 32; Luke 15:17-18; Hosea 2:6-7.
11 Ezekiel 36:31; Isaiah 30:22.
12 Joel 2:12-13.
13 Jeremiah 31:18-19.
14 II Corinthians 7:11.
15 Acts 26:18; Ezekiel 14:6; I Kings 8:47-48.
16 Psalm 119:6, 59, 128; Luke 1:6; II Kings 23:25.
17 I Corinthians 6:11; I Corinthians 1:30.
18 Romans 4:6, 8.
19 Ezekiel 36:27.
20 Romans 3:24-25.
21 Romans 6:6, 14.

90. What shall be done to the righteous on the day of judgment?

On the day of judgment the righteous, being gathered up to Christ in the clouds[1] shall be placed on his right hand and there openly acknowledged and acquitted.[2] They shall join with him in the judging of reprobate angels and men,[3] and shall be received into heaven.[4] There they shall be fully and for ever freed from all sin and misery,[5] filled with inconceivable joys,[6] made perfectly holy and happy both in body and in soul in the company of innumerable saints and holy angels,[7] but especially in the immediate vision and enjoyment of God the Father, of our Lord Jesus Christ and of the Holy Spirit to all eternity.[8] This is the perfect and full communion which the members of the invisible church shall enjoy with Christ in glory at the resurrection and day of judgment.

Having seen what the Scriptures principally teach us to believe concerning God, we now consider what they require as the duty of man.

THE DUTY OF MAN [WLC 91–196 & WSC 39–107]

The Moral Law [WCF 19]

91. What is the duty which God requires of man?

The duty which God requires of man is obedience to his revealed will.[9]

92. What rule did God at first reveal to man for his obedience?

Besides a special command not to eat of the fruit of the tree of the knowledge of good and evil, the rule of obedience revealed to Adam in the state of innocence, and to all mankind in him, was the moral law.[10]

93. What is the moral law?

The moral law is the declaration of the will of God to mankind. It

---

1 I Thessalonians 4:17.
2 Matthew 25:33; Matthew 10:32.
3 I Corinthians 6:2-3.
4 Matthew 25:34 ,46.
5 Ephesians 5:27; Revelation 14:13.
6 Psalm 16:11.
7 Hebrews 12:22-23.
8 I John 3:2; I Corinthians 13:12; I Thessalonians 4:17-18.
9 Romans 12:1-2; Micah 6:8; I Samuel 15:22.
10 Genesis 1:26-27; Romans 2:14-15; Romans 10:5; Genesis 2:17.

directs and binds everyone to personal, perfect and perpetual conformity and obedience to it in the attitude and disposition of the entire person, soul and body,[1] and to the performance of all those duties of holiness and righteousness which he owes to God and man.[2] Life is promised on it being fulfilled and death is threatened on it being broken.[3]

The Law's Use

94. *Is the moral law of any use to man since the fall?*

No person since the fall can attain to righteousness and life by the moral law.[4] Nevertheless, it remains of great use to all people as well as having specific uses for the unregenerate and the regenerate.[5]

Use to All

95. *Of what use is the moral law to all people?*

The moral law is of use to all people to inform them of the holy nature and will of God[6] and of their duty and obligation to conduct themselves accordingly.[7] It is of use to convince them of their inability to keep it, and of the sinful pollution of their nature, hearts and lives.[8] It may humble them in the sense of their sin and misery[9] and so help them to a clearer sight of their need of Christ[10] and of the perfection of his obedience.[11]

Use to Unbelievers

96. *What particular use is the moral law to the unregenerate?*

The moral law is of use to the unregenerate to awaken their consciences to flee from the wrath to come[12] and to drive them to Christ.[13] Alternatively, if they continue in the state and life of sin

---

1 Deuteronomy 5:1-3, 31, 33; Luke 10:26-27; Galatians 3:10; I Thessalonians 5:23.
2 Luke 1:75; Acts 24:16.
3 Romans 10:5; Galatians 3:10, 12.
4 Romans 8:3; Galatians 2:16.
5 I Timothy 1:8.
6 Leviticus 11:44-45; Leviticus 20:7-8; Romans 7:12.
7 Micah 6:8; James 2:10-11.
8 Psalm 19:11-12; Romans 3:20; Romans 7:7.
9 Romans 3:9, 23.
10 Galatians 3:21-22.
11 Romans 10:4.
12 I Timothy 1:9-10.
13 Galatians 3:24.

it leaves them inexcusable[1] and under the law's curse.[2]

Use to Believers

97. *What special use is the moral law to the regenerate?*

Those who are regenerate and believe in Christ are delivered from the moral law considered as a covenant of works[3] so that they are neither justified[4] nor condemned by it.[5] However, as well as the general uses of the law common to everyone, the law is of special use to the regenerate to show them how much they owe to Christ for his fulfilling it, and enduring its curse in their place and for their benefit.[6] Thus it stirs them up to greater thankfulness,[7] and to express this in greater care to conform themselves to the law as the rule of their obedience.[8]

98. *Where is the moral law set out briefly?*

The moral law is set out briefly in the ten commandments. They were delivered by the voice of God on Mount Sinai, written by him on two stone tablets,[9] and are recorded in the twentieth chapter of Exodus. The first four commandments contain our duty to God, and the other six our duty to man.[10]

Rules for Right Interpretation

99. *What rules are to be observed for the right understanding of the ten commandments?*

For the right understanding of the ten commandments the following rules are to be observed:

1. The law is perfect and binds everyone to full conformity in the whole person to the righteousness in it, and to entire obedience for ever, and thus requires the utmost perfection of every duty and forbids the smallest degree of every sin.[11] .
2. The law is spiritual and so reaches the understanding, will, affections and all other powers of the soul, as well as words,

---

1 Romans 1:20 cf. Romans 2:15.
2 Galatians 3:10.
3 Romans 6:14; Romans 7:4, 6; Galatians 4:4-5.
4 Romans 3:20.
5 Galatians 5:23; Romans 8:1.
6 Romans 7:24-25; Galatians 3:13-14; Romans 8:3-4.
7 Luke 1:68-69, 74-75; Colossians 1:12-14.
8 Romans 7:22; Romans 12:2; Titus 2:11-14.
9 Deuteronomy 10:4; Exodus 34:1-4.
10 Matthew 22:37-40.
11 Psalm 19:7; James 2:10; Matthew 5:21-22.

works and gestures.[1]

3. One and the same thing in different respects is required or forbidden in several commandments.[2]
4. Where a duty is commanded the contrary sin is forbidden,[3] and where a sin is forbidden the contrary duty is commanded.[4] Thus, where a promise is attached, the contrary threatening is included,[5] and where a threatening is attached, the contrary promise is included.[6]
5. What God forbids is at no time to be done,[7] and what he commands is always our duty;[8] yet each specific duty is not to be done on every occasion.[9]
6. Under one sin or duty all of the same kind are forbidden or commanded, along with all the causes, means, occasions and appearances of them, and provocations leading to them.[10]
7. In what is forbidden or commanded to ourselves we are bound, according to our position in society, to seek that it may be avoided or performed by others according to the duty of their position in society.[11]
8. In what is commanded to others we are bound to be of assistance to them in ways appropriate to our position and vocation in society, and to take care not to participate with others in what is forbidden to them.[12]

100. What special things are we to consider in the ten commandments?

We are to consider in the ten commandments the preface, the substance of the commandments themselves, and the several reasons attached to some of them, to reinforce them.

---

1 Romans 7:14; Deuteronomy 6:5; cf. Matthew 22:37-39; Matthew 5:21-22, 27-28, 33-34, 37-39, 43-44.
2 Colossians 3:5; Amos 8:5; Proverbs 1:19; I Timothy 6:10.
3 Isaiah 58:13; Deuteronomy 6:13; cf. Matthew 4:9-10; Matthew 15:4-6.
4 Matthew 5:21-25; Ephesians 4:28.
5 Exodus 20:12; cf. Proverbs 30:17.
6 Jeremiah 18:7-8; Exodus 20:7; cf. Psalms 15:1, 4-5, 24:4-5.
7 Job 13:7-8; Romans 3:8; Job 36:21; Hebrews 11:25.
8 Deuteronomy 4:8-9.
9 Matthew 12:7.
10 Matthew 5:21-22, 27-28; Matthew 15:4-6; Hebrews 10:24-25; I Thessalonians 5:22; Jude 23; Galatians 5:26; Colossians 3:21.
11 Exodus 20:10; Leviticus 19:17; Genesis 18:19; Joshua 24:15; Deuteronomy 6:6-7.
12 II Corinthians 1:24; I Timothy 5:22; Ephesians 5:11.

109. *What are the sins forbidden in the second commandment?*

The sins forbidden in the second commandment are: all inventing,[1] recommending,[2] commanding,[3] using[4] and in any way approving any religious worship not instituted by God himself;[5] tolerating a false religion;[6] making any representation of God, of all or any of the three persons, either inwardly in our mind or outwardly in any kind of image or likeness of any creature whatsoever;[7] all worshipping of it,[8] or God in it or by it;[9] the making of any representation of fictitious deities,[10] and all worship of them or service belonging to them;[11] all superstitious practices,[12] corrupting the worship of God,[13] adding to God's worship or taking from it,[14] whether invented and carried on by ourselves[15] or received by tradition from others,[16] even if in the name of antiquity,[17] custom,[18] devotion,[19] good intent, or any other pretext whatsoever;[20] simony;[21] sacrilege;[22] and all neglect,[23] contempt,[24] hindering[25] and opposing of the worship and ordinances which God has appointed.[26]

110. *What are the reasons attached to the second commandment to reinforce it?*

The reasons attached to the second commandment to reinforce it are contained in these words: for I the LORD your God am a jealous God, punishing the children for the sin of the fathers to the third and fourth generations of those who hate me, but showing love to thousands who

---

1 Numbers 15:39.
2 Deuteronomy 13:6-8.
3 Hosea 5:11.
4 I Kings 11:33, 12:33.
5 Deuteronomy 12:30-32.
6 Deuteronomy 13:6-12; Zechariah 13:2-3; Revelation 2:2, 14-15, 20, 17:12, 16-17.
7 Deuteronomy 4:15-19; Acts 17:29; Romans 1:21-23, 25.
8 Daniel 3:18; Galatians 4:8.
9 Exodus 32:5.
10 Exodus 32:8.
11 I Kings 18:26, 28; Isaiah 65:11.
12 Acts 17:22; Colossians 2:21-23.
13 Malachi 1:7-8, 14.
14 Deuteronomy 4:2.
15 Psalm 106:39.
16 Matthew 15:9.
17 I Peter 1:18.
18 Jeremiah 44:17.
19 Isaiah 65:3-5; Galatians 1:13-14.
20 I Samuel 13:11-12; I Samuel 15:21.
21 Acts 8:18.
22 Romans 2:22; Malachi 3:8.
23 Exodus 4:24-26.
24 Matthew 22:5; Malachi 1:7, 13.
25 Matthew 23:13.
26 Acts 13:44-45; I Thessalonians 2:15-16.

love me and keep my commandments.[1] They show that as well as God's authority as our lawgiver, and the fact that we belong to him,[2] he urges his fervent zeal for his own worship,[3] and his punitive indignation against all false worship as spiritual infidelity.[4] He counts those who break this commandment to be those who hate him and threatens to punish them for several generations,[5] but regards those who observe it to be those who love him and keep his commandments, and promises mercy to them for many generations.[6]

Third Commandment: Our attitude to God

111. Which is the third commandment?

The third commandment is: You shall not misuse the name of the LORD your God, for the LORD will not hold anyone guiltless who misuses his name.[7]

112. What is required in the third commandment?

The third commandment requires that the name of God, his titles, attributes,[8] ordinances,[9] the word,[10] sacraments,[11] prayer,[12] oaths,[13] vows,[14] lots,[15] his works[16] and whatever else there is by which he makes himself known, be used in a holy and reverent manner in thought,[17] meditation,[18] word[19] and writing.[20] In short, it requires a holy profession of faith[21] and a correspondingly consistent manner of life,[22] to the glory of God[23] and the good of ourselves[24] and others.[25]

---

1 Exodus 20:5-6.
2 Psalm 45:11; Revelation 15:3-4.
3 Exodus 34:13-14.
4 I Corinthians 10:20-22; Jeremiah 7:18-20; Ezekiel 16:26-27; Deuteronomy 32:16-20.
5 Hosea 2:2-4.
6 Deuteronomy 5:29.
7 Exodus 20:7 [NIV].
8 Matthew 6:9; Deuteronomy 28:58; Psalm 29:2, 68:4; Revelation 15:3-4.
9 Malachi 1:14; Ecclesiastes 5:1.
10 Psalm 138:2.
11 I Corinthians 11:24-25, 28-29.
12 I Timothy 2:8.
13 Jeremiah 4:2.
14 Ecclesiastes 5:2, 4-6.
15 Acts 1:24, 26.
16 Job 36:24.
17 Malachi 3:16.
18 Psalm 8.
19 Colossians 3:17; Psalm 105:2, 5.
20 Psalm 102:18.
21 I Peter 3:15; Micah 4:5.
22 Philippians 1:27.
23 I Corinthians 10:31.
24 Jeremiah 32:39.
25 I Peter 2:12.

113. What are the sins forbidden in the third commandment?

The sins forbidden in the third commandment are: not using God's name as required;[1] its abuse in ignorant,[2] vain,[3] irreverent, godless[4] superstitious[5] or wicked speaking or other use of his titles, attributes,[6] ordinances[7] or works;[8] blasphemy[9] or perjury;[10] all sinful cursing,[11] oaths,[12] vows[13] and lots;[14] the violating of lawful oaths and vows[15] and the fulfilling of unlawful ones;[16] murmuring, complaining,[17] improper inquisitiveness[18] and misapplying of God's decrees[19] and providences;[20] misinterpreting,[21] misapplying[22] or in any way perverting the word or any part of it,[23] to godless jokes,[24] prying or unprofitable questions, foolish discussions or the maintenance of false doctrines;[25] misusing God's creatures or anything belonging to the character of God, for the purpose of the occult[26] or for sinful lusts and practices;[27] speaking evil of,[28] mocking,[29] reviling,[30] or in any way opposing God's truth, grace and ways;[31] making profession of Christianity in hypocrisy or for evil purposes,[32] of being ashamed of it[33] or a shame to it by lack of

---

1 Malachi 2:2.
2 Acts 17:23.
3 Proverbs 30:9.
4 Malachi 1:6-7, 12, 3:14.
5 I Samuel 4:3-5; Jeremiah 7:4, 9-10, 14, 31; Colossians 2:20-22.
6 II Kings 18:30, 35; Exodus 5:2; Psalm 139:20.
7 Psalm 50:16-17.
8 Isaiah 5:12.
9 II Kings 19:22; Leviticus 24:11.
10 Zechariah 5:4, 8:17.
11 I Samuel 17:43; II Samuel 16:5.
12 Jeremiah 5:7, 23:10.
13 Deuteronomy 23:18; Acts 23:12, 14.
14 Esther 3:7, 9:24; Psalm 22:18.
15 Psalm 24:4; Ezekiel 17:16, 18-19.
16 Mark 6:26; I Samuel 25:22, 32-34.
17 Romans 9:14, 19-20.
18 Deuteronomy 29:29.
19 Romans 3:5, 7, 6:1-2.
20 Ecclesiastes 8:11, 9:3; Psalm 39.
21 Matthew 5:21-48.
22 Ezekiel 13:22.
23 II Peter 3:16; Matthew 22:24-31.
24 Isaiah 22:13; Jeremiah 23:34, 36, 38.
25 I Timothy 1:4, 6-7, 6:4-5, 20; II Timothy 2:14; Titus 3:9.
26 Deuteronomy 18:10-14; Acts 19:13.
27 II Timothy 4:3-4; Romans 13:13-14; I Kings 21:9-10; Jude 4.
28 Acts 13:45; I John 3:12.
29 Psalm 1:1; II Peter 3:3.
30 I Peter 4:4.
31 Acts 13:45-46, 50, 4:18, 19:9; I Thessalonians 2:16; Hebrews 10:29.
32 II Timothy 3:5; Matthew 23:14, 6:1-2, 5, 16.
33 Mark 8:38.

compliance,[1] unwise,[2] unfruitful[3] and offensive living,[4] or backsliding.[5]

114. What reasons are attached to the third commandment?

The reasons attached to the third commandment in the words, *The* LORD *your God* and, *For the* LORD *will not hold anyone guiltless who misuses his name,*[6] are to the effect that, since he is our LORD and God, his name is not to be profaned or in any way abused by us.[7] So far is he from acquitting and sparing the breakers of this commandment, that he will not permit them to escape his righteous judgment,[8] although many of them escape the censures and punishments of men.[9]

Forth Commandment: God's Holy Day [WCF 21:7-8]

115. Which is the fourth commandment? [WSC 57 is the same]

The fourth commandment is: Remember the sabbath day by keeping it holy. Six days you shall labour and do all your work, but the seventh day is a sabbath to the LORD your God. On it you shall not do any work, neither you, nor your son or daughter, nor your manservant or maidservant, nor your animals, nor the alien within your gates. For in six days the LORD made the heavens and the earth, the sea and all that is in them, but he rested on the seventh day. Therefore the LORD blessed the seventh day and made it holy.[10]

116. What is required in the fourth commandment?

The fourth commandment requires of all men the sanctifying or keeping holy to God such set times as he has appointed in his word, in particular, one whole day in seven. From the beginning of the world to the resurrection of Christ the seventh day of the week was so appointed, but thereafter he appointed the first day of the week as the Christian Sabbath, so to continue to the end of the world.[11] In the New Testament it is called the Lord's Day.[12]

---

1 Psalm 73:14-15.
2 I Corinthians 6:5-6; Ephesians 5:15-17.
3 Isaiah 5:4; II Peter 1:8-9.
4 Romans 2:23-24.
5 Galatians 3:1, 3; Hebrews 6:6.
6 Exodus 20:7.
7 Leviticus 19:12.
8 Ezekiel 36:21-23; Deuteronomy 28:58-59; Zechariah 5:2-4.
9 I Samuel 2:12, 17, 22-24 compared with I Samuel 3:13.
10 Exodus 20:8-11 [NIV].
11 Deuteronomy 5:12-14; Genesis 2:2-3; I Corinthians 16:1-2; Acts 20:7; Matthew 5:17-18; Isaiah 56:2, 4, 6-7.
12 Revelation 1:10.

117. How is the sabbath or the Lord's Day to be kept holy?

The sabbath or Lord's Day is to be kept holy by a holy resting all the day,[1] not only from such works as are at all times sinful but even from such other work and recreation as are lawful on other days,[2] making it our delight to spend the whole time (except so much of it as is to be taken up in works of necessity and mercy[3]) in the public and private worship of God.[4] Therefore we are to prepare our hearts and arrange and complete our worldly business with such foresight, diligence and care that we may be free and fit for the duties of that day.[5]

118. Why is the direction to keep the sabbath more particularly addressed to heads of families and those with responsibility for others?

The direction to keep the sabbath is more particularly addressed to heads of families and those with responsibility for others because they are not only bound to keep it themselves but to see that it is kept by all those in their charge, and because they often tend to hinder those in their charge by giving them work to do on the sabbath.[6]

119. What are the sins forbidden in the fourth commandment?

The sins forbidden in the fourth commandment are: all omission of the duties required,[7] all careless, negligent and unprofitable performing of them, and being tired of them;[8] as well as the misuse of the day by idleness and doing what is in itself sinful;[9] and by all needless works, words and thoughts about our worldly affairs and recreations.[10]

120. What are the reasons attached to the fourth commandment to reinforce it?

The reasons attached to the fourth commandment to reinforce it are: the equity in God's allowance of six days out of seven for our own affairs and reserving but one to himself, seen in these words: *Six days you shall labour and do all your work,*[11] God's claim to special

---

1 Exodus 20:8.
2 Exodus 16:25-28; Nehemiah 13:15-22; Jeremiah 17:21-22.
3 Matthew 12:1-13.
4 Isaiah 58:13; Luke 4:16; Acts 20:7; I Corinthians 16:1-2; Psalm 92 (title); Isaiah 66:23; Leviticus 23:3.
5 Exodus 20:8; Luke 23:54, 56; Exodus 16:22, 25-26, 29; Nehemiah 13:19.
6 Exodus 20:10; Joshua 24:15; Nehemiah 13:15, 17; Jeremiah 17:20-22; Exodus 23:12.
7 Ezekiel 22:26.
8 Acts 20:7, 9; Ezekiel 33:30-32; Amos 8:5; Malachi 1:13.
9 Ezekiel 23:38.
10 Jeremiah 17:24, 27; Isaiah 58:13.
11 Exodus 20:9.

ownership of the seventh: *the seventh day is a sabbath to the LORD your God;*[1] the example of God who *in six days made the heaven and the earth, the sea and all that is in them, and rested on the seventh day;* and the blessing which God put on that day when he not only set it apart as a day for his service, but appointed it as a means of blessing to us in our holy use of it: *Therefore the LORD blessed the sabbath day and made it holy.*[2]

121. Why is the word 'Remember' placed at the beginning of the fourth commandment?

The word *remember* is placed at the beginning of the fourth commandment[3] in part because of the great benefit of remembering it. Remembrance helps us to prepare to keep the sabbath,[4] and in keeping it to keep all the rest of the commandments[5] and to continue in thankful remembrance of the two great benefits of creation and redemption which are a short summary of our religion.[6] The word *remember* is also placed at the beginning of the fourth commandment because we are very prone to forget the sabbath[7] since it is less clearly established from the light of nature[8] yet it places limits on our natural liberty in things that are lawful at other times;[9] also it comes only once in seven days and many other activities come between and too often keep our minds from thinking about it, either to prepare for it or to use it rightly;[10] and Satan with his agents seeks by all means to blot out the glory and even the memory of it, so as to bring in irreligion and ungodliness.[11]

122. What is the sum of the six commandments which contain our duty to man?

The sum of the six commandments which contain our duty to man is to love our neighbour as ourselves,[12] and to do to others what we would have them do to us.[13]

---

1 Exodus 20:10.
2 Exodus 20:11.
3 Exodus 20:8.
4 Exodus 16:23; Luke 23:54, 56 cf. with Mark 15:42; Nehemiah 13:19.
5 Psalm 92 title, 13-14; Exodus 20:12, 19-20.
6 Genesis 2:2-3; Psalm 118:22, 24 cf. with Acts 4:10-11; Revelation 1:10.
7 Ezekiel 22:26.
8 Nehemiah 9:14.
9 Exodus 34:21.
10 Deuteronomy 5:14-15; Amos 8:5.
11 Lamentations 1:7; Jeremiah 17:21-23; Nehemiah 13:15-23.
12 Matthew 22:39.
13 Matthew 7:12.

COMMANDS 5-10 [SEE WSC 42] [THE COMMANDMENTS ARE QUOTED FROM THE NIV]; [CF. WSC 63 – 81]

Fifth Commandment: Authority

123. Which is the fifth commandment?

The fifth commandment is: Honour your father and your mother so that you may live long in the land the LORD your God is giving you.[1]

124. Who are meant by 'father' and 'mother' in the fifth commandment?

By *father* and *mother* in the fifth commandment are meant not only natural parents[2] but all who are greater in years[3] and gifts,[4] and especially those who are placed over us by God's ordinance, whether in family,[5] church[6] or society.[7]

125. Why are those over us called 'father' and 'mother'?

Those over us are called *father* and *mother* to teach them that in all duties towards those of a more humble position in life they should, like natural parents, express love and tenderness to them appropriate to the particular relationship;[8] and also to bring those under others to a greater willingness and cheerfulness in performing their duties to those over them as they would to their parents.[9]

126. What is the general scope of the fifth commandment?

The general scope of the fifth commandment is the performance of those duties which we mutually owe in our different relationships in life, whether to those under us, over us, or our equals.[10]

127. What is the honour owed by those under others to those over them?

The honour which is owed by those under others to those over them is: all due respect in heart,[11] speech[12] and behaviour;[13] prayer and

1 Exodus 20:12.
2 Proverbs 23:22, 25; Ephesians 6:1-2.
3 I Timothy 5:1-2.
4 Genesis 4:20-22; Genesis 45:8.
5 II Kings 5:13.
6 II Kings 2:12; II Kings 13:14; Galatians 4:19.
7 Isaiah 49:23.
8 Ephesians 6:4; II Corinthians 12:14; I Thessalonians 2:7-8, 11; Numbers 11:11-12.
9 I Corinthians 4:14-16; II Kings 5:13.
10 Ephesians 5:21; I Peter 2:17; Romans 12:10.
11 Malachi 1:6; Leviticus 19:3.
12 Proverbs 31:28; I Peter 3:6.
13 Leviticus 19:32; I Kings 2:19.

thanksgiving for them,[1] imitation of their virtues and graces;[2] willing obedience to their lawful commands and counsels;[3] due submission to correction of faults;[4] faithfulness to[5] and defence[6] and support of their persons and authority according to their position and the nature of their responsibility;[7] bearing with their weaknesses and covering them in love,[8] that thus in everything they may be a credit to those over them and to their authority.[9]

128. What are the sins of those under others towards those over them?

The sins of those under others towards those over them are: all neglect of the duties required,[10] envy,[11] contempt[12] and rebellion[13] against the person[14] and status[15] of those over them in their lawful advice,[16] commands and correction of faults,[17] as well as cursing, mocking,[18] and any unruly and offensive behaviour that brings shame and dishonour to them and their authority.[19]

129. What is required of those who are over others towards those under them?

It is required of those who are over others, according to the authority they have received from God and the relation in which they stand to others, to love,[20] pray for[21] and bless those under them;[22] to instruct,[23] advise and admonish them;[24] to approve,[25] commend[1] and reward those

---

1 I Timothy 2:1-2.
2 Hebrews 13:7; Philippians 3:17.
3 Ephesians 6:1-2, 5-7; I Peter 2:13-14; Romans 13:1-5; Hebrews 13:17; Proverbs 4:34; Proverbs 23:22; Exodus 18:19, 24.
4 Hebrews 12:9; I Peter 2:18-20.
5 Titus 2:9-10.
6 I Samuel 26:15-16; II Samuel 18:3; Esther 6:2.
7 Matthew 22:21; Romans 13:6-7; I Timothy 5:17-18; Galatians 6:6; Genesis 45:11, 47:12.
8 I Peter 2:18; Proverbs 23:22; Genesis 9:23.
9 Psalm 127:3-5; Proverbs 31:23.
10 Matthew 15:4-6.
11 Numbers 11:28-29.
12 I Samuel 8:7; Isaiah 3:5.
13 II Samuel 15:1-12.
14 Exodus 21:15.
15 I Samuel 10:27.
16 I Samuel 2:5.
17 Deuteronomy 21:18-21.
18 Proverbs 30:11, 17.
19 Proverbs 19:26.
20 Colossians 3:19; Titus 2:4.
21 I Samuel 12:23; Job 1:5.
22 I Kings 8:55-56; Hebrews 7:7; Genesis 49:28.
23 Deuteronomy 6:6-7.
24 Ephesians 6:4.
25 I Peter 3:7.

who do well[2] and to disapprove,[3] rebuke and punish those who do wrong;[4] and to protect[5] and provide for them all things necessary for soul[6] and body.[7] By such serious, wise, holy and exemplary behaviour, they are to bring glory to God[8] and honour to themselves,[9] and so preserve the authority which God has given them.[10]

130. *What are the sins of those who are over others?*

Apart from the neglect of their duties,[11] the sins of those who are over others are: an excessive looking out for their own interests,[12] their own glory,[13] comfort, profit or pleasure;[14] ordering things which are unlawful[15] or which those under them have no power to do;[16] persuading,[17] encouraging[18] or favouring those under them in what is evil,[19] and dissuading, discouraging or disapproving them in what is good;[20] correcting them excessively;[21] carelessly exposing or leaving them to wrong, temptation and danger;[22] provoking them to wrath;[23] or in any way dishonouring themselves or lessening their authority by unjust, indiscreet, rigorous or careless behaviour.[24]

131. *What are the duties of equals?*

The duties of equals are: to respect the dignity and worth of each other[25] by giving precedence to another;[26] and to rejoice in each other's gifts and progress as they would in their own.[27]

---

1 I Peter 2:14; Romans 13:3.
2 Esther 6:3.
3 Romans 13:3-4.
4 Pro 29:15; I Peter 2:14.
5 Job 29:12-17; Isaiah 1:10, 17.
6 Ephesians 6:4.
7 I Timothy 5:8.
8 I Timothy 4:12; Titus 2:3-5.
9 I Kings 3:28.
10 Titus 2:15.
11 Ezekiel 34:2-4.
12 Philippians 2:21.
13 John 5:44; John 7:18.
14 Isaiah 66:10-11; Deuteronomy 17:17.
15 Daniel 3:4-6; Acts 4:17-18.
16 Exodus 5:10-18; Matthew 23:2, 4.
17 Matthew 14:8 cf. with Mark 6:24.
18 II Samuel 13:28.
19 I Samuel 3:13.
20 John 7:46-49; Colossians 3:21; Exodus 5:17.
21 I Peter 2:18-20; Hebrews 12:10; Deuteronomy 25:3.
22 Genesis 38:11, 26; Acts 18.17.
23 Ephesians 6:4.
24 Genesis 9:21; I Kings 12:13-16; I Kings 1:6; I Samuel 2:29-31.
25 I Peter 2:17.
26 Romans 12:10.
27 Romans 12:15-16; Philippians 2:3-4.

132. What are the sins of equals?

Apart from the neglect of the duties required,[1] the sins of equals are: undervaluing the worth,[2] envying the gifts[3] and grieving at the progress or prosperity of others,[4] and claiming pre-eminence over them.[5]

133. What is the reason attached to the fifth commandment to reinforce it?

The reason attached to the fifth commandment in the words, *So that you may live long in the land the LORD your God is giving you*,[6] is an explicit promise of long life and prosperity (as far as it shall serve God's glory and their own good) to all those who keep this commandment.[7]

Sixth Commandment: Human Life

134. Which is the sixth commandment?

The sixth commandment is: You shall not murder.[8]

135. What are the duties required in the sixth commandment?

The duties required in the sixth commandment are all due care and legitimate endeavour to preserve the life of ourselves[9] and others:[10] by resisting all thoughts and purposes,[11] subduing all passions[12] and avoiding all occasions,[13] temptations[14] and practices which tend to the unjust taking of human life;[15] by just defence of human life against violence,[16] patient bearing of the hand of God,[17] composure of mind,[18] cheerfulness of spirit;[19] by sober use of food,[20] drink,[1] medicine,[2] sleep,[3]

---

1 Romans 13:8.
2 II Timothy 3:3.
3 Acts 7:9; Galatians 5:26.
4 Numbers 12:2; Esther 6:12-13.
5 III John 9; Luke 22:24.
6 Exodus 20:12.
7 Deuteronomy 5:6; I Kings 8:25; Ephesians 6:2-3.
8 Exodus 20:13.
9 Ephesians 5:28-29.
10 I King 18:4.
11 Jeremiah 26:15-16; Acts 23:12, 16-17, 21, 27.
12 Ephesians 4:26-27.
13 II Samuel 2:22; Deuteronomy 22:8.
14 Matthew 4:6-7; Proverbs 1:10-11, 15-16.
15 I Samuel 24:12; I Samuel 26:9-11; Genesis 37:21-22.
16 Psalm 82:4; Proverbs 24:11-12; I Samuel 14:45.
17 James 5:7-11; Hebrews 12:9.
18 I Thessalonians 4:11; I Peter 3:3-4; Psalm 37:8-11.
19 Proverbs 17:22.
20 Proverbs 25:16, 27.

work[4] and recreations;[5] by charitable thoughts,[6] love,[7] compassion,[8] meekness, gentleness and kindness;[9] by peaceable,[10] mild and courteous speech and behaviour;[11] by forbearance, readiness to be reconciled, patient bearing and forgiving of injuries, and repaying evil with good;[12] by comforting and assisting the distressed, and protecting and defending the innocent.[13]

136. What are the sins forbidden in the sixth commandment?

The sins forbidden in the sixth commandment are: any taking of our own life[14] or that of others[15] except in public justice,[16] lawful war[17] or necessary defence;[18] neglecting or withdrawing the lawful and necessary means of preserving human life;[19] sinful anger,[20] hatred,[21] envy,[22] desire for revenge;[23] all excessive passions[24] and distracting cares;[25] immoderate use of food, drink,[26] work[27] and recreations;[28] provoking words,[29] oppression,[30] quarrelling,[31] striking, wounding,[32] and whatever else tends to the destruction of human life.[33]

---

1 I Timothy 5:23.
2 Isaiah 38:21.
3 Psalm 127:2.
4 Ecclesiastes 5:12; II Thessalonians 3:10, 12; Proverbs 16:26.
5 Ecclesiastes 3:4, 11.
6 I Samuel 19:4-5; I Samuel 22:13-14.
7 Romans 13:10.
8 Luke 10:33-34.
9 Colossians 3:12-13.
10 James 3:17.
11 I Peter 3:8-11; Proverbs 15:1; Judges 8:1-3.
12 Matthew 5:24; Ephesians 4:2,32; Romans 12:17, 20-21.
13 I Thessalonians 5:14; Job 31:19-20; Matthew 25:35-36; Proverbs 31:8-9.
14 Acts 16:28.
15 Genesis 9:6.
16 Numbers 35:31, 33.
17 Jeremiah 48:10; Deuteronomy 20:1ff.
18 Exodus 22:2-3.
19 Matthew 25:42-43; James 2:15-16; Ecclesiastes 6:1-2.
20 Matthew 5:22.
21 I John 3:15; Leviticus 19:17.
22 Proverbs 14:30.
23 Romans 12:19.
24 Ephesians 4:31.
25 Matthew 6:31, 34.
26 Luke 21:34; Romans 13:13.
27 Ecclesiastes 12:12, 2:22-23.
28 Isaiah 5:12.
29 Proverbs 15:1; Proverbs 12:18.
30 Ezekiel 18:18; Exodus 1:14.
31 Galatians 5:15; Proverbs 23:29.
32 Numbers 35:16-18, 21.
33 Exodus 21:18-36.

Seventh Commandment: Purity

137. Which is the seventh commandment?

The seventh commandment is: You shall not commit adultery.[1]

138. What are the duties required in the seventh commandment?

The duties required in the seventh commandment are: chastity in body, mind, affections,[2] words[3] and behaviour;[4] and the preservation of it in ourselves and others;[5] watchfulness over the eyes and all the senses;[6] self-control,[7] keeping chaste company,[8] modesty in dress;[9] marriage by those who do not have the gift of restraint,[10] love within marriage,[11] living together as man and wife;[12] diligent labour in our callings;[13] avoiding all opportunities for impurity, and resisting temptations to it.[14]

139. What are the sins forbidden in the seventh commandment?

Apart from the neglect of the duties required,[15] the sins forbidden in the seventh commandment are: adultery, fornication,[16] rape, incest,[17] sodomy and all unnatural sexual acts;[18] all impure imaginations, thoughts, plans, and desires;[19] all corrupt or obscene talk or listening to such;[20] lustful looks,[21] shameless or unchaste behaviour, immodest dress;[22] prohibiting lawful marriages[23] and allowing unlawful ones;[24] allowing, tolerating or conducting brothels and using them;[25] entangling vows of celibacy,[26] undue delay of marriage;[1] having more

---

1 Exodus 20:14.
2 I Thessalonians 4:4; Job 31:1; I Corinthians 7:34.
3 Colossians 4:6.
4 I Peter 2:3.
5 I Corinthians 7:2, 35-36.
6 Job 31:1.
7 Acts 24:24-25.
8 Proverbs 2:16-20.
9 I Timothy 2:9.
10 I Corinthians 7:2, 9.
11 Proverbs 5:19-20.
12 I Peter 3:7.
13 Proverbs 31:11, 27-28.
14 Proverbs 5:8; Genesis 39:8-10.
15 Proverbs 5:7.
16 Hebrews 13:4; Galatians 5:19.
17 II Samuel 13:14; I Corinthians 5:1.
18 Romans 1:24, 26-27; Leviticus 20:15-16.
19 Matthew 5:28, 15:19; Colossians 3:5.
20 Ephesians 5:3-4; Proverbs 7:5, 21-22.
21 Isaiah 3:16; II Peter 2:14.
22 Proverbs 7:10, 13.
23 I Timothy 4:3.
24 Leviticus 18:1-21; Mark 6:18; Malachi 2:11-12.
25 I Kings 15:12; II Kings 23:7; Deuteronomy 23:17-18; Leviticus 19:29; Jeremiah 5:7; Proverbs 7:24-27.
26 Matthew 19:10-11.

modestly of ourselves or others;[1] denying the gifts and graces of God;[2] exaggerating smaller faults;[3] hiding, excusing or lessening the seriousness of sins when called to make a free confession;[4] unnecessary exposing of weaknesses;[5] raising false reports,[6] receiving and approving evil reports,[7] and refusing to listen to a just defence;[8] evil suspicion;[9] envying or grieving at the deserved good reputation of any one,[10] trying or wishing to impair it,[11] being glad at their disgrace and bad reputation;[12] scornful contempt[13] and foolish admiration of others;[14] breach of lawful promises;[15] neglecting things of good report,[16] and practising, or refusing to avoid ourselves or not preventing where we can in others, such things as bring about a bad name.[17]

Tenth Commandment: Desire

146. Which is the tenth commandment?

The tenth commandment is: You shall not covet your neighbour's house. You shall not covet your neighbour's wife, or his manservant or maidservant, his ox or his donkey, or anything which belongs to your neighbour.[18]

147. What are the duties required in the tenth commandment?

The duties required in the tenth commandment are: such a full contentment with our own condition,[19] and such a charitable attitude of the whole soul to our neighbour that all our inward desires and feelings concerning him tend to and advance his good.[20]

---

1 Luke 18:9, 11; Romans 12:16; I Corinthians 4:6; Acts 12:22; Exodus 4:10-14.
2 Job 27:5-6, 4:6.
3 Matthew 7:3-5.
4 Proverbs 28:13, 30:20; Genesis 3:12-13; Jeremiah 2:35; II Kings 5:25; Genesis 4:9.
5 Genesis 9:22; Proverbs 25:9-10.
6 Exodus 23:1.
7 Proverbs 29:12.
8 Acts 7:56-57; Job 31:13-14.
9 I Corinthians 13:5; I Timothy 6:4.
10 Numbers 11:29; Matthew 21:15.
11 Ezra 4:12-13.
12 Jeremiah 48:27.
13 Psalm 35:15-16, 21; Matthew 27:28-29.
14 Jude 16; Acts 12:22.
15 Romans 1:31; II Timothy 3:3.
16 I Samuel 2:24.
17 II Samuel 13:12-13; Proverbs 5:8-9, 6:33.
18 Exodus 20:17.
19 Hebrews 13:5; I Timothy 6:6.
20 Job 31:29; Romans 12:15; Psalm 122:7-9; I Timothy 1:5; Esther 10:3; I Corinthians 13:4-7.

148. What are the sins forbidden in the tenth commandment?

The sins forbidden in the tenth commandment are: discontent with our own state;[1] envying[2] and grieving at the good of our neighbour,[3] together with all ungoverned longings and desires for things that belong to him.[4]

The Law's Transgression and Penalty

149. Is any person able to keep the commandments of God perfectly?

No person is able, either in his own strength[5] or through any grace received in this life, to keep the commandments of God perfectly,[6] but breaks them daily in thought,[7] word and deed.[8]

150. Are all transgressions of the law equally sinful?

Not all transgressions of the law of God are equally sinful, but some sins, because of their nature and the circumstances, are more sinful in the sight of God than others.[9]

151. What are the circumstances that make some sins more sinful than others?

1. *The person offending:*[10] Sins are rendered more sinful when the person committing them is older,[11] of greater experience or grace,[12] prominent in Christian profession,[13] gifts,[14] position,[15] office,[16] leadership[17] and when his example is likely to be followed by others.[18]
2. *The parties offended:*[19] Sins are rendered more sinful if directly against God,[20] his attributes[1] and worship;[2] against

---

1 I Kings 21:4; Esther 5:13; I Corinthians 10:10.
2 Galatians 5:26; James 3:14, 16.
3 Psalm 112:9-10; Nehemiah 2:10.
4 Romans 7:7-8, 13:9; Colossians 3:5; Deuteronomy 5:21.
5 James 3:2 John 15:5; Romans 8:3.
6 Ecclesiastes 7:20; I John 1:8, 10; Galatians 5:17; Romans 7:18-19.
7 Genesis 6:5; Genesis 8:21.
8 Romans 3:9-19; James 3:2-13.
9 John 19:11; Ezekiel 8:6; I John 5:16; Psalm 78:17, 32, 56.
10 Jeremiah 2:8.
11 Job 32:7, 9; Ecclesiastes 4:13.
12 I Kings 11:4, 9.
13 II Samuel 12:14; I Corinthians 5:1.
14 James 4:17; Luke 12:47-48.
15 Jeremiah 5:4-5.
16 II Samuel 12:7-9; Ezekiel 8:11-12.
17 Romans 2:17-24.
18 Galatians 2:11-14.
19 Matthew 21:38-39.
20 I Samuel 2:25; Acts 5:4; Psalm 51:4.

Christ and his grace;[3] against the Holy Spirit,[4] his witness[5] and his working;[6] against people of a higher position in life, those of eminence,[7] and those to whom we are specially related or bound;[8] against any of the saints,[9] particularly weak believers,[10] their spiritual welfare or the spiritual welfare of any other,[11] and the common good of all or many.[12]

3. *The nature and kind of offence*:[13] Sins are rendered more sinful if they are against the express letter of the law,[14] break many commandments, involve many sins;[15] if they are not only conceived in the heart but are shown in words and actions,[16] cause others to stumble,[17] and cannot be compensated;[18] if against means of grace,[19] mercies,[20] judgments,[21] the natural order,[22] conviction of conscience,[23] public or private warning,[24] church discipline,[25] civil punishments;[26] if against prayers, purposes, promises,[27] vows,[28] covenants[29] or undertakings to God or men;[30] if done deliberately,[31] wilfully,[32] presumptuously,[33] shamelessly,[1] boastfully,[2] maliciously,[3]

---

1 Romans 2:4.
2 Malachi 1:8, 14.
3 Hebrews 2:2-3, 12:25.
4 Hebrews 10:29; Matthew 12:31-32.
5 Ephesians 4:30.
6 Hebrews 6:4-6.
7 Jude 8; Numbers 12:8-9; Isaiah 3:5.
8 Proverbs 30:17; II Corinthians 12:15; Psalm 55:12-15.
9 Zephaniah 2:8, 10-11; Matthew 18:6; I Corinthians 6:8; Revelation 17:6.
10 I Corinthians 8:11-12; Romans 14:13, 15, 21.
11 Ezekiel 13:19; I Corinthians 8:12; Revelation 18:12-13; Matthew 23:15.
12 I Thessalonians 2:15-16; Joshua 22:20.
13 Proverbs 6:30-33.
14 Ezra 9:10-12; I Kings 11:9-10.
15 Colossians 3:5; I Timothy 6:10; Proverbs 5:8-12; Proverbs 6:32-33; Joshua 7:21.
16 James 1:14-15; Matthew 5:22; Micah 2:1.
17 Matthew 18:7; Romans 2:23-24.
18 Deuteronomy 22:22 compared with verses 28-29; Proverbs 6:32-35.
19 Matthew 11:21-24; John 15:22.
20 Isaiah 1:13; Deuteronomy 32:6.
21 Amos 4:8-11; Jeremiah 5:3.
22 Romans 1:26-27.
23 Romans 1:32; Daniel 5:22; Titus 3:10-11.
24 Proverbs 29:1.
25 Titus 3:10; Matthew 18:17.
26 Proverbs 27:22, 23:35.
27 Psalm 78:34-37; Jeremiah 2:20, 42:5-6, 20-21.
28 Ecclesiastes 5:4-6; Proverbs 20:25.
29 Leviticus 26:25.
30 Proverbs 2:17; Ezekiel 17:18-19.
31 Psalm 36:4.
32 Jeremiah 6:16.
33 Numbers 15:30; Exodus 21:14.

frequently,[4] obstinately,[5] with pleasure,[6] constancy[7] or as a repeat offence after repentance.[8]

4. *Circumstances of time*[9] *and place*:[10] Sins are rendered more sinful if on the Lord's Day[11] or other times of divine worship;[12] or immediately before[13] or after these[14] or other helps to prevent or remedy such misdeeds;[15] if in public or in the presence of others likely to be provoked or led to sin because of them.[16]

152. What does every sin deserve at the hands of God?

Every sin, even the least, is against the sovereignty,[17] goodness[18] and holiness of God,[19] and against his righteous law,[20] and therefore deserves his wrath and curse[21] both in this life[22] and the life that is to come.[23] The penalty for sin cannot be paid except by the blood of Christ.[24]

The Way to be Saved

153. What does God require of us that we may escape his wrath and curse due to us for the transgression of the law?

To escape the wrath and curse due to us for the transgression of the law, God requires of us repentance toward himself and faith toward our Lord Jesus Christ,[25] and the diligent use of the outward

1 Jeremiah 3:3; Proverbs 7:13.
2 Psalm 52:1.
3 III John 10.
4 Numbers 14:22.
5 Zechariah 7:11-12.
6 Proverbs 2:14.
7 Isaiah 57:17.
8 Jeremiah 34:8-11; II Peter 2:20-22.
9 II Kings 5:26.
10 Jeremiah 7:10; Isaiah 26:10.
11 Ezekiel 23:37-39.
12 Isaiah 58:3-5; Numbers 25:6-7.
13 I Corinthians 11:20-21.
14 Jeremiah 7:8-10; Proverbs 7:14-15; John 13:27, 30.
15 Ezra 9:13-14.
16 II Samuel 16:22; I Samuel 2:22-24.
17 James 2:10-11.
18 Exodus 20:1-2.
19 Habakkuk 1:13; Leviticus 10:3, 11:44-45.
20 I John 3:4; Romans 7:12.
21 Ephesians 5:6; Galatians 3:10.
22 Lamentations 3:39; Deuteronomy 28:15-68.
23 Matthew 25:41.
24 Hebrews 9:22; I Peter 1:18-19.
25 Acts 20:21; Matthew 3:7-8; Luke 13:3, 5; Acts 16:30-31; John 3:16, 18.

means by which Christ gives us the benefits of his mediation.[1]

154. *What are the outward means by which Christ gives us the benefits of his mediation?*

The outward and ordinary means by which Christ gives to his church the benefits of his mediation are all his ordinances, especially the word, sacraments and prayer, and all these are made effective in the salvation of the elect.[2]

The Bible as a means of Grace

155. *How is the word of God made effective to salvation?*

The Spirit of God makes the reading but especially the preaching of the word, an effective means of enlightening,[3] convincing and humbling sinners;[4] of driving them out of themselves and drawing them to Christ;[5] of conforming them to Christ's image,[6] and subduing them to his will;[7] of strengthening them against temptations and corruptions;[8] of building them up in grace,[9] and establishing their hearts in holiness and comfort, through faith, to salvation.[10]

156. *Is the word of God to be read by everyone?*

Although all are not to be permitted to read the word publicly to the congregation,[11] yet all kinds of people are bound to read it privately by themselves,[12] and with their families,[13] and to this end the Holy Scriptures are to be translated out of the original into the languages of the people.[14]

157. *How is the word of God to be read?*

The Holy Scriptures are to be read with the highest respect for them;[15] with a firm persuasion that they are the very word of

---

1 Proverbs 2:1-5, 8:33-36.
2 Matthew 28:19-20; Acts 2:42, 46-47.
3 Nehemiah 8:8; Acts 26:18; Psalm 19:8.
4 I Corinthians 14:24-25; II Chronicles 34:18-19, 26-28.
5 Acts 2:37, 41; Acts 8:27-39.
6 II Corinthians 3:18.
7 II Corinthians 10:4-6; Romans 6:17.
8 Matthew 4:4, 7, 10; Ephesians 6:16-17; I Corinthians 10:11.
9 Acts 20:32; II Timothy 3:15-17.
10 Romans 16:25; I Thessalonians 3:2, 10-11, 13; Romans 15:4, 10:13-17, 1:16.
11 Deuteronomy 31:9, 11-13; Nehemiah 8:2-3, 9:3-5.
12 Deuteronomy 17:19; Revelation 1:3; John 5:39; Isaiah 34:16.
13 Deuteronomy 6:6-9; Genesis 18:17, 19; Psalm 78:5-7.
14 I Corinthians 14:6, 9, 11-12, 15-16, 24, 27-28.
15 Psalm 19:10; Nehemiah 8:3-10; Exodus 24:7; II Chronicles 34:27; Isaiah 66:2.

God,[1] and that only God can enable us to understand them;[2] with desire to know, believe and obey the will of God revealed in them;[3] with diligence[4] and attention to the content and scope of them;[5] with meditation,[6] application,[7] self-denial[8] and prayer.[9]

158. By whom is the word of God to be preached?

The word of God is to be preached only by those who are sufficiently gifted,[10] and also duly approved and called to that office.[11]

159. How is the word of God to be preached by those who are called?

Those who are called to labour in the ministry of the word are to preach sound doctrine,[12] diligently,[13] in season and out of season;[14] plainly,[15] not with persuasive words of human wisdom, but in demonstration of the Spirit's power;[16] faithfully,[17] making known the whole will of God;[18] wisely,[19] applying themselves to the needs and capacities of the hearers;[20] zealously,[21] with fervent love to God[22] and the souls of his people;[23] sincerely,[24] aiming at God's glory,[25] and the conversion,[26] building up[27] and final salvation of God's people.[28]

---

1 II Peter 1:19-21.
2 Luke 24:45; II Corinthians 3:13-16.
3 Deuteronomy 17:10, 20.
4 Acts 17:11.
5 Acts 8:30, 34; Luke 10:26-28.
6 Psalms 1:2, 119:97.
7 II Chronicles 34:21.
8 Proverbs 3:5; Deuteronomy 33:3.
9 Proverbs 2:1-6; Psalms 119:18; Nehemiah 7:6, 8.
10 I Timothy 3:2, 6; Ephesians 4:8-11; Hosea 4:6; Malachi 2:7; II Corinthians 3:6.
11 Jeremiah 14:15; Romans 10:15; Hebrews 5:4; I Corinthians 12:28-29; I Timothy 3:10, 4:14, 5:22.
12 Titus 2:1, 8.
13 Acts 18:25.
14 II Timothy 4:2.
15 I Corinthians 14:19.
16 I Corinthians 2:4.
17 Jeremiah 23:28; I Corinthians 10 4:1-2.
18 Acts 20:27.
19 Colossians 1:28; II Timothy 2:15.
20 I Corinthians 3:2; Hebrews 5:12-14; Luke 12:42.
21 Acts 18:25.
22 II Corinthians 5:13-14; Philippians 1:15-17.
23 Colossians 4:12; II Corinthians 12:15.
24 II Corinthians 2:17; II Corinthians 17:4:2.
25 I Thessalonians 2:4-6; John 7:18.
26 I Corinthians 9:19-22.
27 II Corinthians 12:19; Ephesians 4:12.
28 I Timothy 4:16; Acts 26:16-18.

160. What is required of those who hear the word preached?

It is required of those who hear the word preached that they attend on it with diligence,[1] preparation[2] and prayer;[3] examine by the Scriptures what they hear;[4] receive the truth with faith,[5] love,[6] meekness[7] and readiness of mind[8] as the word of God;[9] meditate on[10] and discuss it;[11] hide it in their hearts,[12] and bring forth its fruit in their lives.[13]

The Sacraments as a means of Grace [WCF 27]

161. How do the sacraments become effective means of salvation?

The sacraments become effective means of salvation not by any power in themselves or virtue derived from the piety or intention of the one who administers them, but only by the working of the Holy Spirit and the blessing of Christ, by whom they are instituted.[14]

162. What is a sacrament?

A sacrament is a holy ordinance appointed by Christ in his church[15] to signify, seal and set forth[16] to those who are within the covenant of grace,[17] the benefits of his mediation;[18] to strengthen and increase their faith and all other graces;[19] to oblige them to obedience[20] to testify and cherish their love and communion with one another;[21] and to mark them off from those who are outside.[22]

---

1 Proverbs 8:34.
2 I Peter 2:1-2; Luke 8:18.
3 Psalms 119:18; Ephesians 6:18-19.
4 Acts 17:11.
5 Hebrews 4:2.
6 II Thessalonians 2:10.
7 James 1:21.
8 Acts 17:11.
9 I Thessalonians 2:13.
10 Luke 9:44; Hebrews 2:1.
11 Luke 24:14; Deuteronomy 6:6-7.
12 Proverbs 2:1; Psalm 119:11.
13 Luke 8:15; James 1:25.
14 Peter 3:21; Acts 8:13 comp. v23; I Corinthians 3:6-7; I Corinthians 12:13.
15 Genesis 17:7,10; Exodus 12; Matthew 28:19; Matthew 26:26-28.
16 Romans 4:11; I Corinthians 11:24-25.
17 Romans 15:8; Exodus 12:48.
18 Acts 2:38; I Corinthians 10:16.
19 Romans 4:11; Galatians 3:27.
20 Romans 6:3-4; I Corinthians 10:21.
21 Ephesians 4:2-5; I Corinthians 12:13.
22 Ephesians 2:11-12; Genesis 34:14.

163. What are the parts of a sacrament?

A sacrament has two parts: the one, an outward and visible sign used according to Christ's own appointment; the other, an inward and spiritual grace signified by it.[1]

164. How many sacraments has Christ instituted in his Church under the New Testament?

Under the New Testament Christ has instituted in his church only two sacraments, Baptism and the Lord's Supper.[2]

Baptism [WCF 28]

165. What is Baptism?

Baptism is a sacrament of the New Testament in which Christ has appointed the washing with water in the name of the Father, and of the Son, and of the Holy Spirit,[3] to be a sign and seal of being grafted into himself,[4] of remission of sins by his blood,[5] and regeneration by his Spirit;[6] of adoption,[7] and resurrection to everlasting life.[8] By it the parties baptised are solemnly admitted into the visible church,[9] and enter into an open and professed pledge to belong only and completely to the Lord.[10]

166. To whom is Baptism to be administered?

Baptism is not to be administered to any who are outside membership of the church on earth,[11] and therefore strangers to the covenant of promise, until they profess their faith in Christ and obedience to him;[12] but infants descending from parents, one or both, professing faith in Christ and obedience to him, are for that reason within the covenant and are to be baptised.[13]

---

1 Matthew 3:11; I Peter 3:21; Romans 2:28-29.
2 Matthew 28:19; I Corinthians 11:20, 23; Matthew 26:26-28.
3 Matthew 28:19.
4 Galatians 3:27.
5 Mark 1:4; Revelation 1:5.
6 Titus 3:5; Ephesians 5:26.
7 Galatians 3:26-27.
8 I Corinthians 15:29; Romans 6:5.
9 I Corinthians 12:13.
10 Romans 6:4.
11 [The phrase 'the church on earth' here and in Question 166 is 'the visible church' in the 1647 text: see also WLC 61-63].
12 Acts 8:36-37; Acts 2:38.
13 Genesis 17:7, 9 compared with Galatians 3:9, 14; and Colossians 2:11-12 and Acts 2:38-39 and Romans 4:11-12; I Corinthians 7:14; Matthew 28:19; Luke 18:15-16; Romans 11:16.

consciences in both aspects they are to wait for the benefit of it in due time.[1] However, if in either preparation or conduct they see they have failed, they are to be humbled,[2] and next time to receive the sacrament with more care and diligence.[3]

Baptism and the Lord's Supper compared

176. In what do the sacraments of Baptism and the Lord's Supper agree?

The sacraments of Baptism and the Lord's Supper agree, in that the author of both is God;[4] the spiritual part of both is Christ and his benefits;[5] both are seals of the same covenant,[6] are to be dispensed by ministers of the gospel, and by no-one else;[7] and both are to be continued in the church of Christ until his second coming.[8]

177. In what do the sacraments of Baptism and the Lord's Supper differ?

The sacraments of Baptism and the Lord's Supper differ in that baptism is to be administered once only, with water, as a sign and seal of our regeneration and grafting into Christ,[9] and that even to infants;[10] whereas the Lord's Supper is to be administered often, in the elements of bread and wine, to represent and set forth Christ as spiritual nourishment to the soul,[11] and to confirm our continuance and growth in him,[12] but only to such as are of sufficient age and ability to examine themselves.[13]

---

1 Psalms 123:1-2, 42:5, 8, 43:3-5.
2 II Chronicles 30:18-19; Isaiah 1:16, 18.
3 II Corinthians 7:11; I Chronicles 15:12-14.
4 Matthew 28:19; I Corinthians 11:23.
5 Romans 6:3-4; I Corinthians 10:16.
6 Romans 4:11 compare with Colossians 2:12; Matthew 26:27-28.
7 John 1:33; Matthew 28:19; I Corinthians 11:23; I Corinthians 4:1; Hebrews 5:4.
8 Matthew 28:19-20; I Corinthians 11:26.
9 Matthew 3:11; Titus 3:5; Galatians 3:27.
10 Genesis 17:7, 9; Acts 2:38-39; I Corinthians 7:14.
11 I Corinthians 11:23-26.
12 I Corinthians 10:16.
13 I Corinthians 11:28-29.

PRAYER AS A MEANS OF GRACE [WCF 21:1-6]

178. What is prayer?

Prayer is an offering up of our desires to God,[1] in the name of Christ,[2] by the help of his Spirit,[3] with confession of our sins[4] and thankful acknowledgment of his mercies.[5]

179. Are we to pray only to God?

God alone is able to search the hearts,[6] hear the requests,[7] pardon the sins,[8] and fulfil the desires of all;[9] and he alone is to be believed in[10] and worshipped with religious worship.[11] Therefore prayer, which is a special part of religious worship,[12] is to be made by all to him alone,[13] and to no one else.[14]

180. What is it to pray in the name of Christ?

To pray in the name of Christ is, in obedience to his command and with confidence in his promises, to ask mercy for his sake,[15] and this not by a mere mentioning of Christ's name,[16] but by drawing our encouragement to pray, and our boldness, strength and hope of acceptance in prayer, from Christ and his mediation.[17]

181. Why are we to pray in the name of Christ?

Since the sinfulness of man and his distance from God because of it are so great, we can have no access into his presence without a mediator;[18] and since no one in heaven or earth is appointed to or qualified for that glorious work but Christ alone,[19] we are to pray in no other name but his alone.[20]

---

1 Psalm 62:8.
2 John 16:23.
3 Romans 8:26.
4 Psalm 32:5-6; Daniel 9:4.
5 Philippians 4:6.
6 I Kings 8:39; Acts 1:24; Romans 8:27.
7 Psalm 65:2.
8 Micah 7:18.
9 Psalm 145:18-19.
10 Romans 10:14.
11 Matthew 4:10.
12 I Corinthians 1:2.
13 Psalm 50:15.
14 Romans 10:14.
15 John 14:13-14; John16:24; Daniel 9:17.
16 Matthew 7:21.
17 Hebrews 4:14-16; I John 5:13-15.
18 John 14:6; Isaiah 59:2; Ephesians 3:12.
19 John 6:27; Hebrews 7:25-27; I Timothy 2:5.
20 Colossians 3:17; Hebrews 13:15.

182. How does the Spirit help us to pray?

We do not know what we ought to pray for, but the Spirit helps our weakness by enabling us to understand for whom, for what and how prayer is to be made, and by working and strengthening in our hearts (although not in all persons nor at all times to the same extent) those perceptions, dispositions of heart and graces which are necessary for the right performance of the duty of prayer.[1]

183. For whom are we to pray?

We are to pray for the whole church of Christ on the earth;[2] for civil authorities,[3] for Christian ministers;[4] for ourselves,[5] our brethren,[6] even our enemies;[7] and for all kinds of people living now[8] or who may live in the future.[9] But prayer is not to be offered for the dead,[10] nor for those of whom it is known that they are guilty of 'the sin that leads to death'.[11]

184. For what are we to pray?

We are to pray for all things that aim at the glory of God,[12] the welfare of the church,[13] our own[14] or others' good,[15] but not for any thing that is unlawful.[16]

185. How are we to pray?

We are to pray with reverent recognition of the majesty of God,[17] and a deep sense of our own unworthiness,[18] our specific needs[19] and our sins;[20] with penitent,[21] thankful[22] and full hearts;[23] with understandings,[24] faith,[1] sincerity,[2] fervour,[3] love[4] and perseverance,[5]

---

1 Romans 8:26-27; Psalm 10:17; Zechariah 12:10.
2 Ephesians 6:18; Psalm 28:9.
3 I Timothy 2:1-2.
4 Colossians 4:3.
5 Genesis 32:11.
6 James 5:16.
7 Matthew 5:44.
8 I Timothy 2:1-2.
9 John 17:20; II Samuel 7:29.
10 II Samuel 12:21-23.
11 I John 5:16.
12 Matthew 6:9.
13 Psalm 51:18, 122:6.
14 Matthew 7:11.
15 Psalm 125:4.
16 I John 5:14.
17 Ecclesiastes 5:1.
18 Genesis 18:27; Genesis 32:10.
19 Luke 15:17-19.
20 Luke 18:13-14.
21 Psalm 51:17.
22 Philippians 4:6.
23 I Samuel 1:15; I Samuel 2:1.
24 I Corinthians 14:15.

waiting expectantly on him,[6] with humble submission to his will.[7]

The Lord's Prayer

186. What rule has God given for our direction in the duty of prayer?

The whole word of God is of use to direct us in the duty of prayer,[8] but the special rule of direction is that form of prayer which our Saviour Christ taught his disciples, commonly called the Lord's prayer.[9]

187. How is the Lord's Prayer to be used?

The Lord's Prayer is not only for our guidance as a pattern for making other prayers; but may also be used as a prayer itself, provided it be done with understanding, faith, reverence, and the other graces necessary to the right carrying out of the duty of prayer.[10]

188. How many parts are there in the Lord's Prayer?

The Lord's Prayer consists of three parts: a preface, requests and a conclusion.

189. What does the preface of the Lord's Prayer teach us?

The preface of the Lord's Prayer (contained in the words, *Our Father in heaven*[11]) teaches us that when we pray, we are to draw near to God with confidence in his fatherly goodness, and our right to share in it;[12] with reverence and all other child-like attitudes,[13] heavenly desires,[14] and due recognition of his sovereign power, majesty and gracious condescension.[15] It also teaches that we should pray with and for others.[16]

---

1 Mark 11:24; James 1:6.
2 Psalms 145:18, 17:1.
3 James 5:16.
4 I Timothy 2:8.
5 Ephesians 6:18.
6 Micah 7:7.
7 Matthew 26:39.
8 I John 5:14.
9 Matthew 6:9-13; Luke 11:2-4.
10 Matthew 6:9 compared with Luke 11:2.
11 Matthew 6:9.
12 Luke 11:13; Romans 8:15.
13 Isaiah 64:9.
14 Psalm 123:1; Lamentations 3:41.
15 Isaiah 63:15-16; Nehemiah 1:4-6.
16 Acts 12:5.

190. What do we pray for in the first request?

In the first request (which is, *Hallowed be your name*[1]) we acknowledge the complete inability and lack of inclination to honour God rightly that is in ourselves and all people,[2] and we pray that by his grace God would enable and persuade us and others to know, acknowledge, and highly regard him,[3] his titles,[4] attributes,[5] ordinances, word,[6] works and all that through which he is pleased to make himself known,[7] and enable us to glorify him in thought, word[8] and deed.[9] We also pray that he would prevent and remove atheism,[10] spiritual ignorance,[11] idolatry,[12] contempt for holy things,[13] and whatever dishonours him,[14] and that, by his over-ruling providence, he would direct and arrange all things to his own glory.[15]

191. What do we pray for in the second request?

In the second request (which is, *Your kingdom come*[16]) we acknowledge ourselves and all mankind to be by nature under the dominion of sin and Satan,[17] and we pray that the kingdom of sin and Satan may be destroyed,[18] the gospel spread throughout the world,[19] the Jews called,[20] the fulness of the Gentiles brought in,[21] and that the church may be provided with all the New Testament officer-bearers and ordinances,[22] cleansed from corruption,[23] and countenanced and maintained by the civil authorities.[24] Our prayer

---

1 Matthew 6:9.
2 II Corinthians 3:5; Psalm 51:15.
3 Psalm 67:2-3.
4 Psalm 83:18.
5 Psalm 86:10-13, 15.
6 II Thessalonians 3:1; Psalms 147:19-20, 138:1-3; II Corinthians 2:14-15.
7 Psalms 145, and 8.
8 Psalms 103:1, 19:14.
9 Philippians 1:9, 11.
10 Psalms 67:1- 4.
11 Ephesians 1:17-18.
12 Psalms 97:7.
13 Psalms 74:18, 22-23.
14 II Kings 19:15-16.
15 II Chronicles 20:6, 10-12; Psalms 83, 140:4, 8.
16 Matthew 6:10.
17 Ephesians 2:2-3.
18 Psalm 68:1, 18; Revelation 12:10-11.
19 II Thessalonians 3:1.
20 Romans 10:1.
21 John 17:9, 20; Romans 11:25-26; Psalm 67.
22 Matthew 9:38; II Thessalonians 3:1.
23 Malachi 1:11; Zephaniah 3:9.
24 I Timothy 2:1-2.

is that by these means the ordinances of Christ may be purely dispensed, and made effective to the converting of those who are yet in their sins, and the confirming, comforting and building up of those who are already converted;[1] and that Christ would rule in our hearts here,[2] and that the time of his second coming and our reigning with him for ever may come quickly.[3] And so we pray that God would be pleased to exert the kingdom of his power in all the world as may best serve to achieve these ends.[4]

192. What do we pray for in the third request?

In the third request (which is, *Your will be done on earth as it is in heaven*[5]) we acknowledge that by nature we and all people are not only completely unable and unwilling to know and do the will of God,[6] but are prone to rebel against his word,[7] to fret and complain against his providence,[8] and to be wholly inclined to do the will of the flesh and of the devil.[9] Therefore we pray that God by his Spirit may take away from ourselves and others all spiritual blindness,[10] weakness,[11] unwillingness[12] and perversity of heart,[13] and by his grace make us able and willing to know, do and submit to his will in all things[14] with humility,[15] cheerfulness,[16] faithfulness,[17] diligence,[18] zeal,[19] sincerity[20] and constancy,[21] like that of the angels in heaven.[22]

---

1 Acts 4:29-30; Ephesians 6:18-20; Romans 15:29-30, 32; II Thessalonians 1:11, II Thessalonians 2:16-17.
2 Ephesians 3:14-20.
3 Revelation 22:20.
4 Isaiah 64:1-2; Revelation 4:8-11.
5 Matthew 6:10.
6 Romans 7:18; Job 21:14; I Corinthians 2:14.
7 Romans 8:7.
8 Exodus 17:7; Numbers 14:2.
9 Ephesians 2:2.
10 Ephesians 1:17-18.
11 Ephesians 3:16.
12 Matthew 26:40-41.
13 Jeremiah 31:18-19.
14 Psalm 119:1, 8, 35-36; Acts 21:14.
15 Micah 6:8.
16 Psalm 100:2; Job 1:21; II Samuel 15:25-26.
17 Isaiah 38:3.
18 Psalm 119:4-5.
19 Romans 12:11.
20 Psalm 119:80.
21 Psalm 119:112.
22 Isaiah 6:23; Psalm 103:20-21; Matthew 18:10.

193. What do we pray for in the fourth request?

In the fourth request (which is, *Give us today our daily bread*[1]) we acknowledge that in Adam, and by our own sin, we have forfeited our right to all the outward blessings of this life, and deserve to be wholly deprived of them by God, and to have his curse on them even as we use them;[2] and we acknowledge that they cannot by themselves sustain us[3] nor can we merit[4] or obtain them by our own industry,[5] but are prone to desire,[6] obtain[7] and use them unlawfully.[8] Therefore we pray for ourselves and others, that both they and we, looking to the providence of God from day to day as we use the lawful means, may by his free gift and as it shall seem best to his fatherly wisdom, enjoy a sufficient share of them.[9] We also pray that we may have that share continued and blessed to us in our holy and beneficial use of it,[10] and contentment in it,[11] and that we be kept from all things that are contrary to our material support and welfare.[12]

194. What do we pray for in the fifth request?

In the fifth request (which is, *Forgive us our debts as we also have forgiven our debtors*[13]) we acknowledge that we and all others are guilty both of original and actual sin, and thus have become debtors to the justice of God, which debt neither we nor any other creature can pay, even to the smallest extent.[14] Therefore we pray for ourselves and others, that God of his free grace and through the obedience and satisfaction of Christ, grasped and applied by faith, may acquit us from both the guilt and the punishment of sin,[15] accept us in his Beloved,[16] continue his grace and favour to us,[17] pardon our daily failings,[1] and fill us

---

1 Matthew 6:11.
2 Genesis 2:17, 3:17; Romans 8:20-22; Jeremiah 5:25; Deuteronomy 28:15-68.
3 Deuteronomy 8:3.
4 Genesis 32:10.
5 Deuteronomy 8:17-18.
6 Jeremiah 6:13; Mark 7:21-22.
7 Hosea 12:7.
8 James 4:3.
9 Genesis 43:12-14; Genesis 28:20; Ephesians 4:28; II Thessalonians 3:11-12; Philippians 4:6.
10 I Timothy 4:3-5.
11 I Timothy 6:6-8.
12 Proverbs 30:8-9.
13 Matthew 6:12.
14 Romans 3:9-22; Matthew 18:24-25; Psalm 130:3-4.
15 Romans 3:24-26; Hebrews 9:22.
16 Ephesians 1:6-7.
17 II Peter 1:2.

with peace and joy as he gives us daily more and more assurance of forgiveness.[2] And we are more bold to ask for this and encouraged to expect it, when we have this testimony in ourselves, that we from the heart forgive others their offences.[3]

195. *What do we pray for in the sixth request?*

In the sixth request (which is, *And lead us not into temptation but deliver us from the evil one*[4]) we acknowledge that the most wise, righteous and gracious God, for various wise and holy reasons, may so arrange things that we may be attacked, confused and for a time led captive by temptations;[5] we acknowledge that Satan,[6] the world[7] and the flesh are ready powerfully to draw us aside and ensnare us;[8] and we acknowledge that because of our corruption[9] weakness, and lack of vigilance,[10] even after the pardon of our sins, we are not only subject to temptations and ready to expose ourselves to them,[11] but are also of ourselves unable and unwilling to resist them, to recover ourselves from them, or to learn from them,[12] and so we deserve to be left under their power.[13] Therefore we pray that God would so over-rule the world and all in it,[14] subdue the flesh[15] and restrain Satan,[16] direct all things,[17] give and bless all means of grace[18] and awaken us to watchfulness as we use them, that we and all his people may by his providence be kept from being tempted to sin.[19] We further pray that if we are tempted, that by his Spirit we may be powerfully supported and enabled to stand in the hour of temptation,[20] or when we fall, that we may be raised and restored,[21]

---

1 Hosea 14:2; Jeremiah 14:7.
2 Romans 15:13; Psalm 51:7-10, 12.
3 Luke 11:4; Matthew 6:14-15; Matthew 18:35.
4 Matthew 6:13.
5 II Chronicles 32:31.
6 I Chronicles 21:1.
7 Luke 21:34; Mark 4:19.
8 James 1:14.
9 Galatians 5:17.
10 Matthew 26:41.
11 Matthew 26:69-72; Galatians 2:11-14; II Chronicles 18:3 compared with II Chronicles 19:2.
12 Romans 7:23-24; I Chronicles 21:1-4; II Chronicles 16:7-10.
13 Psalm 81:11-12.
14 John 17:15.
15 Psalms 51:10, 119:133.
16 II Corinthians 12:7-8.
17 I Corinthians 10:12-13.
18 Hebrews 13:20-21.
19 Matthew 26:41; Psalm 19:13.
20 Ephesians 3:14-17; I Thessalonians 3:13; Jude 24.
21 Psalm 51:12.

and have the experience sanctified to us for our future good.[1] In short, we pray that our sanctification and salvation may be perfected,[2] Satan trodden under our feet,[3] and we be fully freed from sin, temptation and all evil, for ever.[4]

196. What does the conclusion attached to the Lord's Prayer teach us?[5]

The conclusion attached to the Lord's Prayer (which is, *For yours is the kingdom and the power and the glory for ever, Amen.*[6]) teaches us to strengthen our requests with arguments,[7] taken not from any worthiness in ourselves or in any other creature, but from God;[8] and with our prayers to join praises,[9] ascribing to God alone eternal sovereignty, omnipotence and glorious excellence.[10] Thus, as he is able and willing to help us,[11] so we by faith are the more bold to plead with him that he would,[12] and calmly to rely on him that he will fulfil our requests.[13] And to testify this as our desire and assurance we say, Amen.[14]

To God be the Glory

1 I Peter 5:8-10.
2 II Corinthians 13:7, 9.
3 Romans 16:20; Zechariah 3:2; Luke 22:31-32.
4 John 17:15; I Thessalonians 5:23.
5 The conclusion does not appear in Luke's record (Luke 11) and is omitted in several important manuscripts of Matthew 6. However, it is a perfectly scriptural kind of conclusion – see the texts cited.
6 Matthew 6:13.
7 Romans 15:30.
8 Daniel 9:4, 7-9, 16-19.
9 Philippians 4:6.
10 I Chronicles 29:10-13.
11 Ephesians 3:20-21; Luke 11:13.
12 II Chronicles 20:6, 11.
13 II Chronicles 14:11.
14 I Corinthians 14:16; Revelation 22:20-21.

THE WESTMINSTER SHORTER CATECHISM IN MODERN ENGLISH

THE SHORTER CATECHISM

INTRODUCTORY –WSC 1-3 CF. WLC 1-5

Life's purpose and Holy Scripture [WCF 1]

1. ***What is the chief purpose for which man is made?***

The chief purpose for which man is made is to glorify God, and to enjoy him forever.

2. ***What rule has God given to direct us how to glorify and enjoy him?***

The word of God, which consists of the Scriptures of the Old and New Testaments, is the only rule to direct us how to glorify and enjoy him.

3. ***What do the Scriptures principally teach?***

The Scriptures principally teach what man is to believe concerning God, and what duty God requires of man.

WHAT MAN OUGHT TO BELIEVE CONCERNING GOD – WSC 4-38 CF. WLC 6-90

The One and Triune God [WCF 2]

4. ***What is God?***

God is a Spirit, infinite, eternal and unchangeable in his being, wisdom, power, holiness, justice, goodness and truth.

5. ***Are there more Gods than one?***

There is only one God, the living and true God.

6. ***How many persons are there in the Godhead?***

There are three persons in the Godhead: the Father, the Son and the Holy Spirit; and these three are one God, the same in substance, equal in power and glory.

God's Eternal Plan [WCF 3]

7. ***What are the decrees of God?***

The decrees of God are his eternal plan, according to the purpose of his will, by which, for his own glory, he has foreordained what ever comes to pass; /yet in such a manner as to be in no way the author of sin.\

8. How does God carry out his decrees?

God carries out his decrees in the works of creation and providence.

Creation [WCF 4]

9. What is the work of creation?

The work of creation is the making by God of all things from nothing, by his powerful word, in the space of six days, and all very good.

10. How did God create man?

God created man, male and female, in his own image, in knowledge, righteousness and holiness, with rule over the creatures.

Providence [WCF 5 & 7:1-2]

11. What are God's works of providence?

God's works of providence are his most holy, wise and powerful preservation and control of all his creatures, and all their actions.

12. What special act of providence did God exercise towards man in the state in which he was created?

When God had created man, he entered into a covenant of life with him, on condition of perfect obedience, forbidding him to eat of the tree of the knowledge of good and evil on penalty of death.

Sin in the human race [WCF 6]

13. Did our first parents continue in the state in which they were created?

Our first parents, being left to the freedom of their own will, fell from the state in which they were created by sinning against God.

14. What is sin? [WLC 24]

Sin is any failure to measure up to what God requires, or any disobedience to his commands.

15. What was the sin by which our first parents fell from the state in which they were created?

The sin by which our first parents fell from the state in which they were created, was their eating the fruit that God had forbidden.

16. Did all mankind fall in Adam's first disobedience?

Since the covenant of life was made with Adam for his

descendants as well as for himself, all mankind descending from him in the ordinary manner, sinned in him, and fell with him in his first transgression.

17. ***Into what state did the fall bring mankind?***

The fall brought mankind into a state of sin and misery.

18. ***What is the sinfulness of that state into which man fell?***

The sinfulness of the state into which man fell includes the guilt of Adam's first sin, the lack of the righteousness which he had at first, and the corruption of every part of his nature, which is commonly called Original Sin, together with all actual sins which flow from it.

19. ***What misery did the fall bring upon mankind?***

The fall brought upon mankind loss of communion with God, and his wrath and curse, so that we are justly liable to all miseries in this life, to death itself, and to punishment in hell for ever.

GOD'S COVENANT OF GRACE [WCF 7:3-6]

20. ***Did God leave all mankind to perish in the state of sin and misery?***

God, solely of his love and mercy, from all eternity elected some to everlasting life, and entered into a covenant of grace to deliver them out of the state of sin and misery, and to bring them into a state of salvation by a Redeemer.

CHRIST THE MEDIATOR [WCF 8]

The Person of Christ

21. ***Who is the Redeemer of God's elect?***

The only Redeemer of God's elect is the Lord Jesus Christ, who, being the eternal Son of God became man, and so was and continues to be God and man, in two distinct natures and one person for ever.

22. ***How did Christ, the Son of God, become man?***

Christ, the Son of God, became man by taking to himself a body and a soul like ours, being conceived by the power of the Holy Spirit in the womb of the Virgin Mary, and born of her, yet without sin.

The Offices of Christ

23. What offices does Christ fill as our Redeemer?

Christ as our Redeemer fills the offices of a prophet, of a priest and of a king, in his states both of humiliation and exaltation.

24. How does Christ fill the office of a prophet?

Christ fills the office of a prophet in revealing to us by his word and Spirit the will of God for our complete salvation.

25. How does Christ fill the office of a priest?

Christ fills the office of a priest in his once offering up of himself to God as a sacrifice, to satisfy divine justice and reconcile us to God; and in making constant intercession for us.

26. How does Christ fill the office of a king?

Christ fills the office of a king in making us his willing subjects, in ruling and defending us, and in restraining and conquering all his and our enemies.

Christ's State of Humiliation

27. In what did Christ's humiliation consist?

Christ's humiliation consisted in being born, and that in poor circumstances; in being subject to God's law; in undergoing the miseries of this life, the wrath of God and the curse of death on the cross; in being buried; and in continuing under the power of death for a time.

Christ's State of Exaltation

28. In what does Christ's exaltation consist?

Christ's exaltation consists in his rising again from the dead on the third day; in ascending into heaven; in sitting at the right hand of God the Father; and in coming to judge the world at the last day.

God's Effective Call and the Church [WCF 10:1-4; 25:1-6; 26:1]

29. How are we made to share in the redemption purchased by Christ?

We are made to share in the redemption purchased by Christ by the effective application of it to us by his Holy Spirit.

30. *How does the Spirit apply to us the redemption purchased by Christ?*

The Spirit applies to us the redemption purchased by Christ by producing faith in us, and by this uniting us to Christ in our effective calling.

31. *What is effective calling?*

Effective calling is the work of God's Spirit by which he convinces us of our sin and misery, enlightens our minds in the knowledge of Christ, and renews our wills, and so persuades and enables us to embrace Jesus Christ, freely offered to us in the gospel.

32. *What benefits in this life are shared by those who are effectively called?*

In this life those who are effectively called share in justification, adoption and sanctification, and the further benefits in this life which accompany or flow from them.

Justification and Faith [WCF 11 & 14]

33. *What is justification?*

Justification is an act of God's free grace in which he pardons all our sins and accepts us as righteous in his sight for the sake of the righteousness of Christ alone, which is credited to us and received by faith alone.

Adoption [WCF 12]

34. *What is adoption?*

Adoption is an act of God's free grace by which we are received into the number and have a right to all the privileges of the sons of God.

Sanctification [WCF 13]

35. *What is sanctification?*

Sanctification is the work of God's free grace by which we are renewed throughout in the image of God and are enabled more and more to die to sin and live to righteousness.

FURTHER BENEFITS IN THIS LIFE AND AT DEATH

36. *What benefits in this life accompany or flow from justification, adoption and sanctification?*

The benefits in this life which accompany or flow from

justification, adoption and sanctification are: assurance of God's love, peace of conscience, joy in the Holy Spirit, progress in holiness, and perseverance in it to this life's end.

37. What benefits do believers receive from Christ at death?

The souls of believers are at their death made perfect in holiness and immediately pass into glory; and their bodies, being still united to Christ, rest in their graves until the resurrection.

Benefits at the Resurrection

38. What benefits do believers receive from Christ at the resurrection?

At the resurrection of Christ will immediately raise up in glory all believers; he will openly acknowledge and acquit them in the day of judgment, /graciously rewarding them according to their works of faith,\ and they will enter into the full enjoyment of God for all eternity.

Having seen what the Scriptures principally teach us to believe concerning God, we now consider what they require as the duty of man.

THE DUTY OF MAN [WSC 39–107 & WLC 91–196]

The Moral Law [WCF 19]

39. What is the duty which God requires of man?

The duty which God requires of man is obedience to his revealed will.

40. What rule did God at first reveal to man for his obedience?

The rule which God at first revealed to man for his obedience was the moral law.

41. Where is the moral law set out briefly?

The moral law is set out briefly in the ten commandments.

42. What is the sum of the ten commandments?

The sum of the ten commandments is to love the Lord your God with all your heart, with all your soul, with all your strength and with all your mind; and your neighbour as yourself.
[See WLC 102 and 122.]

Preface

43. What is the preface to the ten commandments?

The preface to the ten commandments is: I am the Lord your God who brought you out of Egypt, out of the land of slavery.

44. What does the preface to the ten commandments teach us?

The preface to the ten commandments teaches us that because God is the Lord and our God and Redeemer, therefore we are bound to keep all his commandments.

COMMANDS 1-4 [SEE WSC 42 AND WLC 122] [CF. WLC 103 – 122]

First Commandment: The One to be worshipped

45. Which is the first commandment?

The first commandment is: You shall have no other gods before me.

46. What is required in the first commandment?

The first commandment requires us to know and acknowledge God to be the only true God and our God; and to worship and glorify him accordingly.

47. What is forbidden in the first commandment?

The first commandment forbids the denial of or failure to worship and glorify, the true God as God and our God; and it forbids giving that worship and glory to any other which is due to God alone.

48. What do the words 'before me' in the first commandment teach us?

These words 'before me' in the first commandment teach us that God, who sees all things, takes notice of and is much displeased with the sin of having any other god.

Second Commandment: The manner of worship

49. Which is the second commandment?

The second commandment is: You shall not make for yourself an idol in the form of anything in heaven above or on the earth beneath or in the waters below. You shall not bow down to them or worship them; for I the Lord your God am a jealous God, punishing the children for the sin of the fathers to the third and fourth generations of those who hate me, but showing love to thousands who love me and keep my commandments.

50. What are the duties required in the second commandment?

The second commandment requires us to receive, observe, and

keep pure and entire all such religious worship and ordinances as God has appointed in his word.
[See WCF 21 and 22]

51. *What is forbidden in the second commandment?*

The second commandment forbids the worship of God by images, or any other way not appointed in his word.

52. *What are the reasons attached to the second commandment?*

The reasons attached to the second commandment are God's authority as our lawgiver, the fact that we belong to him, and the zeal he has for his own worship.

Third Commandment: Our attitude to God

53. *Which is the third commandment?*

The third commandment is: You shall not misuse the name of the Lord your God, for the Lord will not hold anyone guiltless who misuses his name.

54. *What is required in the third commandment?*

The third commandment requires the holy and reverent use of God's name, titles, ordinances, word, and works.
[See WCF 22]

55. *What is forbidden in the third commandment?*

The third commandment forbids all unworthy use of anything by which God makes himself known.

56. *What is the reason attached to the third commandment?*

The reason attached to the third commandment is that though the breakers of this commandment may escape punishment from men, yet the Lord your God will not suffer them to escape his righteous judgment.

Fourth Commandment: God's Holy Day [WCF 21:7-8]

57. *Which is the fourth commandment?*

The fourth commandment is: Remember the sabbath day by keeping it holy. Six days you shall labour and do all your work, but the seventh day is a sabbath of the Lord your God. On it you shall not do any work, neither you, nor your son or daughter, nor your manservant or maidservant, nor your animals, nor the alien within your gates. For in six days the Lord made the heavens and the earth, the sea and all that is in them, but he rested on the seventh day. Therefore the Lord blessed the seventh day and made it holy.

58. What is required in the fourth commandment?

The fourth commandment requires the keeping holy to God such set times as he has appointed in his word, in particular, one whole day in seven.

59. Which day of the seven has God appointed to be the weekly sabbath?

From the beginning of the world to the resurrection of Christ God appointed the seventh day of the week to be the weekly sabbath, but thereafter he appointed the first day of the week, to continue to the end of the world, which is the Christian sabbath /or Lord's day.\

60. How is the sabbath /or Lord's day\ to be kept holy?

This Sabbath /or Lord's day, which is given for man's good and as a pointer to his eternal destiny,[1]\ is to be kept holy by resting all that day from our work and recreations, and spending the whole time in public and private worship, except the time spent in works of necessity and mercy.

61. What is forbidden in the fourth commandment?

The fourth commandment forbids the omission or careless performance of the duties required, and the misuse of the day by idleness, sinful acts, or unnecessary thoughts, words or works about our worldly affairs and recreations.

62. What are the reasons attached to the fourth commandment?

The reasons attached to the fourth commandment are God's allowance of six days worldly tasks, his claim to special ownership of the seventh, his own example, and his blessing of the sabbath day.

COMMANDS 5-10 [SEE WSC 42] [THE COMMANDMENTS ARE QUOTED FROM THE NIV]; [CF. WLC 123 – 148]

Fifth Commandment: Authority

63. Which is the fifth commandment?

The fifth commandment is: Honour your father and your mother so that you may live long in the land the Lord your God is giving you.

64. What is required in the fifth commandment?

The fifth commandment requires us to preserve the honour and

---

1 Mark 2:27, Hebrew 4: 4-5, 9-11.

perform the duties belonging to everyone in their different positions and relationships in life.

65. What is forbidden in the fifth commandment?

The fifth commandment forbids us to neglect or to do anything against the honour and duty which belongs to everyone in their various positions and relationships in life.

66. What is the reason attached to the fifth commandment?

The reason attached to the fifth commandment is a promise of long life and prosperity (so far as it shall serve God's glory and their own good) to all those who keep this commandment.

Sixth Commandment: Human life

67. Which is the sixth commandment?

The sixth commandment is: You shall not murder.

68. What is required in the sixth commandment?

The sixth commandment requires all lawful endeavours to preserve our own life and the life of others.

69. What is forbidden in the sixth commandment?

The sixth commandment forbids us to take our own life or to take unjustly the life of our neighbour, or anything tending to these ends.

Seventh Commandment: Purity

70. Which is the seventh commandment?

The seventh commandment is: You shall not commit adultery.

71. What is required in the seventh commandment?

The seventh commandment requires us to preserve our own and our neighbour's chastity in heart, speech and behaviour.

72. What is forbidden in the seventh commandment?

The seventh commandment forbids all impure thoughts, words and actions.

Eighth Commandment: Property

73. Which is the eighth commandment?

The eighth commandment is: You shall not steal.

74. What is required in the eighth commandment?

The eighth commandment requires us to obtain lawfully, and to further, the wealth and material well being of ourselves and others.

75. What is forbidden in the eighth commandment?

The eighth commandment forbids whatever does or may unjustly hinder our own or our neighbour's wealth and material well being.

Ninth Commandment: Speech

76. Which is the ninth commandment?

The ninth commandment is: You shall not give false testimony against your neighbour.

77. What is required in the ninth commandment?

The ninth commandment requires us to maintain and promote truth between men, and our own and our neighbour's good name, especially when called upon to bear witness.

78. What is forbidden in the ninth commandment?

The ninth commandment forbids whatever misrepresents truth, or is injurious to our own or our neighbour's good name.

Tenth Commandment: Desire

79. Which is the tenth commandment?

The tenth commandment is: You shall not covet your neighbour's house. You shall not covet your neighbour's wife, or his manservant or maidservant, his ox or his donkey, or anything which belongs to your neighbour.

80. What is required in the tenth commandment?

The tenth commandment requires full contentment with our own condition, and a right and charitable attitude to our neighbour and all that is his.

81. What is forbidden in the tenth commandment?

The tenth commandment forbids all discontent with our own state; envying and grieving at the good of our neighbour, together with all ungoverned longings and desires for things that belong to him.

The Law's Transgression and Penalty

82. Is any man able to keep the commandments of God perfectly?

No mere human person, since the fall, is able to keep the commandments of God perfectly in this life, but breaks them daily in thought, word and deed.

83. Are all transgressions of the law equally sinful?

Some sins, because of their nature and the circumstances, are more sinful in the sight of God than others.

84. What does every sin deserve?

/Although some sins will be more severely punished than others,[1]\ yet every sin deserves God's wrath and curse, both in this life and the life that is to come.

The Way to be Saved

85. What does God require of us that we may escape his wrath and curse due to us for sin?

To escape the wrath and curse due to us for sin, God requires of us faith in our Lord Jesus Christ and repentance leading to life together with the diligent use of all the outward means by which Christ gives to us the benefits of redemption.

86. What is faith in Jesus Christ?

Faith in Jesus Christ is a saving grace by which we receive and rest upon him alone for salvation as he is freely offered to us in the gospel. [See WLC 72-73]

Repentance leading to Life [WCF 15 & WLC 76]

87. What is repentance leading to life?

Repentance leading to life is a saving grace by which a sinner having truly realised his sin and grasped the mercy of God in Christ, turns from his sin with grief and hatred and turns to God with full resolve and effort after new obedience. [See WLC 76]

88. What are the outward means by which Christ gives to us the benefits of redemption?

The outward and ordinary means by which Christ gives to us the benefits of redemption are his ordinances, especially the word, sacraments and prayer, and all these are made effective in the salvation of the elect.

The Bible as a means of Grace

89. How is the word of God made effective to salvation?

The Spirit of God makes the reading but especially the preaching of the word, an effective means of convincing and converting sinners, and building them up in holiness and comfort, through faith, to salvation.

---

1 Matthew 11:21-24; Luke 12:47-48.

90. How is the word to be read and heard, that it may become effective to salvation?

We must attend to the word with diligence, preparation and prayer, receive it with faith and love, lay it up in our hearts, and practise it in our lives, so that it may become effective to salvation. [see also WLC 160]

The Sacraments as a means of Grace [WCF 27]

91. How do the sacraments become effective means of salvation?

The sacraments become effective means of salvation not because of any power in them or in him who administers them, but only by the blessing of Christ and the working of his Spirit in those who receive them in faith.

92. What is a sacrament?

A sacrament is a holy ordinance appointed by Christ, by which, by visible signs, Christ, and the benefits of the new covenant, are represented, sealed and applied to believers.

93. Which are the sacraments of the New Testament?

The sacraments of the New Testament are two only, Baptism and the Lord's supper, /and these take the place of Circumcision and the Passover in the Old Testament.\ [see WCF 27:5]

Baptism [WCF 28]

94. What is Baptism?

Baptism is the sacrament /of solemn admission into the church on earth\ in which the washing with water in the name of the Father, and of the Son, and of the Holy Spirit, signifies and seals our being grafted into Christ, our having a share in the benefits of the covenant of grace, and our pledge to be the Lord's.

95. To whom is Baptism to be administered?

Baptism is not to be administered to any outside membership of the church on earth, until they profess their faith in Christ and obedience to him; but infants descending from parents (one or both) professing faith in Christ and obedience to him, /are, for that reason, within the covenant and\ are to be baptised.

The Lord's Supper [WCF 29]

96. What is the Lord's Supper?

The Lord's supper is a sacrament in which, by giving and receiving bread and wine according to Christ's appointment, his death is proclaimed, and those who receive rightly are by faith (and not by the mouth in a physical manner) made partakers of his body and blood, with all his benefits, to their spiritual nourishment and growth in grace.

97. What is required to receive rightly the Lord's Supper?

It is required of those who would receive rightly the Lord's Supper, that they examine themselves as to their knowledge of the meaning and object of this sacrament, their faith to feed upon Christ, and their repentance, love and new obedience; for coming in an unworthy manner would bring judgment on themselves.

Prayer as a means of Grace [WCF 21:1-6]

98. What is prayer?

Prayer is an offering up of our desires to God, for things agreeable to his will, in the name of Christ, with confession of our sins and thankful acknowledgement of his mercies. [see also WCF 21:3]

The Lord's Prayer

99. What rule has God given for our direction in prayer?

The whole word of God is of use to direct us in prayer, but this special rule of direction is that form of prayer which Christ taught his disciples, commonly called the Lord's Prayer.

100. What does the preface of Lord's Prayer teach us?

The preface of Lord's Prayer (which is, *Our Father in heaven*) teaches us firstly to draw near to God with all holy reverence and confidence as children to a father able and ready to help us; and secondly, that we should pray with and for others.

101. What do we pray for in the first request?

In the first request (which is, *Hallowed be your name*) we pray that God may enable us and others to glorify him in all in which he makes himself known; and that he would over-rule all things for his own glory.

102. What do we pray for in the second request?

In the second request (which is, *Your kingdom come*) we pray that Satan's kingdom may be destroyed, that the Kingdom of grace may be advanced and ourselves and others brought into it and kept in it; and that /Christ's return and\ the kingdom of glory may come quickly.

103. What do we pray for in the third request?

In the third request (which is, *Your will be done on earth as it is in heaven*) we pray that God, by his grace, would make us able and willing to know, obey and submit to his will in all things, as the angels do in heaven.

104. What do we pray for in the fourth request?

In the fourth request (which is, *Gives us today our daily bread*) we pray that by God's free gift we may receive a sufficient share of the good things of this life, and enjoy his blessing with them.

105. What do we pray for in the fifth request?

In the fifth request (which is, *Forgive us our debts as we also have forgiven our debtors*) we pray that God, for Christ's sake, would freely pardon all our sins; and we are encouraged to ask this because, by his grace, we are enabled from the heart to forgive others.

106. What do we pray for in the sixth request?

In this sixth request (which is, *And lead us not into temptation but deliver us from the evil one*) we pray that God would either keep us from being tempted to sin, or support and deliver us when we are tempted.

107. What does the conclusion attached to the Lord's Prayer teach us?[1]

The conclusion attached to the Lord's Prayer (which is, *For yours is the kingdom and the power and the glory forever, Amen.*) teaches us to take our encouragement in prayer from God alone, and in our prayers to praise him, ascribing kingdom, power and glory to him. And in testimony of our desire and assurance, we say, Amen.

To God be the Glory

[1] The conclusion does not appear in Luke's record (Luke 11) and is omitted in several important manuscripts of Matthew 6. However, it is a perfectly scriptural kind of conclusion – see the texts cited.

THE FOLLOWING NOTE APPEARED IN THE ORIGINAL EDITION:

"So much of every question, both in the Larger and Shorter Catechism, is repeated in the answer, as maketh every answer an entire proposition or sentence in itself; to the end that the learner may further improve it upon all occasions, for his increase in knowledge and piety, even out of the course of catechising, as well as in it.

And albeit the substance of the doctrine comprised in that abridgement, commonly called *The Apostles' Creed*, be fully set forth in each of the Catechisms, so as there is no necessity of inserting the Creed itself; yet it is here annexed, not as though it were composed by the Apostles or ought to be esteemed canonical scripture, as the Ten Commandments and the Lord's Prayer, (much less a prayer, as ignorant people have been apt to make both it and the Decalogue), but because it is a brief sum of the Christian faith, agreeable to the word of God, and anciently received in the churches of Christ".

THE CREED

I believe in God the Father almighty,
Creator of heaven and earth,

and in Jesus Christ, his only Son, our Lord,
who was conceived by the Holy Spirit,
born of the Virgin Mary,
suffered under Pontius Pilate,
was crucified, dead, and buried;
he descended into hell;[1]
the third day he rose again from the dead;
he ascended into heaven,
and is seated at the right hand
of God the Father almighty;
from there he shall come to judge
the living and the dead.

I believe in the Holy Spirit,
the holy catholic Church,
the communion of saints,
the forgiveness of sins,
the resurrection of the body,
and the life everlasting. Amen.

---

1 That is, continued in the state of the dead, and under the power of death till the third day. [*Note in 1648 edition – compare also WLC 50*].

FURTHER READING

The books marked * deal with the topic in greater depth and are more difficult. These are suggested for the more mature reader or those with deeper insight.

The books marked # denote an e-book.

Some of the books may be out of print and only available on the second hand market or as an e-book.

COMMENTARIES ON THE CONFESSION OF FAITH

HODGE, A. A. — Westminster Confession, A Commentary, Banner of Truth, June 1, (2004).

PHILIP, James. — The Westminster Confession of Faith, An Exposition - Part 1, Publisher unknown, (1966).

SHAW, R. *# — An Exposition of the Westminster Confession of Faith, Christian Heritage, (1998-06).

Van DIXHOORN Chad. — Confessing the Faith, A Reader's Guide To The Westminster Confession of Faith, Banner of Truth, United States, (2014).

WARD, Rowland S. — The Westminster Confession of Faith, A Study Guide: New Expanded Edition New Melbourne Press, (2004).

WILLIAMSON, G. I. — The Westminster Confession of Faith for study classes, Presbyterian and Reformed Pub. Co., Philadelphia (1964).

EXPOSITIONS ON THE DOCTRINES OF THE REFORMED FAITH

BERKHOF, L. — A summary of Christian Doctrine, Banner of Truth; 4th edition (December 1, 1960).

BERKHOF, L. * — Systematic Theology Wm. B. Eerdmans (8 Nov 2011).

BOICE, J. M. — Foundations of the Christian Faith (Master Reference Collection) IVP Academic (1986-05).

BOICE, J. M. — Whatever Happened to The Gospel of Grace?: Rediscovering the Doctrines That Shook the World, Crossway Books, USA, (2009).

CALVIN, J. * — Institutes of the Christian Religion (edited by John T McNeill, translated and indexed by Ford Lewis Battles) Westminster John Knox Press (1960).

MURRAY, J. — Collected Writings of John Murray Volume 2: Lectures in Systematic Theology, Banner of Truth, (October 1977).

PACKER, J I. — Concise Theology, Tyndale House, (1993).

PACKER, J I. — God's Words: Key Bible Themes you need to know, Baker Book House (Nov 1988).

REYMOND, R. L. * — A New Systematic Theology of the Christian Faith, Thomas Nelson; 2nd Revised & enlarged edition (9 Aug 1998).

UPRICHARD, R.E.H. — What Presbyterians Believe, The Oaks (1 Jun 2011).

CHAPTER I – OUR GREAT GOD

On Scripture:

PACKER, J. I. God Has Spoken: Revelation and the Bible, Baker Academic (1 May 1994).
YOUNG, E. J. Thy Word Is Truth, Banner of Truth (1997)

On God and his Plan:

BAVINCK, H. * Doctrine of God (Students Reformed Theological Library) Banner of Truth, (1996)
BOETTNER, L. The Reformed Doctrine of Predestination, EERDMAN, (1965)
FERGUSON, S. B. A Heart for God, Banner of Truth (May 1st 1987).
MACLEOD, D. Behold Your God (Revised and Expanded Edition), Christian Focus, (1995).
PINK, A. W. The Sovereignty of God, Wilder (15 Jan, 2009).

On Creation:

Refer to sections in Systematic Theologies above as there is much material on this.

Creationist:

http://creation.com; https://answersingenesis.org

On Intelligent Design:

http://www.intelligentdesign.org

CHAPTER II – MAN – THE CROWN OF CREATION

BOSTON, T. Human Nature in its Fourfold State, Create Space Independent Publishing Platform (March 3, 2011).
HOEKEMA, A. A. * Created in God's Image, William B Eerdmans Reprint edition (31 Dec 1996).

On Covenant

ROBERTSON, O. Palmer: * The Christ of the Covenants, Presbyterian and Reformed; First edition (22 Dec 1987).

See also Systematic Theologies and books on Infant Baptism.

Chapter III – OUR GREAT SALVATION

On the Mediator

BLANCHARD, J. Meet the Real Jesus, EP Books (10 Jan 2014).
MURRAY, J. Redemption Accomplish and Applied, William B Eerdmans, New edition (1 Dec, 1989).
STOTT, J. The Cross of Christ (with Study Guide), IVP Books (2006).

On Salvation

BROOKS, T. Heaven on Earth (assurance), The Banner of Truth (Dec 1982)
BUCHANAN, J. * The Doctrine of Justification (An Outline of Its History in the Church and Its Exposition from Scripture), ASIN: B003V4B3JY.
FERGUSON, S. B. Children of the Living God, The Banner of Truth; (May 1989).
FERGUSON, S. B. Grow in grace, The Banner of Truth; (Sep 1989).
FERGUSON, S. B. The Christian Life (A Doctrinal Introduction), Banner of Truth (1981).
HELM, Paul The Beginnings (Word and Spirit), Banner of Truth (June 1986).
HOEKEMA, Anthony A. * Saved by grace, William B Eerdmans (31 Dec 1996).
JOHNSTON Mark Child of a King, (What joining God's Family really means) Christian Focus (October 5, 2001).

Chapter IV – LIVING THE CHRISTIAN LIFE

ADAMS, Jay E. Marriage, Divorce and Re-marriage in the Bible, Zondervan (May 20, 1986)
CHANTRY, Walter J. God's Righteous Kingdom, The Banner of Truth (Dec 1980)
CHANTRY, Walter J. Call the Sabbath a Delight, The Banner of Truth (1 April 1991)
HELM, Paul: The Callings, (The Gospel in the World), The Banner of Truth (August 1, 1987).
KEVAN, E. * The Grace of the Law, Soli Deo Gloria Publications; (June 1, 2003).
MURRAY, J. * Principles of Conduct, Wm. B. Eerdmans Publishing Company (July 17, 1957).
MURRAY, J. * Divorce, P & R Publishing (August 1, 1987).

Chapter V – THE CHURCH OF CHRIST

On the Church in General

BANNERMAN, J. * The Church of Christ (2 vols) Solid Ground Christian Books (September 22, 2009).
CLOWNEY, E.P. * The Doctrine of the Church Inter Varsity Press (October 24, 1995).
GORDON, T. David Why Johnny can't sing hymns P&R Publishing (June 1, 2010).
HYDE Daniel E. Welcome to the Reformed Church, Reformation Trust Publishing (March 17, 2010).
KUIPER, R. B. The Glorious Body of Christ, Banner of Truth (June 1, 1967)
WITHEROW, T. The Apostolic Church, Biblio Life (3 Oct 2009).

On the Eldership:

EYRES, L. R. Elders of the Church, P & R Publishing (June 1, 1975).

On the Sacraments:

CROOKS, Rodger M. Salvation's Sign and Seal, What do Paedo-Baptists really believe? Christian Focus.

LEAHY, F. Biblical Baptism, Crown & Covenant Publications.

LETHAM, Robert Christian's Pocket Guide to Baptism, Christian Focus Publications (9 July 2012).

MURRAY, J. * Christian Baptism, Philadelphia: (1952).

SPROUL, R. C. # What is Baptism, (free e-book) Reformation Trust Publishing; (August 24, 2011).

SPROUL, R. C. # What is the Lord's Supper (free e-book) Reformation Trust Publishing; (October 7, 2013).

R.C. Sproul has several books on Baptism (see Evangelical Book Shop Websites).

CHAPTER VI – OUR GREAT FUTURE

BLANCHARD, J. What ever Happened to Hell? Evangelical Press & Services Ltd; (1 Jun 2004).

BOETTNER, L. * The Millennium, Presbyterian & Reformed. (1984).

DONNELLY, Edward Biblical Teaching on the Doctrines of Heaven and Hell, The Banner of Truth Trust (24 Sep 2001).

GRIER, W. J. The Momentous Event: A Discussion of Scripture Teaching on the Second Advent, Banner of Truth Trust, (1970).

HELM, Paul The Last Things (DEATH, JUDGMENT, HEAVEN AND HELL), The Banner of Truth; (Jan 1989).

HENDRIKSEN, W. The Bible on the Life Hereafter, Revell, a division of Baker Publishing Group (31 Dec 1995).

HOEKEMA, A. A. * The Bible and the Future, Wm. B. Eerdmans Publishing Company (September 6, 1994).

MOTYER, J. Alec Life 2: The Sequel, Christian Focus Publications (May 31, 2008).

RIDDLEBARGER, Kim A Case for Amillennialism: Understanding the End Times, Baker Books (March 1, 2003)

EXTRA NOTE ON CONFESSIONS & CREEDS

BARRETT, Lee C., III * The Heidelberg Catechism, A New Translation for the Twenty-First Century, United Church Press (June 30, 2007).

De YOUNG, KEVIN The Good News We Almost Forgot, Rediscovering the Gospel in a 16th Century Catechism, Moody Publishers (March 17, 2010).

JOHNSTON, Mark G. Our Creed, For Every Culture and Every Generation, Presbyterian and Reformed (October 19, 2012).

KELLY, Douglas F.; ROLLINSON, Phillip The Westminster Shorter Catechism in Modern English Presbyterian and Reformed; (1 Oct 2012)

PACKER, J. I. & PARRET, Gary A. Grounded in the Gospel, Building Believers the Old-Fashioned Way, Baker Books (1 April 2010).

TRUEMAN Carl The Creedal Imperative, Crossway (19 Oct 2012).

About the Author

William McKeown, a retired minister of the Presbyterian Church in Ireland, came to faith in his late teens. After leaving school at age fifteen, he worked in industry for a number of years. On being called to the ministry, he studied Electrical Engineering at Queens University and then Theology at Union Theological College, Belfast.

William's first charge was Clogher and Glenhoy congregations in Co. Tyrone, followed by Ballysally Church Extension, Coleraine and then Ravenhill in Belfast where he served for eighteen years.

William is married to Anne and they have three adult children and four grandchildren. Apart from reading Christian theology, biography and history, William's other interests include photography, cycling and computers.